National Fifth Edition

EVERYBODY'S GUIDE TO

SMALL CLAIMS COURT

by Attorney Ralph Warner

Edited by Annie Tillery and Cora Jordan

Illustrated by Linda Allison

NOLO PRESS   BERKELEY, CALIFORNIA

YOUR RESPONSIBILITY WHEN USING A SELF-HELP LAW BOOK

We've done our best to give you useful and accurate information in this book. But this book does not take the place of a lawyer licensed to practice law in your state. If you want legal advice, see a lawyer. If you use any information contained in this book, it's your personal responsibility to make sure that the facts and general information contained in it are applicable to your situation.

KEEPING UP-TO-DATE

To keep its books up-to-date, Nolo Press issues new printings and new editions periodically. New printings reflect minor legal changes and technical corrections. New editions contain major legal changes, major text additions or major reorganizations. To find out if a later printing or edition of any Nolo book is available, call Nolo Press at (510) 549-1976 or check the catalog in the *Nolo News*, our quarterly newspaper.

To stay current, follow the "Update" service in the *Nolo News*. You can get the paper free by sending us the registration card in the back of the book. In another effort to help you use Nolo's latest materials, we offer a 25% discount off the purchase of any new Nolo book if you turn in any earlier printing or edition. (See the "Recycle Offer" in the back of the book.)

Fifth Edition	
Third Printing	February 1994
Legal Editing	David Brown, Lisa Guerin and Robin Leonard
Illustrations	Linda Allison
Production	Jackie Clark Stephanie Harolde
Graphics	Amy Ihara
Printing	Delta Lithograph

Warner, Ralph E.
        Everybody's guide to small claims court / by Ralph Warner;
illustrations by Linda Allison. -- 5th national ed.
        p. cm.
        Includes index.
        ISBN 0-87337-161-5
        1. Small claims courts—United States. I. Title
KF8769.W37   1991
347.73'04--dc20
[347.3074]   91-3145
                                                                 CIP

THANK YOU

A number of talented friends have helped me improve this book. With enough help, even a tarnished penny can be made to shine.

Special thanks to Annie Tillery and Cora Jordan, who struggled mightily to update and improve this new edition. Thanks, too, to Judge Roderic Duncan and to Mary Alice Coleman of the State of California Department of Consumer Affairs, who don't always agree with what I write, but are nonetheless, unfailingly helpful.

Over the years, Dave Brown, Lisa Guerin, Robin Leonard and Mary Randolph have helped compile all the material appearing in the Appendix. Their thorough, patient and dedicated work have made this a better book.

Lisa Goldoftas provided numerous useful suggestions in helping rewrite Chapter 24, "Collecting Your Money."

Linda Allison's wonderful drawings speak for themselves. Working with her is like catching the first ray of sunshine on a clear morning.

ABOUT THE AUTHOR

Ralph Warner is the publisher and co-founder of Nolo Press. During a few-year stint as a legal aid lawyer in the late 1960s, it occurred to him that most Americans—not just the poor—were alienated from and oppressed by the legal system. Deciding to make a career out of working to provide better legal services, he helped found what is now known as the self-help law movement.

Ralph has authored or co-authored a number of Nolo Press books, including *The Independent Paralegal's Handbook, The Landlord's Law Book: Rights and Responsibilities, Tenants' Rights, The Partnership Book* and *29 Reasons Not to Go to Law School.*

GET 25% OFF YOUR NEXT PURCHASE

RECYCLE YOUR OUT-OF-DATE BOOKS

It's important to have the most current legal information. Because laws and legal procedures change often, we update our books regularly. To help keep you up-to-date we are extending this special offer. Cut out and mail the title portion of the cover of any old Nolo book with your next order and we'll give you a 25% discount off the retail price of ANY new Nolo book you purchase directly from us. For current prices and editions call us at 1-800-992-6656.

This offer is to individuals only.

For Toni,
the light, the heart, and the love of my life

TO OUR READERS

This book can be of great help to you and your family. The advice it offers about Small Claims Court is as sound as I have been able to make it, after much study of, and experience in, the area. Many knowledgeable people have reviewed these materials and many of their suggestions for change and clarification have been included. But advice will not always work. Like well-meaning recommendations of all kind, some of the advice I present here may not be helpful. So here are some qualifications. If you have access to a lawyer's advice and it is contrary to that given here, follow your lawyer's advice; the individual characteristics of your problem can better be considered by someone in possession of all the facts. Laws and procedures vary considerably from one state to the next and it's impossible to guarantee that every bit of information and advice contained here will be accurate. It is your responsibility to get a copy of the rules governing your local Small Claims Court and to make sure that the facts and general advice contained in this book are applicable in your state and to your situation. Small Claims Court rules and regulations change constantly, and you should check with your Small Claims Court clerk to make sure that information printed here is still current. And finally, please pay attention to this general disclaimer: Of necessity, neither the author nor the publisher of this book makes any guarantees regarding the outcome of the uses to which this material is put. Thank you, and good luck!

R.W.
Berkeley, California

CONTENTS

CHAPTER 1

In the Beginning

A. First Things

Small Claims procedures are established by state law. This means that there are differences in the operating rules of Small Claims Courts from state to state.[1] Differences include such things as the maximum amount for which you can sue, who can sue, and what papers must be filed where and when. The Appendix includes the information you will need no matter where you are using these materials.

While the details of using Small Claims Courts vary state to state, the basic approach necessary to prepare and present a case

---

[1]There are also differences among names used for Small Claims Court (or its equivalent) in the different states. As you will see in the Appendix, "Justice of the Peace," "Conciliation," "District," "Justice," "Municipal," "City," and "County" courts are among the names commonly used. Often, Small Claims Courts will be listed in the telephone directory under these names, and not as "Small Claims Courts."

properly is remarkably similar everywhere. But details are important, and you will wish to obtain from your local Small Claims Court clerk a copy of its procedural rules to supplement what you read here. Many times in this book I will advise you to check a particular detail in your state's law. If you can't find the answer in your local rules, call the Small Claims Court clerk and ask. Remember, your tax money pays for the court system, and . you have a right to be completely informed.

The purpose of Small Claims Court is to hear disputes involving modest amounts of money, without long delays and formal rules of evidence. Disputes are normally presented by the people involved. Lawyers are not prohibited in most states, but the limited dollar amounts involved usually make it uneconomical for people to hire them.[2] The maximum amount of money for which you can sue (in legal jargon, this is called the "jurisdictional amount") is $5,000 in California and $2,000 in New York. These amounts are about average, although there is considerable variation. Some states allow Small Claims Court cases up to $10,000, while others limit cases to no more than $1,000. (See Appendix.)

In recent years, the maximum amount for which suits can be brought has been on the rise almost everywhere. Don't rely on your memory, or what a friend tells you, or even what you read here. Call the local Small Claims Court clerk and find out exactly how much you can sue for. You may be pleasantly surprised to find that the maximum is more than you thought.

There are three great advantages of Small Claims Court:

• First, you get to prepare and present your own case without having to pay a lawyer more than your claim is worth.

• Second, bringing a dispute to Small Claims Court is simple. The gobbledygook of complicated legal forms and language prevalent in other courts is kept to a minimum. To start your

---

[2]The trend, however, is to eliminate lawyers completely (see Appendix for state-by-state rules). In California and Michigan, for example, lawyers may appear in Small Claims Court only when they are suing (or being sued) on their own case, but may not represent others.

case, you need only fill out a few lines on a simple form (e.g., "Honest Al's Used Chariots owes me $2,000 because the 1982 Chevette they sold me in supposedly 'excellent condition' died less than a mile from the car lot"). When you get to court, you can talk to the judge without a whole lot of "res ipsa loquiturs" and "pendente lites." If you have documents or witnesses, you may present them for what they are worth, with no requirement that you comply with the thousand years' accumulation of rusty, musty procedures, habits and so-called rules of evidence of which the legal profession is so proud.

• Third, and perhaps most important, Small Claims Court doesn't take long. Most disputes are heard in court within a month or two from the time the complaint is filed. The hearing itself seldom takes more than 15 minutes. The judge announces her decision either right there in the courtroom, or mails it out within a few days.

But before you decide that Small Claims Court sounds like just the place to bring your case, you will want to answer a basic question. Are the results you are likely to achieve in proportion to, or greater than, the effort you will have to expend? This must be answered by looking at each dispute individually. It is all too easy to get so involved in a particular dispute that you lose sight of the fact that the time, trouble and expense of bringing it to court are way out of balance with any likely return.

In order to think profitably about whether your case is worth the effort, you will want to understand the details of how Small Claims Court works—who can sue, where, for how much, etc. You will also want to learn a little law—are you entitled to relief, how much, and how do you compute the exact amount? Finally and most importantly comes the detail that so many people overlook to their later dismay. Assuming that you prepare and present your case brilliantly, and get a judgment for everything you request, can you collect? This seems a silly thing to overlook, doesn't it? Sad to say, however, it is often done. Plaintiffs commonly go through the entire Small Claims procedure with no chance of collecting a dime because they have sued a person who has neither money nor any reasonable prospect of getting any.

The purpose of the first dozen chapters of this book is to help you decide whether or not you have a case worth pursuing. These are not the sections where grand strategies are brilliantly unrolled to baffle and confound the opposition—that comes later. Here we are more concerned with such mundane tasks as locating the person you want to sue, suing in the right court, filling out the necessary forms and getting them properly served. Perhaps it will disappoint those of you with a dramatic turn of mind, but most cases are won or lost before anyone enters the courtroom.

Throughout this book we reproduce forms used in California and New York. Forms used elsewhere will sometimes look quite different, but you will find that the differences are usually more a matter of graphics than of substance. The basic information requested—who is suing whom about what—is very similar everywhere. Blank copies of all forms are available at your local Small Claims clerk's office.

B. Checklist of Things to Think Out Before Initiating or Defending Your Case

Here is a preliminary checklist of things you will want to think about at this initial stage. As you read further, we will go into each of these areas in more detail. But let me remind you again, if you haven't already gotten a copy of your local Small Claims Court rules, do it now. It's silly to come to bat with two out in the ninth and the bases loaded and not know if you are supposed to run to first or third.

Plaintiffs' (Filers') Checklist

1. Does the other person owe you the money, or, put another way, "Is there liability"? (See Chapter 2)

2. How many dollars is your claim for? If it is for more than the Small Claims maximum, do you wish to waive the excess and still use Small Claims Court? (See Chapter 4)

3. Is your suit brought within the proper time period (Statute of Limitations)? (See Chapter 5)

4. Which Small Claims Court should you bring your suit in? (See Chapter 9)

5. Whom do you sue? As you will see in many cases, especially those involving businesses and automobiles, this can be a little more technical and tricky than you might have guessed. (See Chapter 8)

6. Have you made a reasonable effort to contact the other party to offer a compromise? (See Chapter 6)

7. And again, the most important question—assuming that you can win, is there a reasonable chance that you can collect? (See Chapters 3 and 24)

Defendants' Checklist

1. Do you have a good legal defense against the claim of the plaintiff? (See Chapters 2 and 12)

2. Has the plaintiff sued for a reasonable or an excessive amount? (See Chapter 4)

3. Has the plaintiff brought his suit within the proper time limit (Statute of Limitation)? (See Chapter 5)

4. Has the plaintiff followed reasonably correct procedures in bringing suit and serving you with the court papers? (See Chapters 11 and 12)

5. Have you made a reasonable effort to contact the plaintiff in order to arrive at a compromise settlement? (See Chapters 6 and 12)

Defendant's Note: In addition to your right to defend a case, you also have the right to file your own claim (Chapters 10 and 12). You will want to do this if you believe that you suffered damage arising from the same incident or transaction that forms the basis of the plaintiff's suit against you, and that the plaintiff is responsible for your loss. If your claim is for less than the Small Claims Court maximum, you can file your claim of defendant (called a "counterclaim" in many states) in Small Claims Court. But if it is for more, you will probably want to get the case transferred to a formal court.[3] Before making any decision, read your local rules carefully.

C. Legal Jargon Defined

Mercifully, there is not a great deal of technical language in use in Small Claim Courts. But there are a few terms that may be new to you and with which you will have to become familiar.

---

[3]A few states require that even claims over the Small Claims Court limit be first presented to a Small Claims Court judge to see if they have merit before transfer to a formal court is allowed. Some states will refuse to accept counterclaims over the dollar limit at all, and transfer to a higher court is not allowed on this basis. In these states, a defendant must initiate a new action in formal court if her claim is for more than the Small Claims Court maximum (see the Appendix).

Don't try to learn all of these terms now. Refer back to these definitions when you need them. Here we give you the most widely used version of most terms. In some states jargon may vary slightly, but the substance will be remarkably similar everywhere.

Abstract of Judgment: An official document which you get from the Small Claims Court clerk's office which indicates that you have a money judgment against another person. Filing it with the County Recorder places a lien on real property owned by the judgment debtor. Some states may use slightly different terminology.

Appeal: Some states only allow a defendant to appeal; others allow appeals based only on law—not facts. Many require a bond to be posted (see Chapter 23 and Appendix).

Arbitration: A voluntary system under which a case is heard by arbitrators rather than in a court setting. Not available in most states, but used widely in New York City night courts. Ask your court clerk for local rules, if any.

Calendar: List of cases to be heard by a Small Claims Court on a particular day. A case taken off calendar is removed from the list. This usually occurs because the defendant has not been served or because the parties jointly request that it be heard on another day.

Civil Code (CC) and Code of Civil Procedure (CCP): The Civil Code contains much of a state's substantive law. The Code of Civil contains its legal procedures. These books are available at all public libraries and at law libraries (which are located at the county courthouse and open to the public). A number of states call these legal codes by other names, such as "Revised Statutes," "Rules of Civil Procedure" (RCP), and "Rules of Court." Ask the law librarian for help if you have trouble finding the right book.

Claim of Defendant: A claim by a defendant that the plaintiff owes him money. A Claim of Defendant, also called a "Defendant's Claim," is filed as part of the same Small Claims action that the plaintiff has started.

Claim of Exemption: A procedure by which a "judgment debtor" can claim that, under federal and/or state law, certain of his money or other property is exempt from being grabbed to satisfy a debt.

Continuance: A court order that a hearing be postponed to a later date.

Counterclaim: Basically the same as a "claim of defendant" or a "cross complaint." Different states use different names.

Default Judgment: A court decision given to the plaintiff (the person filing suit) when the defendant fails to show up (defaults).

Defendant: The person being sued.

Dismissed Case: A dismissal usually occurs when a case is dropped by the plaintiff. If the defendant has not filed a claim, the plaintiff can do this by filing a written request. If the defendant has filed a claim, they must agree in writing before a dismissal will be allowed. If a plaintiff does not show up in court on the appointed day, the judge may dismiss the case.

Equity: The value of a particular piece of property that you actually own. For example, if a car has a fair market value of $2,000 and you owe a bank $750 on it, your equity is $1,250.

Formal Court: As used here, this term refers to the regular "lawyer-dominated" state courts. The states call their trial courts by all sorts of names (municipal, superior, district, circuit, supreme, civil, etc.).For example, in California, claims of up to $25,000 that are not eligible for Small Claims Court are heard in Municipal Court, and claims over that amount are heard in Superior Court. All of these courts require a knowledge of confusing language and procedure, and you will want to avoid them if possible.

Garnish: To attach (legally take) money—usually wages, or commissions, or a bank account—for payment of a debt.

Hearing: The court trial.

Homestead: Homestead laws allow homeowners to protect the equity in their homes up to a certain amount from attachment and sale to satisfy most debts. Homestead laws can work in one of two ways. In some states, the homeowner must file a paper called a "Declaration of Homestead." In other states, simply owning a home (and having the deed recorded) is enough to entitle the homeowner to homestead protection.

Judgment: The decision rendered by the court.

Judgment Creditor: A person to whom money is owed under a court decision.

Judgment Debtor: A person who owes money under a court decision.

Jurisdiction: Jurisdiction refers generally to the authority a court has to hear a case. A Small Claims Court has jurisdiction to hear cases involving money damages up to a certain amount (e.g., Alaska is $5,000, Kansas is $1,000). (This is often called the "jurisdictional amount.") Some Small Claims Courts also have jurisdiction over certain types of non-money cases, such as unlawful detainer (eviction) actions, and some may award non-money remedies, including rescission, restitution, reformation and specific performance, as discussed in Chapter 4.

Levy: A legal method to seize property or money for unpaid debts under court order. For example, a sheriff can levy on (sell) your automobile if you refuse to pay a judgment.

Lien: A legal right to an interest in the real estate of another for payment of a debt. To get a lien, you first must get a court judgment and then take proper steps to have the court enter an "Abstract of Judgment." You can then take the Abstract to the county office where property deeds are recorded in a county where the judgment debtor has real estate to establish the lien.

Motion to Vacate a Judgment: The motion the defendant must file to reopen a proceeding because she did not appear in court to defend a case on the proper date and the judge has entered a Default Judgment. See Chapter 10.

Order of Examination: A court procedure allowing a judgment creditor to question a debtor about the extent and location of his assets. It is very common in California, and other states have similar procedures, but names may vary somewhat. Often it is referred to as "Supplemental Proceedings."

Plaintiff: The person who starts a lawsuit.

Process Server: Person who delivers court papers to a party or witness. See Chapter 14.

Recorder (Office of the County Recorder): The person employed by the county to make and record documents. The County Recorder's office is usually located in the main county courthouse.

Satisfaction of Judgment: A written statement filed by the judgment creditor when the judgment is paid. See Chapter 23.

Statute of Limitations: The time period in which you must file your lawsuit. It is normally figured from the date the act or omission giving rise to the lawsuit occurs, and varies depending on the type of suit. See Chapter 5.

Stay of Enforcement: When a Small Claims Court judgment is appealed by a defendant, enforcement (collection) of the judgment is stayed (stopped) until the time for appeal has expired.

Stipulation: An agreement to compromise a case which is entered into by the parties and then presented to the judge.

Submission: When a judge wants to delay decision on a case until a later time, she "takes it under submission." Some judges announce their decision as to who won and who lost right in the courtroom. More often, they take cases under submission and mail out decisions later.

Subpoena: Court order requiring a witness to appear in court. It must be served on the person subpoenaed to be valid. See Chapter 14.

Subpoena Duces Tecum: A court order requiring that certain documents be produced in court.

Substituted Service: A method by which court papers may be served on a defendant who is difficult to serve by other means. See Chapter 11.

Transfer: The procedure by which the defendant can have a Small Claims case transferred to a "formal court." In most states this can be done when the defendant has a claim against the plaintiff for an amount more than the Small Claims maximum. In a few states, it can also be done because the defendant simply doesn't want to be in Small Claims Court. In many states, a defendant who wants a jury trial can also transfer to formal court. See Appendix for details.

Trial De Novo: The rehearing of a Small Claims case from scratch when an appeal has been taken by a defendant. In this situation, the previous decision by the Small Claims judge has no effect and the appeal takes the form of a new trial (trial de novo). This is allowed only in some states. Check the Appendix.

Unlawful Detainer (known as "summary dispossess" and "forcible entry and detainer" in some states): Legalese for "eviction." Unlawful detainers may be brought in Small Claims Court in some states. Check the Appendix.

Venue: This basically refers to the proper location (court) to bring a suit, and is discussed in detail in Chapter 9. If a suit is brought in the wrong place, it can be transferred to the right court or dismissed, in which case the plaintiff must refile in the right court.

Wage Garnishment: After a judgment has been issued (and the defendant's time to appeal, if any, has elapsed), the Small Claims Court clerk will issue a writ of execution upon request. This may be turned over to a sheriff, marshal or constable with orders to collect (garnish) a portion of the judgment debtor's wages directly from his employer.

Writ Of Execution: An order by a court to the sheriff, marshal or constable of a specific area (in most states, this is either a city or county) to collect a specific amount of money due.

D.   Legal Research

As part of using Small Claims Court, you may need to look up a state law or city or county ordinance. In many states, laws are roughly divided by subject matter, often into sets of books that are usually called "codes" or "statutes." Thus, there will be a Civil Code, Probate Code, Penal Code, Vehicle Code, and many more. Other states follow a somewhat different organizational system under which all laws are lumped together in one seemingly endless numerical sequence. In either case, a subject index (often in the last volume) will be available.

You can get access to state laws at any large public library, publicly-funded law school library or county law library (which, in many states, are located in main county courthouses and often in larger branch courthouses) and are open to the public.

Ordinances are passed by cities and counties and have the force of law in that municipality. Among other things, ordinances often include zoning rules, building codes, leash laws, parking restrictions, view and tree-cutting rules and often minor vehicle violations. Usually, you can get copies of local ordinances from city or county offices, and collected sets are commonly available at the public library.

If you do your research at a law library, you may have an opportunity to look up state laws in the annotated codes. In addition to the basic laws, these codes also list relevant court decisions (called "cases") interpreting each law. If you find a court case that seems to fit your situation, you may want to read it, and if it still seems relevant, point it out to the judge as part of your Small Claims presentation. (See Chapter 23, Section D, for an example of an appropriate written presentation.)

For a more thorough exploration of how to use the law library, see one or both of the following resources, which are available at most libraries:

• *Legal Research: How to Find and Understand the Law*, by Stephen Elias and Susan Levinkind (Nolo Press), an easy-to-read book that provides step-by-step instructions on how to find legal information.

• *Legal Research Made Easy*, a 2-1/2 hour video tape, hosted by Robert Berring, an experienced law librarian and legal research professor, that clearly explains what resources to use and how to go about efficiently researching a legal problem.

CHAPTER 2

Do You Have a Case?

Before you even start thinking about going to court—any court—you must answer a basic question: Do you have a good case? Before you can collect for a loss you have suffered, you must show that the other party is legally responsible for it. Put into legal slang, this means that you must show that there is "liability." Obvious, you say. Perhaps it is to you, but apparently not to lots of others.

Here is what often seems to happen. People focus on their own loss—the amount of money that they are out as a result of whatever incident occurred. They think that because they have been damaged, they must have a right of recovery against someone. But the fact that a loss has occurred isn't enough to make a winning case. You must state facts that indicate to the judge that the person you are suing should legally be held accountable.

If you have suffered monetary damage as a result of the conduct of someone else, and you feel that person was in the wrong, by all means pursue your case to court. But as you do, understand that the judge will be trying to see if what happened to you ("your loss") can be made to fit the requirements of one or another legal theory that justifies your recovery. The rest of this chapter constitutes a discussion of the theories most commonly used to do this. The point of my presenting these to you is not to give you a mini law school course, although at times I fear it may seem like one, but to give you an opportunity to think about how to best present the story of what happened to you in a way that will make it easy for the judge to rule in your favor.

Let's now look at the relevant legal theories, one by one, to see if you can make your loss fit at least one of them:

1. A valid contract (written, oral or implied) has been broken by the person you are suing and, as a result, you have suffered a monetary loss (see Section A below for more);

2. The negligent behavior of the person you are suing has caused you to suffer property damage resulting in a monetary loss (see Section B below for more);

3. The intentional behavior of the person you are suing has caused you to suffer property damage resulting in a monetary loss (see Section B below for more);

4. The negligent or intentional behavior of the person you are suing has caused you to suffer personal injury (see Section C below for more);

5. You were injured by a defective product and qualify for recovery under the doctrine of "strict liability" (see Section D below for more);

6. A written or implied warranty extended to you by a merchant has been breached and as a result, you have suffered a monetary loss (e.g., a new car suffers mechanical problems shortly after purchase). (See Section E below for more on this.)

7. A right created by statute has been violated and as a result, you have suffered a monetary loss. This would be the case if a consumer protection law was violated resulting in your being out some money (see Section F below for more).

Now, before we consider each of these legal theories individually, here is an example of why it's so important to establish not only that you have suffered a loss, but that someone is legally liable to make it good. One night someone entered the garage in the plaintiff's apartment complex, smashed her car window and stole a fancy AM-FM radio and tape deck worth $528. Upon discovery of the theft, the plaintiff (let's call her Sue) immediately got several witnesses to the fact that her car had been broken into. She took pictures and then called the police. After the police investigation was complete, Sue obtained a copy of their investigation report. She also got several estimates as to the cost of repairing the damage to the car window, the lowest of which was $157. Sue added the cost of the window to the value of the tape deck and filed suit in Small Claims Court against the building owner for $685.

Sue overlooked only one thing. Unfortunately for her, it was an important one. Under the circumstances the building owner wasn't liable. He had never promised (orally or in writing) to keep the garage locked, had never done so, had never led Sue to believe that he would do so, and indeed could point to requests from other tenants that the garage be kept open. All the tenants were reasonably on notice that it was easy to gain access to the garage either from inside or outside the building. Put simply, the building owner was neither in violation of a contract, nor guilty of any negligent behavior in failing to lock the garage. The situation facing Sue was no different than it would have been if her car had been damaged on the street.

Now let's take this same situation, but change a few facts. Instead of a situation where the door was always open and no one ever expected it to be closed, let's now assume that the lease contract signed by the landlord and tenant stated that the tenant would be assigned a parking place in a "secured garage." Let's also assume that the garage had always been locked until the lock broke seven days before the theft occurred. Finally, let's assume that Sue and other tenants had asked the owner to fix the lock the day after it broke, but that he hadn't "gotten around to it."

In this situation, Sue should win. The landlord made certain promises to the tenant (to keep the garage locked) and then failed to keep them in a situation where he had ample opportunity to do so. The failure presumably allowed the thief access to the car.

Note: In both fact situations above, the total amount of damage $685.50, was the same. But in the first, there was no right of recovery (the defendant wasn't liable), and in the second, the apartment owner's failure to keep the door locked violated the defendant's lease contract. In addition, the failure of the apartment owner to fix the lock within a reasonable time constituted negligence.

A. How to Approach a Breach of Contract Case

In broad outline, a contract is any agreement between parties where one person agrees to do something for the other in exchange for something in return. The agreement may be written, oral, or implied.[1] (An implied contract is one created by law so as to avoid injustice.)

---

[1]Generally speaking, contracts that can't be performed within a year must be in writing. The great majority of consumer-type contracts, however, can be performed in a year and therefore oral contracts are normally enforceable. Also, a person who lacks mental capacity cannot

Note: See Section E below for breach of warranty information, which is often based on a written or oral contract.

Example 1: "I promise to give you $750 on the first of January." This is not a contract because you have promised to do nothing for me in return. I have only indicated that I will give you a gift in the future. This sort of promise is not enforceable.[2]

Example 2: "I promise to pay you $750 on January 1 in exchange for your promise to shine my door knob every morning before 7 o'clock." This is a valid contract. If I refuse to pay you, you can go to court and get a judgment for the $750.

Example 3: I ask you if you want your house painted. You say "yes." I paint the house. You refuse to pay, claiming that since you never agreed on a price, there was no contract. You are wrong. A court will use the doctrine of "quantum meruit" (as much as is deserved for labor) to rule that when one person does work for another that the second person consents to (implied consent is often enough), a contract exists. In other words, the law will require that a person getting the benefit of work, where there is a reasonable expectation that such work should be paid for, is contractually obligated to pay for it.

Perhaps the largest number of cases coming before Small Claims Court involve the breach of a contract. Often the contract that has not been honored involves a failure to pay money. Hardly a day goes by when someone isn't sued for failing to pay the phone company, the milkman, the local hospital, or even book fines to the public library. But sometimes a breach of contract suit stems, not from failure to pay a bill, but because one party has performed his duties under the contract badly, or not at all, and the other person has been damaged as a result. Such might be the case if an apartment owner accepted a deposit and

---

make an enforceable contract and contracts made by minors can be cancelled (disaffirmed) under some circumstances.

[2]If the promise was based on an underlying loan—that is, "I promise to give you $750 on the first of January because you lent me that amount last year," it would be a valid contract.

agreed to rent an apartment to a tenant and then rented it to someone else.[3]

Damages resulting from a breach of contract are normally not difficult to prove. You must show that the contract existed; if it is written, the document should be presented to the court, and if it's oral or implied from the circumstances, the facts necessary to establish it should be stated. You must then testify as to the circumstances of the other person's breach of the contract and the amount of damages you have suffered. In many situations this involves no more than stating that a legitimate bill for X dollars has not been paid.

The fact that many contract cases are easy to win doesn't mean that all are won. I have seen a good number of plaintiffs lose what to them seemed to be open and shut cases. Why? Simply because they failed to show that the defendant owed them any money. Put another way: they failed to show either that a contract existed (see *Example 2* below) or that it was breached if it did exist (see *Example 1* below).

Example 1: Let's look at the facts of a situation that I witnessed recently in Small Claims Court in Oakland, California. Plaintiff sued defendant for $650, the cost of replacing a pigskin suede jacket that was ruined (it shrunk dramatically) by the defendant's cleaning establishment. Plaintiff had taken the jacket to defendant for cleaning and given him a $50 fee. Defendant, by accepting the jacket and the fee, clearly implied that he would properly clean the jacket. A contract existed.

Plaintiff was very sure of his loss. He stood in the courtroom, a great bear of a man, looking as if he had just escaped from a professional football team and slowly put the jacket on. As he wiggled into the coat, the whole courtroom, including the judge who almost choked trying to keep a straight face, burst out laughing. The sleeves barely came to the man's elbows and the coat itself didn't reach his waist. With a little luck the jacket would have fit a good-sized jockey.

---

[3]Leases and rental agreements, whether written or oral, are contracts. See footnote 5 below.

As I sat watching, I thought that the case was over and that the plaintiff had won easily. Certainly by putting on the jacket he had made his point more effectively than he could have with ten minutes of testimony. I was wrong. The plaintiff had overlooked two things, one obvious, and one not so obvious. By the time the defendant finished his presentation, the plaintiff's case had shrunk almost as much as the jacket.

THIS, YOUR HONOR WAS MY BEST JACKET PRIOR TO ITS VISIT TO ACME CLEANERS...

The obvious thing that the plaintiff overlooked in asking for the $650 replacement value of the jacket was that the jacket was eight months old and had been worn a good bit. Valuation is a common problem in clothing cases and we discuss it in detail in Chapters 4 and 21. Let's just say here that the jacket was worth no more than $400 in its used condition and that, in any situation where your property is damaged or destroyed, the amount of your recovery will be limited to the fair market value of the goods at the time the damage occurs—not their replacement value.

Now let's look at defendant's other defense. He testified that, when he saw the jacket after cleaning, he had been amazed. His cleaning shop specialized in leather goods and the cleaning process used should have resulted in no such shrinking problem.

What's more, he testified that he had examined a number of other leather goods in the same cleaning batch and found no shrinking problem with any of them. To find out what happened, he sent the jacket to an "independent testing laboratory." Their report, which he presented to the court, stated that the problem was not in the cleaning, but in the jacket. It was poorly made in that the leather had been severely overstretched prior to assembly. When it had been placed in the cleaning fluid, it had shrunk as a result of this poor original workmanship.

What happened? The judge was convinced by the testing lab report and felt that defendant had breached no contract as far as the cleaning was concerned.[4] However, the judge also felt that the defendant, as a leather cleaning specialist, had some responsibility to notify plaintiff that the jacket should not have been cleaned in the first place. Therefore, the judge held mostly for the defendant, but did award the plaintiff $100 in damages.

Example 2: A few weeks later I saw another contract case where the plaintiff had suffered an obvious loss, but failed to show that the defendant was responsible for making it good. This time it was a landlord suing the parent of a tenant for damages that the tenant had caused to her apartment. The parent was sued because he had co-signed his daughter's lease. The plaintiff easily convinced the judge that the damage had, in fact, occurred and the judge seemed disposed toward giving judgment for the $580 requested until the parent presented his defense. He showed that the lease between his daughter and the landlord had been rewritten three times after he originally co-signed the agreement without his again adding his signature and that the changes, which included the replacement of several of his daughter's original roommates with others, were significant.

---

[4]Plaintiff could bring suit against the person who made the jacket for defective workmanship. It could be argued that, by using inferior material, they had breached an implied warranty (contract) that the goods sold were reasonably fit for the purpose they were designed to fulfill. Warranty actions must, however, be filed promptly (see Section E below).

He claimed that, because he had not co-signed any of the subsequent leases, he wasn't liable. The judge agreed.[5]

Note: We will go further into individual fact situations that commonly arise in the area of contracts in Chapters 16-21. You will want to read these chapters before you decide whether or not you have a good case. Also, if your breach of contract situation involves fraud or undue influence committed by the other party, or you received little or nothing for your money through the direct fault of the seller, you may have a right to have the contract ended (rescinded) and get your money or goods back. I discuss this "recission" remedy in Chapter 4, under the section entitled "Equitable Relief."

Equitable relief and actions for fraud, however, are not available in every state, so read Chapter 4 and the Appendix to this book before deciding to pursue them.

---

[5]Leases, rental agreements, and the rights and responsibilities of co-signers are discussed in more detail in Moskovitz & Warner, *California Tenants' Rights,* (Nolo Press). While this book relates specifically to California, it contains much general information of value in all states.

B. How to Approach a Case Where Your Property Has Been Damaged By the Negligent or Intentional Acts of Someone Else

After cases involving breach of contract, the most common disputes that come to Small Claims Court involve damage to one person's property caused by the negligent actions of another. Less often, the plaintiff claims that he suffered loss because the defendant intended to damage his belongings.

A technical definition of what constitutes negligence could easily fill the next few pages. Indeed, whole law texts have been written on the subject. I remember thinking in law school that the more scholarly professors wrote about the subject of negligence, the more mixed up they got. Like good taste or bad wine, negligence seems to be easy to recognize, but hard to define.

Despite the problems involved, let me try and give you a one-sentence definition: If, as a result of another person's conduct, your property is injured and that person didn't act with reasonable care in the circumstances, you have a case based on his or her negligence.[6] It's as simple—or complex—as that. If you want to get into the gory details of the subject, go to your nearest law library and get any recent legal text on "Torts." "Torts" are wrongful acts or injuries.

Example: Jake knows the brakes on his ancient Saab are in serious need of repair, but does nothing about it. One night when the car is parked on a hill, the brakes fail and the car rolls across the street and destroys Keija's persimmon tree. Keija sues Jake for $125, which is the reasonable value of the tree. Jake would lose because he did not act with reasonable care under the circumstance.

Another obvious situation involving negligence would be one where a car or bus swerves into your driving lane and side-swipes your fender. The driver of the offending vehicle has a duty to operate it in such a way as to not harm you. By swerving into your lane, it is extremely likely that he has failed to do so. A situation where negligence could be difficult to show, however, might involve your neighbor's tree that falls on a car parked in your driveway. Here you have to be ready to prove that for some reason (age, disease, an obviously bad root system, etc.) the tree was in a weakened condition, and the neighbor was negligent in failing to do something about it. If the tree had looked to be in good health, you would have a tough time proving that your neighbor was negligent in not cutting it down or propping it up.

Another situation which you should keep in mind is that of "compound negligence," that is, where more than one person is responsible for the damages you suffer.

Example: Sandy comes home from work one day to find Fred and his '72 Mustang in the middle of her front lawn and her new fence knocked over. Fred admits his car knocked over the fence. Simple case against Fred? Maybe not.

---

[6]Sometimes negligence can occur when a person who has a duty or responsibility to act fails to do so. For example, a car mechanic who fails to check your brakes after you tell him they have been working poorly and he promises to do so would be negligent.

What if Fred had just picked up his car from Atomic Auto Repair where he had had his brakes worked on and they failed when he attempted to stop across from Sandy's house? Fred's liability may range from minimal (Atomic is only 50 feet away; he just left the shop and they assured him the brakes were fixed) to extensive (Atomic is across town and at the last two stop signs, Fred's brakes acted "funny" but he continued to drive anyway).

Or, what if Fred's brakes are fine, but he claims he was rear-ended at the stop sign by Dana and shoved into Sandy's fence? Again, Fred's liability may be minimal (Dana was drunk and speeding) or it may be extensive (Fred ran a stop sign while turning and was rear-ended by Dana who had the right of way.) In any event, remember to sue both parties (Fred and Atomic or Fred and Dana) and let them fight it out.

There is no fool-proof way to determine in advance if someone is or is not negligent. It's often a close question—a matter of judgment. If you are in doubt, bring your case and let the judge decide. After all, he or she gets paid (by you, the taxpayer) to do it.

Here are a couple of questions which may help you make a decision as to whether you have a good case based on someone else's negligence.

• Did the person whose act (or failure to act) injured you behave in a reasonable way? Or to put it another way, would you have behaved differently if you were in her shoes?

• How much did your conduct contribute to causing the injury?

If you believe that the person who caused you to suffer a monetary loss behaved in an unreasonable way (ran a red light when drunk) and that you were acting sensibly (driving at 30 mph in the proper lane), you probably have a good case. If you were a little at fault (slightly negligent), but the other fellow was much more at fault (very negligent), you can still recover in California, New Jersey, New York, Wisconsin, and most other states. If a judge finds that one person (drunk and speeding) was 80 percent at fault, and that the other (slightly inattentive) was 20 percent at fault, the slightly inattentive party can recover 80 percent of her loss.[7]

A situation slightly less common, but often involving injury to your personal property is where your property has been intentionally damaged by someone.

Example: Basil and Shirley are neighbors who can't stand the sight of each other. Both, however, are champion tulip growers and this year Basil took first, second and third place in the local garden club contest for his exotic tulips. Shirley, angry, frustrated and jealous, destroys all of Basil's tulips. Basil should be able to recover the value of his tulips from Shirley and possibly "punitive" (meant to punish) damages.

Punitive damages are related to both the amount of harm done and the worth of the defendant. (Because they are meant to punish, a $50 fine against a millionaire would be meaningless; but don't expect a lot of money just because someone is rich. The punitive damage award must bear a relation to your injury and must not make your total award exceed the Small Claims dollar limit.)

Punitive damages are more common in formal courts because they can often amount to a great deal of money. But if you have been intentionally damaged by someone and the amount you're asking for is less than the limit for your Small Claims Court, mention punitive damages to the judge. If the defendant acted maliciously and you're able to show it, the judge may be inclined to grant your request. (Do keep in mind, however, that a few states prohibit giving punitive damages in Small Claims Court, so check your local rules and the Appendix.)

---

[7]This system of allowing recovery even if the injured party was himself negligent is called "comparative negligence." Certain states have modified this theory somewhat; some, for example, only allow a negligent party to recover if she was less than 50 percent negligent. See Chapter 3 of Heft and Heft, *Comparative Negligence Manual* (Callaghan). The comparative negligence scheme replaces the old "contributory negligence" doctrine, which barred any recovery by anyone who was the least bit negligent. Some states still use contributory negligence. You can check your local law library to find out which system your state uses.

C. How to Approach a Personal Injury (and Mental Distress) Case

The considerations here are much the same as outlined in Section B just above. You must show not only that you were injured but that someone's intentional or negligent behavior caused your injury, unless your case qualifies as one where the law applies the doctrine of strict liability (see Section D below). Most personal injury cases involve amounts of money which are clearly over the Small Claims maximum and should therefore be pursued in formal courts, but occasionally a minor personal injury case will be appropriate for Small Claims.

Example 1: Keija and Soto are playing softball in a picnic area of a park, where many families are picnicking in the sun. Soto, never a star fielder, misses a batted ball which hits seven year old Willie in the face (as he's eating some potato salad) and chips his tooth. As Willie was in a picnic area where he had a right to be, we can safely assume that Keija and Soto were negligent. Why? Because as a society, we have decided that picnic areas are for picnickers, and if your actions aren't designed for the picnic area and you hurt someone, you're going to have to pay.

Example 2: Now assume that Keija and Soto wandered over to the softball field for their game of bat and catch. Their skills still haven't improved and Soto again misses. The ball again hits Willie, who had escaped his parents and had wandered onto the field unobserved. Are Keija and Soto liable? Probably not. Keija and Soto took reasonable precautions to avoid hitting picnickers by playing on the ballfield. They have a much less duty of care to people who wander into the middle of their game on the ball field.

Suggestion: Before you sue someone for a personal injury (or for property damage), think not only about your loss, but whether the other party acted reasonably under the circumstances. In other words, were they negligent? If they were not, you have no right to recover, no matter what your injury, unless your situation qualifies under Section D, below. If in doubt, go ahead and sue, but be prepared to deal with the liability question, as well as simply showing the extent of your injury. In later chapters I will give you some practical advice as to how to prove your case.

Mental Distress Note: As discussed further in Chapter 4, you do not have to suffer a physical injury to successfully recover in court as a result of someone else's negligent or intentionally obnoxious behavior. Invasion of privacy and the intentional infliction of mental distress are but two of the types of lawsuits that can be based on non-physical injuries. For example, if your landlord enters your apartment without permission several times and you request that she cease doing so, but she persists, causing you to become genuinely upset and anxious, you have a good case. Obviously, not every instance of obnoxious behavior that makes you mad qualifies as being serious enough to bring a successful lawsuit. Generally, to recover, the other person's actions must:

- Be truly obnoxious;

- Violate a state law or local ordinance (such as noise);

- Continue after you have asked the person to stop (it's best to do this in writing and to do it more than once).

In addition, you must be able to convince a judge that you have genuinely suffered mental distress as a result of the other person's conduct. (Therapy bills or loss of weight would be evidence to present to the judge, if that were your situation.)

D. How to Approach a Case When You are Injured By a Defective Product (Doctrine of Strict Liability)

There is a legal concept called "strict liability." When this doctrine applies, there is no need to prove negligence. It's enough that an injury occurred as a result of something going wrong with the defendant's product or activity. This concept is traditionally applied to such things as nuclear reactors, munitions storage, people who keep wild and inherently dangerous animals (a cheetah in the city) and other extremely hazardous activities.

Strict liability also applies in the situation of a defective product. (This is generally referred to as "products liability.")[8] Here, your vacuum cleaner, hair dryer, steam iron, lawnmower, car, etc. malfunctions and you get hurt. As an injured person, you are entitled to recover from the manufacturer or other strictly liable defendant (usually the person you bought or rented the product from) without having to prove negligence. Of course, most product liability cases will end up in formal courts, but now and then a defect in a product will cause an injury small enough that the damage caused falls within the Small Claims Court maximum.

---

[8]Efforts are being made nationwide to expand the application of strict liability. In California, for example, strict liability has been held to apply to a landlord's responsibility for injury-causing defects in rented property. There, a landlord is held to a strict duty of care toward tenants when a defective condition which existed at the time the tenant moved in caused the injury (e.g., a tenant slips in the shower and is injured when she cuts herself on a non-shatter resistant glass door). This is true even though the landlord didn't know about the condition that caused the defect.

E. How to Approach a Breach of Warranty Case

First you need to understand that warranty law is extremely confusing, even to lawyers. A principal reason for this is that, in every state, at least two separate and distinct warranty laws can apply to the retail sale of goods.[9] The sad result is that, short of presenting you with a major treatise, it's impossible to thoroughly explain warranty law. The best I can do in the short space I have here is to give you several general rules of thumb.

Note: I discuss warranties as they apply to new and used car transactions in Chapter 17.

1. If a new or used product comes with a written warranty, you have the right to rely on it.

2. If a seller makes written or oral statements describing a product's features (e.g., "these tires will last at least 25,000 miles") or what it will do, and you rely on these statements as part of your decision to purchase the product, these statements constitute an express warranty that you have a right to rely on. This is true even though the written warranty states there are no other warranties.

3. In most situations an implied warranty of general fitness for the intended use or "merchantability" is also present (e.g., that a lawnmower will cut grass, a tire will hold air, a calculator will subtract, etc.). This warranty exists in addition to the written and express warranties discussed just above and applies even though there is a statement (often called a "warranty disclaimer") saying no warranties exist beyond the written warranty, or that no warranty exists at all, or that all implied warranties are specifically disclaimed.

---

[9]The Magnuson-Moss Consumer Warranty Act (15 USC 2302) is a federal law which applies in every state. In addition, every state has adopted a "commercial code" which includes other protections for consumers. Some states have enacted separate consumer protection laws which go beyond the Magnuson-Moss Act and the "Commercial Code." For example, California has the Song-Beverly Credit Card Act (Civil Code Secs. 1747-1748.5).

4. If a warranty is breached (e.g., a TV set with a six-month warranty on parts and labor breaks the day after purchase), you should notify the seller and manufacturer in writing, keeping a copy of your letter. Give them a reasonable chance to make necessary repairs or replace the defective product. Thirty days to accomplish this is usually considered to be reasonable. If they don't, it's time to think about filing in Small Claims.

5. In considering whether and how to pursue a breach of warranty case, realize that Small Claims Court judges usually consider this type of dispute based on a broad view of fairness. In other words, if you purchase goods that are clearly defective, or do not accomplish the task they were represented by the seller to handle (either in an advertisement or a personal statement to you), and you have made and documented a good faith effort to have the seller or manufacturer either fix or replace the goods or refund your money, file in Small Claims Court and let the judge worry about the details of warranty law.

Example: Alan purchases a computer and some expensive accounting software from ABC Computer. He explains his bookkeeping needs to the salesperson in detail and is assured that the computer and software will do the job. The computer contains a written warranty against defects in parts and labor for 90 days. The warranty statement says that all implied warranties are disclaimed. The software contains no written warranty statement. It is apparent to Alan after a couple of days work that the software simply is not sophisticated enough to meet the book-keeping needs he had explained to the salesperson and that the salesperson didn't know what he was talking about when he said it was "perfect for the job."

Two days later the computer breaks. Alan calls ABC and asks for the computer to be fixed or replaced and for his money back on the software. As to the computer, Alan should have no problem—it broke within the written warranty period. The software raises a different problem. In asking for his money back Alan can claim a breach of an express warranty (the salesperson's statement that it would meet his needs), and the implied warranty of general fitness or merchantability (it simply doesn't meet the reasonable standard of accounting packages). This latter

claim would be hard to prove, however, if the software is
adequate to accomplish more routine accounting tasks, just not
sophisticated enough for Alan's special needs. If the seller won't
make good and Alan prepares to go to court, he should give
considerable thought to how he can prove that he relied on the
salesperson's statements that the software would meet his
specific bookkeeping needs as part of his decision to purchase it.
If he had given the salesperson written specifications as to his
accounting needs and had a copy, or if he had a witness to the
salesperson's grandiose promises, he would be in good shape.
Otherwise, it might come down to his word against the
salesperson's.

F. How to Approach a Case When Your Rights Under State Law Have Been Breached

There are thousands of laws which purport to protect
consumers. Everything from the construction of home swimming
pools, to regulation of retail sales, to the moving of household
goods, to the types of contracts that you can be offered by a
health studio are covered. These laws are too extensive to outline
here; however, you should be aware that they exist.

One of the most common consumer complaints (for which specific laws exist providing remedies for consumers) is false or deceptive advertising. In general, these laws provide that private parties may recover the money they spent for goods or services advertised falsely. The point is simple: if you believe that the person you have a claim against has violated a state law and that this violation is directly related to the monetary damage you have suffered, call the judge's attention to the law in question as part of your oral presentation in Small Claims Court.

Here is an example specific to California, but which may be generalized for any state.

Example: Steve E. of San Francisco, California purchased a set of cookware from a very persuasive door-to-door salesperson. That afternoon he checked at a discount store and found a very similar cookware set for half the price. Realizing that he had been talked into a bad deal, Steve wondered if he had any rights to cancel the door-to-door purchase. On the way home he stopped at a local law library and looked up door-to-door sales in the index to the West California Codes.[10] He found nothing. Being a persistent sort, Steve next looked up the word home. Sure enough, he found an entry for "Home Solicitation Contracts," and under that a subheading for "Cancellations." He was referred to Section 1689.6 of the California Civil Code. Looking up this section, Steve read that, "the buyer has the right to cancel a home solicitation contract or offer until midnight of the third business day after the day on which the buyer signs an agreement or offer to purchase." Steve immediately wrote a letter cancelling his contract and asking the sales company to refund his money and pick up the cookware. When it refused, Steve filed an action in Small Claims Court, pointed the statute out to the judge, and walked away with a judgment for the amount of the purchase.

---

[10]Your local law library will probably be located in the building which houses the county courthouse. Ask a librarian to point you to your state codes or statutes, which will contain a fairly extensive index. Be creative and exhaustive in looking through the index. Remember that it was put together by people with legal training and may not seem logical to you.

In addition to the specific consumer protection rights embedded in literally thousands of state laws, there are several general legal rules you should know about. One of the most important of these deals with fraud. Generally speaking, if fraud is present as part of a transaction (contract, sale, etc.), the deal can be cancelled. Fraud can take the form of intentional misrepresentation; negligent misrepresentation (a positive assertion without adequate information that it is true); fraudulent concealment (suppression of what is true); a false promise (a promise with no intention to perform); or any other act designed to deceive. If you think you have been defrauded, make sure the judge knows about your claim. The judge has the power to "rescind" the sale or other contract that forms the basis of the fraudulent conduct and order that your money be refunded, along with any damages you have suffered as a result of the fraud.[11]

G. Stating Your Claim on Your Court Papers

Before you get too far into theories of law, let me bring you back to earth. While it is helpful to have a good grasp of what's involved in proving a contract or other type of negligence case (the judge, after all, is a lawyer), it is more important that you stay grounded on the facts of your grievance. One of the joys of Small Claims Court is that you don't plead theories of law—you

---

[11]Keep in mind, however, the note in this chapter at the end of Section A. Not all Small Claims Courts will allow actions for fraud or requests to rescind contracts.

state facts. So, even if you are not sure that what happened to you fully matches one of the legal theories discussed here, bring your case anyway if you have suffered real monetary damage and you believe the person you are suing caused that damage.

Let's jump ahead and take a look at the form you will fill out when you file your case. Turn to Chapter 10 and find the form entitled "Plaintiff's Statement." Look at Line 5. As you can see, there is little space for theory. Indeed, there is barely room to set down the facts of your dispute. You should state your case like this:

"I took my coat to John's Dry Cleaners and it was returned in a damaged (shrunken) condition."

"Defendant's dog bit me on the corner of Rose and Peach Streets in Dover, Pennsylvania."

"The car repairs that Joe's Garage did on my car were done wrong, resulting in my engine burning."

"Defendant refused to return the cleaning deposit for my apartment even though I left it clean."

Note: When you state your case on the court papers, your only goal is to notify the other party and the court as to the broad outline of your dispute. You don't want to try to argue the facts of your case or the law that you believe applies to it. Your chance to do this will come later in court.

Important: Now is a good time to start organizing your materials in one place. Get a couple of manila envelopes or file folders, label them carefully, and find a safe place for storage. One folder or envelope should be used to store all documentary evidence such as receipts, letters, photographs, etc. The other is for your court papers, filing fee receipts, etc. It's no secret that more than one case has been won or lost because of good (or bad) record keeping.

CHAPTER 3

Can You Recover
If You Win?

This is the shortest chapter and the most important. In it, I ask all of you who are thinking of filing a Small Claims suit to focus on a very simple question—can you collect if you win? Collecting from many individuals or businesses isn't a problem as they are solvent and will routinely pay any judgments entered against them. But all too often, the main problem you face in Small Claims Court is not winning your case, but collecting your money when you do.

Nolo Press publishes *Money Troubles: Legal Strategies to Cope with Your Debts,* which contains information for Californians who are over their heads in legal debts and don't know how they are going to keep the roof over their heads and clothes on their kids' backs. The message of the book is that, surprisingly, there are many ways for a debtor to protect himself. A creditor can't legally take the food from the debtor's table, or the TV from his living room, or even (in many cases) the car from his driveway.[1]

What do these facts mean to you? Simply that many people who are not completely without money are nevertheless "judgment proof." You can sue and get judgments against them until red cows dance on the yellow moon, but you can't collect a dime. Unfortunately, just this sort of frustrating thing happens ever day—people go to lots of trouble to win cases only to realize that the judgment is uncollectible. This, of course, compounds the misery. Not only has the person suing lost the money from the original debt or injury, but also the time, trouble and expense of the Small Claims suit. As my grandmother used to say, "no one ever got to live in the big house on the hill by throwing a good quarter after a bad dime."

Whenever a dispute develops, it is all too easy to get caught up in thinking and arguing about who was wrong—so easy that perspective is lost and the problems of collection are forgotten. I emphasize this because I have so often observed people bringing cases to court in which there was never a hope of collecting. How can I tell ahead of time? I can't always, but in many situations, it's not hard. One thing I look for is whether or not the defendant is working. If a person fails to voluntarily pay a judgment, the easiest way to collect it is to garnish his wages.[2] Thus, if the person sued is working, there is an excellent chance of collecting if payment is not made voluntarily. But you can't garnish a welfare, social security, unemployment, pension or

---

[1] In most states, a debtor's motor vehicles are protected, at least to some extent. It is common to allow between $1,000 to $2,500 in equity to be exempt depending on state law. If the debtor uses the vehicle as a tool of his trade, the car is completely exempt from attachment in some states, while in others the exempt amount is higher.

[2] If a person has a very low income, the amount you can recover can be considerably less than 25%. Wage garnishments are not allowed in Texas. Some other states make it difficult to garnish wages of a head of family in a situation where the family has a low income and needs all of its income to survive. A few states, such as New York, limit garnishments to 10% of a person's wages. The sheriff or marshal can supply you with rules.

disability check. So, if the person sued gets his income from one of these sources, red flags should be flying.

But what about other assets? Can't a judgment be collected from sources other than wages? Yes, it can—bank accounts, securities, motor vehicles and real estate are other common collection sources. But remember, as stated above, many types of property are exempt from attachment.In New York, for example among a long list of exemptions, we find "all stoves kept for use in the judgment debtor's dwelling house," a "pew occupied by the judgment debtor in a place of public worship" and a TV set. Many states say that a portion, or all, of the equity in a debtor's home is exempt. In California, a creditor can't effectively get at the equity in a family house unless it exceeds $50,000 ($100,000 if owner is disabled or over 65): In Arizona, the amount is $100,000 and in Massachusetts it's $100,000 ($150,000 if over 65 or disabled).

So before you file your papers, ask yourself these questions:

1. Does the person you wish to sue voluntarily pay debts—or are you dealing with a person who will make it as difficult as possible to collect if you win?

2. Does he have a job or is he likely to get one?[3]

3. If this person doesn't have a job, does she have some other means of support or assets that convince you that you can collect?

4. If you have your doubts about voluntary payment and the person you are suing doesn't have a job, can you identify some non-exempt assets that you can attach, such as a bank account, or real property other than the place where the person lives?

5. If a business is involved, is it solvent and does it have a good reputation for paying debts?

---

[3]In many states you will have the right to collect a judgment for a number of years after it was entered (and often may renew this right). It's common to allow collection up to ten years after the judgment was entered. You are also entitled the collect interest as long as the debt is not paid.

6. Is the person or business you wish to sue living or doing business outside of your state? In some states, you may not be able to get a Small Claims judgment against out-of-staters unless they are present or actively do business in your state.

Note: If a person or a business declares a straight bankruptcy under Chapter 7 and lists you as a creditor, your right to recover is cut off. If you are owed money on a secured debt (there was a security agreement as in the case of a car or major appliance), you are entitled to recover your security. If the judgment was obtained because you or your property was injured by the malicious behavior of the person declaring bankruptcy (e.g., they hit you when drunk), your right to collect is not cut off.

In Chapter 24, we deal in detail with the mechanics of collecting after you get your judgment. If you think that collection may pose a problem, read this chapter now. But remember what my canny old grandmother said about bad dimes and good quarters and don't waste your time chasing people who have no money.

CHAPTER 4

How Much Can You Sue For?

The maximum amount for which you can sue in Small Claims Court varies from state to state. It's $1,500 in Arizona, $1,500 in Kentucky, $1,750 in Michigan, $2,000 in New York and $2,500 in Oregon. As suggested in Chapter 1, to get a copy of the rules that affect you, call your local Small Claims Court clerk. With some exceptions, Small Claims Court does not hear cases unless they are for money damages. Thus, you can't use Small Claims Court to get a divorce, stop ("enjoin") the city from cutting down your favorite oak tree, change your name, or do any of the thousands of other things that require some solution other than the payment of money.[1]

Note: California, Alabama, North Dakota, and a number of other states, allow the judge to grant equitable relief in the form

---

[1] In a number of states, you can use Small Claims Court to handle certain types of evictions. See Chapter 20 and the Appendix.

of rescission, restitution, reformation, and specific performance
instead of, or in addition to, money damages. See "Equitable
Relief" in this chapter for details.

A. Cutting Down a Claim That's Over the Limit to Fit Into Small Claims Court

It is legal to reduce an excessive claim so that it will fit into
Small Claims Court. Thus, you could take a $2,100 debt in New
Jersey (where the dollar limit is $1,500) and bring it into Small
Claims Court, claiming only $1,500.[2] But if you do this, you
forever waive the $600 difference between $1,500 and $2,100. In
legal parlance, this is called "waiving the excess." Why might you
want to do this? Because the alternative to Small Claims Court
involves filing your suit in a formal court with dozens of complicated rules and the considerable expense involved in having a
lawyer fill out the papers, etc. A lawyer would probably charge
considerably more than $600 to represent you. It is possible to
represent yourself in formal court, but doing so requires a good
bit of homework and the guts to walk into an unfamiliar and
sometimes hostile arena. Law libraries exist in most major courthouses and are open to the public. Law librarians are usually
very helpful in assisting you to find materials. However, neither
the librarians nor the court clerks will help you decipher the
numerous confusing procedural rules that you must follow in
the "formal" courts.

I don't mean to discourage you. Lots of people have successfully handled their cases in our formal courts, but you should be
aware before you start that your path may be lonely and frustrating. If you wish to take your case to a formal court yourself,
you might start by looking at the legal form books which are

---

[2]Costs, such as filing fees, service of process, fees where witnesses are
subpoenaed, etc., are recoverable in addition to the dollar limit in most
states.

available for most states. These encyclopedia-like books show you
how to prepare most necessary paperwork. For help in finding
your way around the law library, and interpreting what you find
there, I recommend you obtain a copy of *Legal Research: How to
Find and Understand the Law*, Elias & Levinkind (Nolo Press).

B. Splitting Small Claims Court Cases

It is not legal to split an over-the-limit claim into two or more
pieces to fit each into Small Claims Court. Taking the $2,100
figure we used above, this means that you couldn't sue the same
person separately for $1,200 and $900.[3] As with most rules, however, a little creative thought will take you a long way. While you
can't split a case that's too big to fit it into Small Claims Court,
you can bring multiple suits against the same person as long as
they are based on different claims. This is where the creativity
comes in. There is often a large gray area in which it is genuinely
difficult to differentiate between one divided claim and several
independent ones. If you can reasonably argue that a $2,100 case
actually involves two or more separate contracts, or injuries to
your person or property, you may as well try dividing it. The
worst that will happen is that a judge will disagree and tell you to
make a choice between taking the entire claim to a formal court,
or waiving any claim for money in excess of the dollar limit and
staying in Small Claims.

---

[3]Defendant's claims that are over the Small Claims limit are discussed
in Chapters 10 and 12.

Example 1: Recently I watched a man in the private telephone business come into Small Claims Court with three separate lawsuits against the same defendant for a combined total of $2,000 in a state where the Small Claims Court maximum is $1,000. One claim, he said, was for failure to pay for phone installation, another was for failure to pay for phone maintenance, and the third was for failure to pay for moving several phones to a different location. The man claimed that each suit was based on the breach of a separate contract. The judge, after asking a few questions, told the man that he was on the borderline between one divided (no good) and several separate (okay) claims, but decided to give him the benefit of the doubt and allowed him to present each case. The man won all three and got two judgments for $700 and a third for $600.

Example 2: Another morning in the same state, a woman alleged that she had lent a business acquaintance $1,000 twice and was therefore bringing two separate suits, each for $1,000. The defendant said that this wasn't true. She claimed that she had borrowed $2,000 to be repaid in two installments. A different judge, after listening to each person briefly, told the plaintiff that only one claim was involved and that, if she didn't want to waive all money over $1,000, she should go to formal court.

Suggestion: If you wish to sue someone on two related claims, which you believe can be viewed as separate, you may be better off to file your actions a few days apart. This will result in their being heard on different days, and in most metropolitan areas, by different judges. Unless the defendant shows up and argues that you have split one claim, you will likely get your judgments without difficulty. There is, however, one possible drawback to this approach. If you bring your claims to court on the same day and the judge rules that they are one claim, he will normally give you a choice as to whether to waive the excess over the Small Claims maximum in your state, or go to a formal court. However, if you go to court on different days and the question of split claims is raised on the second or third day, you may have a problem. If the judge decides that your action in splitting the claims was improper, he may throw the second and third claims out of court with no opportunity to refile in a formal court. This is because you have already sued and won, and you are not entitled to sue the same person twice for the same claim.

C. How to Compute the Exact Amount of Your Claim

Sometimes it's easy to understand exactly what dollar amount to sue for, but it's often tricky. Before we get to the tricky part, let's go over the basic rule. When in doubt, always bring your suit a little on the high side. Why? Because the court has the power to award you less than you request, but can't give you more, even if the judge feels that you are entitled to it. But don't go overboard—if you sue for $1,500 on a $500 claim, you are likely to spur your opponent to furious opposition, ruin any chance for an out-of-court compromise, and lose the respect of the judge.

1. Computing the Exact Amount
   —Contract Cases

To arrive at the exact figure to sue on in contract cases, compute the difference between the amount you were supposed to receive under the contract and what you actually received. For example, if Jeannie Goodday agrees to pay Homer Brightspot $1,200 to paint her house to look like a rainbow, but then only gives him $800, Homer has a claim for $400 plus the cost of filing suit and serving Jeannie with the papers (costs are discussed in more detail in Chapter 15). The fact that Jeannie and Homer made their agreement orally does not bar Homer from suing. Oral contracts are generally legal as long as they can be carried out in a year. Of course, people tend to remember oral contracts differently and this can lead to serious proof problems once you get to court. It is always wise to reduce agreements to writing, even if only to a note or letter agreement dated and signed by both parties.[4]

Where the contract involves lending money in exchange for interest, don't forget to include the interest due in the amount for which you sue.[5] I have seen several disappointed people sue for the exact amount of the debt (say $500) and not include interest (say $50), thinking that they could have the judge add the

---

[4]Many useful consumer-oriented agreements, including one for home repair and maintenance situations, can be found in *Simple Contracts for Personal Use*, Elias & Stewart (Nolo Press).

[5]As a general rule, you can only recover interest when it is called for in a written or oral contract. If you loaned a friend $100, but never mentioned interest, you can sue only for the return of the $100.

interest when they got to court. This can't normally be done—the judge doesn't have the power to make an award larger than the amount you request.[6] Of course, you can't sue for interest if the interest amount would make your claim larger than the Small Claims maximum.[7]

Unfortunately, not all claims based on breach of contract are easy to reduce to a money amount. This is often due to a legal doctrine known as "mitigation of damages." Don't let the fancy term throw you. As with so much of our law, the concept behind the "mumbo jumbo" is simple. "Mitigation of damages" means simply that the person bringing suit for breach of contract must himself take all reasonable steps to limit the amount of damages he suffers. Let's take an example from the landlord-tenant field. Tillie the tenant moves out three months before the end of her lease (remember a lease is a contract). Her monthly rent is $350. Can Lothar the landlord recover the full $1,050 ($350 x 3 months) from Tillie in Small Claims Court, assuming that the Small Claims Court limit in the state in which Tillie and Lothar live is at least that high? Probably not. Why? Because Lothar has control of the empty apartment and must take reasonable steps to attempt to find a new tenant. If Lothar can rerent the apartment to someone else for $350 or more per month, he has suffered no damage. Put another way, if Lothar rerents the apartment, he has fulfilled his responsibility to "mitigate damages." In a typical situation, it might take Lothar several weeks (unless he had plenty of advance notice, or Tillie herself found a new tenant) to find a suitable new tenant. If it took three weeks and $25 worth of newspaper ads, Lothar could recover approximately $300 from Tillie.

---

[6] If you find yourself in court and realize you have asked for too little, you should request that the judge allow you to amend your claim. Some judges will do this and offer the defendant a continuance to deal with defending against the higher amount if they wish it.

[7] This is the general rule. In some states, you may collect interest in situations where your underlying claim equals the Small Claims maximum and the interest brings the total over the maximum. Check your local rules.

The "mitigation of damages" concept isn't applicable only to landlord-tenant situations, but applies to every contract case in which the person damaged can take reasonable steps to protect himself. In the earlier example, if Jeannie Goodday had agreed to pay Homer Brightspot $100 per day for seven days to paint her house and then had canceled after the first day, Homer could sue her for the remaining $600, but, if he did, he would surely be asked whether he had earned any other money during the six days. If he had, it would be subtracted from the $600. But what if Homer refused other work and slept in his hammock all week? If Jeannie could show that he had turned down other jobs, or had refused to make reasonable efforts to seek available work, this too would be used to reduce Homer's recovery.

Suggestion: Sue only for the amount of money you are out. Don't try to collect money in court that you have already recovered from someone else.

2. Computing the Exact Amount —Property Damage Cases

When your property has been damaged by the negligent or intentional act of someone else, you have a right to recover for your loss.[8] This amount is often, but not always, the amount of money that it would take to fix the damaged item.

Example: John Quickstop bashes into Melissa Caretaker's new Dodge, smashing in the left rear. How much can Melissa recover? The amount that it would cost to fix, or, if necessary, replace the damaged part of her car. Melissa should get several estimates from responsible body and fender shops and sue for the amount of the lowest one if John won't pay voluntarily (see Chapter 19).

There is, however, a big exception to the rule that a person who has had property damaged can recover the cost of fixing the damaged item. This occurs when the cost to fix the item exceeds its actual cash market value. You are not entitled to a new or better object—only to have your loss made good. Had Melissa Caretaker been driving a 1971 Dodge, the cost to fix the fender might well have exceeded the value of the car. If this was the case, she would be entitled to the value of the car, not the value of the fender repair.

Think of it this way. In any situation where the value of the repair exceeds the value of the object, you are limited to the fair market value of the object (the amount you could have sold it for) a minute before the damage occurred. From this figure, you have to subtract the value, if any, of the object after the injury. Of course, in deciding how much to claim, you should give yourself the benefit of the doubt as to how much a piece of property is worth, but don't be ridiculous. A $300 motor scooter might conceivably be worth $450 to $500, but it's not worth $750.

Example: Let's return to Melissa. If her 1971 Dodge was worth $700 and the fender would cost $800 to replace, she would be limited to a $700 recovery, less what the car could be sold for in its damaged state. If this was $50 for scrap, she would be entitled to $650. However, if Melissa had just gotten a new engine and transmission and her car was worth $1,200, she would legally be

---

[8]If you haven't already done so, read Chapter 2. It is important to remember that you not only have to establish the amount of your loss, but that the person you are suing is legally responsible ("liable") to pay your damages.

entitled to recover and sue for the entire $800 needed to get her Dodge fixed.

Note: Many people insist on believing that they can recover the cost of getting a replacement object when theirs has been totaled. As you should now understand, this isn't necessarily true. If Melissa's $700 car was totaled and she claimed that she simply couldn't get another decent car for less than $1,500, she would still be limited to recovering $700. To get $1,500, she would have to show that her car had a sale value of that much just before the accident. This rule can cause you a real hardship when an older object that is in great shape is destroyed. The fair market value may be low, while the cost of replacement high.

Knowing what something is worth and proving it are quite different. A car that you are sure is worth $1,800 may look like it's only worth $1,200 to someone else. In court, you will want to be prepared to show that your piece of property is worth every bit of the $1,800. The best way to do this is to get some estimates (opinions) from experts in the field (i.e., a car dealer if your car was ruined). This is best done by having the expert come to court and testify, but can also be done in writing. You will also want to check newspaper and flea market ads for the prices asked for comparable goods and creatively explore any other approaches that make sense, given the type of damage you have suffered. We talk more about proving your case in court in Chapters 16-21.

3. Computing the Exact Amount— Cases Involving Damage to Clothing

Clothing is property, so why am I separating it out for special treatment? For two reasons. Cases involving clothing are extremely common in Small Claims Court, and judges seem to apply a logic to them that they apply to no other property damage cases. The reason for this is that clothing is personal to its owner and often has small or little value to anyone else even though it may be in good condition. If the rules that we just learned (i.e., you can recover the repair cost of a damaged item unless this would be more than its market value before the damage occurred, in which case you are limited to recovering its total value) were strictly applied to clothing, there would often be little or no recovery. This is because there is not much market for used clothing.

When suing for damage to new or almost new clothing, sue for its cost. If it is older, sue for the percentage of the value of the clothing which reflects how worn it was when the damage occurred. For example, if your two-year-old suit which cost $400 new were destroyed, sue for $200 if you feel the suit would have lasted another two years. In clothing cases, most judges want answers to these questions:

• How much did the clothing cost originally?

• How much of its useful life was consumed at the time the damage occurred?

• Does the damaged item still have some value to the owner, or has it been ruined?[9]

Example 1: Wendy took her new $250 coat to Rudolph, a tailor, to have alterations made. Rudolph cut part of the back of the coat in the wrong place and ruined it. How much should Wendy sue for? $250—as the coat was almost new. She could probably expect to recover close to this amount.

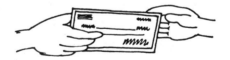

---

[9]The International Fabricare Institute publishes a very useful pamphlet called the *Fair Claims Guide for Consumer Textile Products,* which contains a number of tables designed to tell you what any object of used clothing is worth. It's available from IFI, 12251 Tech Road, Silver Spring, MD 20904 for 50¢.

Example 2: The same facts as just above, but the coat was two years old and had been well worn, although it was still in good condition. Here Wendy would be wise to sue for $200 and hope to recover between $100 and $150.

Example 3: This time we will return Wendy's coat to its almost new condition, but have Rudolph only slightly deface the back, instead of completely destroying it. I would still advise Wendy to sue for the full $250. Whether she could recover that much would depend on the judge. Most would probably award her a little less on the theory that the coat retained some value. Were I Wendy, however, I would strongly argue that I didn't buy the coat with the expectation that I could only wear it in a closet and that as far as I was concerned, the coat was ruined.

4.   Computing the Exact Amount— Personal Injury Cases

Lawyers quickly take over the great majority of cases where someone is injured. These claims are routinely inflated (a mildly-sprained back might be worth $3,000-$5,000 or more), because it is in everyone's selfish interest to do so. The insurance adjusters and insurance company lawyers are as much a part of this something-for-nothing syndrome, as are the ambulance-chasing plaintiff's attorneys. If there aren't lots of claims, lots of lawsuits, lots of depositions and negotiations, it wouldn't take lots of people making lots of money to run the system. Even in states with so-called "no-fault" automobile insurance, the dispute resolution bureaucracy has managed to protect itself very well.

Some small personal injury cases do get to Small Claims Court, however. Dog bite cases are one common example, and there are others. You figure the amount to sue for by adding:

- Out of pocket medical costs, including transportation to medical care providers _____

- Loss of pay, or vacation time for missing work _____

- Pain and suffering[10] _____

- Damage to property[11] _____
  TOTAL _____

Medical and hospital bills, including transportation to and from the doctor, are routinely recoverable as long as you have established that the person you are suing is at fault. However, if you are covered by health insurance and the insurance company has already paid your medical costs, you will find that your policy says that any money that you recover for these costs must be turned over to the company. Often, insurance companies don't make much effort to keep track of, or recover, Small Claims Court judgments as the amounts of money involved don't make it worthwhile. Knowing this, many judges are reluctant to grant judgments for medical bills unless the individual can show that he is personally out-of-pocket the money.

Loss of pay or vacation time is viewed in a similar way. If the cocker spaniel down the block lies in wait for you behind a hedge and grabs a piece of your derriere for breakfast, and as a result you miss a day of work getting yourself patched up, you are entitled to recover the loss of any pay, commissions or vacation time. However, if you are on a job with unlimited paid

---

[10]In more serious cases you would also have to figure the monetary value of any permanent injury. These cases do not, however, get to Small Claims Court.

[11]Often a personal injury is accompanied by injury to property. Thus, a dog bite might also ruin your pants. You add all of your damages together as part of the same suit. You can't sue separately for your pants and your behind.

sick time, so that you suffer no loss for missing work, you have nothing to recover.

The third area of recovery is for what is euphemistically known as "pain and suffering." This is a catch-all phrase that simultaneously means a great deal and nothing at all. Generations of lawyers have made a good living mumbling it. Their idea is often to take a minor injury (sprained ankle) and inflate its value as much as possible by claiming that the injured party underwent great "pain and suffering." "How much is every single minute that my poor client suffered an unbearably painful ankle worth—one dollar, five dollars, ten thousand dollars?" etc. When you read about million dollar settlements, a good chunk of the recovery routinely falls into the "pain and suffering" category. I don't mean to suggest that recovery for "pain and suffering" is always wrong—just that it is often abused.

But back to the case of the nasty cocker spaniel. If you received a painful bite, spent the morning getting your rump attended to, had to take several pain killers and then make sure that the dog was free of rabies, you would very likely feel that you were entitled to some recovery. One judge I know doesn't pay much attention to the evidence in this type of case. He simply awards $500 for a painful bite by a medium-sized dog, adds $100 for anything the size of a lion, and subtracts $100 if the dog looks like a mouse.

Suggestion: In thinking about how much you wish to sue for, be aware that lawyers often bring suit for three to four times the amount of the out-of-pocket damages (medical bills and loss of work). Therefore, if you were out of pocket $500, you might wish to ask for $1,500, the overage being for "pain and suffering." If you have no medical bills (there is no blood or at least x-rays), you will find it difficult to recover anything for "pain and suffering." This is why lawyers routinely encourage their clients to get as much medical attention as possible.

Example 1: Mary Tendertummy is drinking a bottle of pop when a mouse foot floats to the surface. She is greatly nauseated, loses her lunch and goes to the doctor for medication. As a result, she loses an afternoon's pay. She sues the pop company for $500. This is reasonable. She will probably recover most of this amount.

Example 2: The same thing happens to Roy Toughguy. He just throws the pop away in disgust and goes back to work. A few weeks later he hears about Mary's recovery and decides that he too could use $500. How much is he likely to recover? Probably not much more than the price of the soda—he apparently suffered little or no injury.

More Help: Obviously, deciding exactly how much to sue for in a personal injury case can be tricky. If you are in any doubt, I recommend *How To Win Your Personal Injury Claim*, Matthews (Nolo Press). In addition to detailed information on how much a claim is worth, it explains how to negotiate with an insurance company.

5. Computing the Exact Amount—Emotional or Mental Distress

As noted in Chapter 2, in our increasingly crowded urban environment, there are all sorts of ways we can cause one another real pain without making physical contact. For example, if I live in the apartment above you and wake up every morning and pound on my floor (your ceiling) for an hour, I will probably quickly reduce you to the status of a raving maniac. What can you do about it besides bashing me over the head? One remedy is for you to sue me in Small Claims Court based on the fact that my actions constitute the intentional infliction of emotional distress. But how much should you sue for? Unfortunately, there is no good rule of thumb I can give you. It depends on how obnoxious my behavior is, how long it has gone on, how clearly you have asked me to cease it (this should be done in writing), the extent to which you convince the judge you have suffered and, probably at least as important, the personality of the judge. My gut reaction is that in this type of case you do better if you sue for a very reasonable amount. Thus, if you are in a state which permits Small Claims cases up to $1,500, I would normally advise against suing for any amount over $1,000, unless the other person's behavior clearly makes him out to be first cousin to Attila the Hun.

D. Bad Checks

There are several major exceptions to the information on how to compute the amount of your claim set out in Section C, just above. These involve situations where a statute establishes the right to receive extra damages, over and above the amount of the financial injury. The most common of these involves bad checks, where you receive a bad check (or a check on which the writer stops payment in bad faith) and the person giving it to you does not make it good within the time period allowed by the statute— usually 30 days—of your demand to do so.

Over a dozen states have bad-check laws, including Oregon, Arizona, Colorado, California, Montana, Illinois, and Texas. The basic scheme of the laws allow you to recover the amount of the check plus a penalty of three times the amount of the check, up to a certain maximum penalty (California and Oregon allow a maximum penalty of $500.)[12]

In addition, there are usually some minimum and maximum penalties allowed:

1. You can usually sue for some minimum amount in damages, no matter how small the bad check. Thus, in California and Oregon, which both have minimum penalties of $100, if you get a $25 bad check, you can sue for $125.

2. There is usually a top limit on the damages you can sue for, no matter how large the check. Thus, in California, where the maximum penalty is $500, for a $400 bad check, the most you can sue for is $900 (the amount of the check plus the $500 maximum).

E. Equitable Relief (Or Money Can't Always Solve the Problem)

Nearly half the states allow judges to grant relief (provided you ask for it) in ways that do not involve the payment of money, if equity (fairness) demands it. "Equitable relief" is usually limited to one or more of four categories: "rescission," "restitution," "reformation," and "specific performance." Let's translate these into English.[13]

---

[12]In California, this law is mandatory —the judge must award the penalty. See *Mughrabi v. Suzuki;* 243 Cal. Rptr. 438 (1988).

[13]If you think you may want to sue "in equity," where the payment of money just isn't enough, start by looking in the Appendix for your state. For example, Alabama, Arizona, California, Louisiana, Maine and Nebraska expressly allow equitable relief in Small Claims Court. If the law says recovery is limited to "payment of money only" or similar words, equitable relief isn't allowed. If you can't tell from the

Rescission: This is a remedy that is used when a grossly unfair or fraudulent contract is discovered, where a contract was based on a mistake as to an important fact, was induced by duress or undue influence, or one party simply didn't receive what was promised through the fault of the other. Thus, if a merchant sued you for failure to pay for aluminum siding that you contended had been misrepresented and was a total rip-off, you could ask that the contract be rescinded, and that any money you paid be returned to you.

Restitution: This is an important remedy. It gives a judge the power to order that a particular piece of property be transferred to its original owner when fairness requires that the contracting parties be restored to their original positions. It can be used in the common situation in which one person sells another a piece of property (say a motor scooter) and the other fails to pay. Instead of simply giving the seller a money judgment which might be hard to collect, the judge has the power to order the scooter restored to its original owner. Where money has been paid under a contract that is rescinded, the judge can order it to be returned, plus damages. Thus, if a used car purchase was rescinded based on the fraud of the seller, the buyer could get a judgment for the amount paid for the car, plus money spent for repairs, alternate transportation, financing, etc.

Reformation: This remedy is somewhat unusual. It has to do with changing (reforming) a contract to meet the original intent of the parties in a situation where some term or condition agreed to by the parties has been left out or misstated and where fairness dictates that the contract be reformed. Thus, if Arthur the Author and Peter the Publisher orally agree that Peter will publish Arthur's 200-page book and then they write a contract inadvertently leaving out the number of pages, a court would very likely "reform" the contract to include this provision if Arthur showed up with a 2,000-page manuscript. Reformation is most commonly used when an oral agreement is written down incorrectly.

Appendix, look up your state law by referring to the statute in the Appendix.

Specific Performance: This is an important remedy that comes into play where a contract involving an unusual or "one-of-a-kind" object has not been carried out. Say you agree to buy a unique antique jade ring for your mother's birthday that is exactly like the one she lost years before, and then the seller refuses to go through with the deal. A court could cite the doctrine of "specific performance" to order that the ring be turned over to you. "Specific performance" will only be ordered in situations where the payment of money will not adequately compensate the person bringing suit.

Note: In filing out your court papers you will still be required to indicate that the value of the item for which you want equitable relief is under the Small Claims maximum (see Appendix). Thus, you might describe the nature of your claim (Chapter 10, Step 1) as follows: "I want the delivery of a "one-of-a-kind" antique jade ring worth approximately $700 according to my contract with defendant."

Conditional Judgments: In California and in some other states, it's common for judges to issue conditional judgments in cases involving equitable relief. That is, they can order a party to perform or stop a certain act or else pay a money judgment. For example, you agree to sell your baby grand piano for $1,000. The buyer fails to pay and you sue. The judge orders the buyer to either return the piano or fork over the $1,000. If this doesn't occur within a short period, the money judgment may be enforced. (See Chapter 24.)

CHAPTER 5

Is the Suit Brought Within the Proper Time Limits (Statute of Limitations)?

Each state has time limits within which lawsuits must be filed. These are called Statutes of Limitations. Time limits are different for different types of cases. If you wait too long, your right to sue will be barred by these statutes. Why have a Statute of Limitations? Because it has been found that disputes are best settled relatively soon after they develop. Unlike wine, lawsuits don't improve with age. Memories fade and witnesses die or move away, and once-clear details tend to blur together. As a general rule, it is wise to sue as soon after your dispute arises as is reasonably possible. Statutes of Limitations are almost never less than one year, so if you file promptly, you should have little to worry about. Often suits against governments can't be brought unless the government is notified almost immediately of your claim. So, if your dispute is with a city, county, or state, check the rules as quickly as possible.

Almost all disputes brought to Small Claims Court are brought promptly, so the question of whether the person suing has waited too long usually doesn't come up. If your case is one of the rare ones in which the statute of limitations is, or may be, an issue, you will want to check out the statute of limitations for your state. Check your state's laws under the headings "Limitations" or "Statute of Limitations." Read the material carefully— the time periods in which a suit must be brought will vary, depending on the type of suit (e.g., oral contract, written contract, personal injury, etc.).

A. Statute of Limitations Periods— California and Texas

I include here Statute of Limitation periods for two of our largest states. As stated above, time limits for starting legal actions in other states will vary, and you should check the rules that apply to you. But don't get so bogged down with the Statute of Limitations that you miss the major point, which is to sue as promptly as possible after you have suffered a loss. You will find a set of your state's laws at a public library or a law library, which, in most states, will be located at the local courthouse. If you have trouble finding what you need, ask the librarian for help. Librarians positively enjoy finding things.

CALIFORNIA

Personal Injury: One year from the injury, or, if the injury is not immediately discovered, one year from the date it is discovered.

Oral Contracts: Two years from the day the contract is broken.

Written Contracts: Four years from the day the contract is broken.

Damage to Personal or Real Property: Three years from the date the damage occurs.[1]

Fraud: Three years from the date of the discovery of the fraud.

Professional Negligence Against Health Care Providers: Three years after the date of the injury or one year from its discovery.

Suits Against Public Agencies: Before you can sue a city, county or the state government, you must file an administrative claim form. The time period in which this must be done is six months. This is not precisely a Statute of Limitations, but it has the same effect. (See Chapter 8 for a more complete discussion of how to sue governments in Small Claims Court.)

TEXAS

Libel and Slander: One year from the date of the libel or slander.

Evictions (Forcible Entry and Detainer): Two years.

Oral Contracts: Two years from the day the contract was broken.

Personal Injuries: Two years from the injury or, if the injury was not immediately discovered, two years from the date of discovery.

Written Contracts: Four years from the day the contract was broken (but the limitation period for actions upon stated or open accounts is only two years).

---

[1]The statute of limitations is ten years for property damage which results from latent defects in the planning, construction or improvement of real property.

Note: Some contracts which you may assume to be oral may actually be written. People often forget that they signed papers when they first arranged for goods or services. For example, your charge accounts, telephone service, insurance policies as well as most major purchases of goods and services, involve a written contract, even though you haven't signed any papers for years. And another thing—to have a written contract you need not have signed a document full of "whereas's" and "therefores." Any signed writing can be a contract, even if it's written on toilet paper with lipstick. When you go to a car repair shop and they make out a work order and you sign it—that's a contract. (See Chapter 2A for more about contracts.)

B.   Computing the Statute of Limitations

Okay, now let's assume that you have found out what the relevant limitations period is. How do you know what date to start your counting from? That's easy. Start with the day the injury to your person or property occurred, or, if a contract is involved, start with the day that the failure to perform under the terms of the contract occurred. Where a contract to pay in installments is involved, start with the day that the first payment was missed.[2]

---

[2]The Statute of Limitations applies separately to each installment of a contract. Thus, if you agree to pay $5,000 in five installments commencing January 1, 1985 and continuing on January 1 of each succeeding year and never agree in writing to waive the Statute of Limitations, and the Statute of Limitations for written contracts in your state is four years), the creditor's lawsuit can successfully be defended

Example: Doolittle owes Crabapple $500, payable in five monthly installments of $100. Both live in San Jose, California. They never wrote down any of the terms of their agreement. Doolittle misses his third monthly payment which was due on January 1, 1991. Crabapple should compute his Statute of Limitations period from January 2, 1991, assuming, of course, that Doolittle doesn't later catch up on his payments. Since the Statute of Limitations for oral contracts in California is two years, this means that Crabapple has until January 1, 1993 to file his suit. If a written contract had been involved, Crabapple could file until January 1, 1995, as the Statute of Limitations on written contracts in California is four years.

I am frequently asked to explain the legal implications of the following situation. After the Statute of Limitations runs out (say two years on an oral contract to pay for having a fence painted), the debtor commences voluntarily to make payments. Does the voluntary payment have the effect of creating a new two-year Statute of Limitations period, allowing the person who is owed the money to sue if the debtor again stops paying? In most states, including California, simply starting to pay on an obligation barred by the Statute of Limitations doesn't create a new period for suit.[3] All the creditor can do is to keep his toes crossed and hope that the debtor's belated streak of honesty continues. However, if the debtor signs a written agreement promising to make the payments, this does create a new Statute of Limitations period. In legal slang, this is called "reaffirming the debt."

Example: Back to the drama of Doolittle and Crabapple. Let's assume that in February, 1993, Doolittle experiences a burst of energy, gets a job and decides to pay off all of his old debts. He sends Crabapple $50. A week later, suffering terrible strain from

---

(in legalese it is often said his suit is "barred") on the basis that the statute of limitations has expired on January 2, 1994 Your second payment will not be barred until January 2, 1995 and so on.

[3]See California Code of Civil Procedure Section 360. If you live outside California, check your state laws to see if they are the same. Look in the index under "reviving" a Statute of Limitations, or "reaffirming" a debt.

getting up before noon, he quits his job and reverts to his old ways of sleeping in the sun when not reading the racing form. Is the Statute of Limitations allowing Crabapple to sue reinstated? No. As we learned above, once the limitation period of two years has run out, it can't be revived by simply making a payment. However, if Doolittle had sent Crabapple the $50 and had also included a letter saying that he would pay the remainder of the debt, Crabapple would again be able to sue and get a judgment if he failed to pay. Why? Because a written promise to pay a debt barred by the Statute of Limitations has the legal effect of reestablishing the debt.

Debtor's Note: If a creditor and debtor discuss an unpaid bill and the debtor asks the creditor to give her more time to pay, to lower payments, or make some other accommodation, the creditor, assuming he is willing to agree, will almost always require that the debtor waive the Statute of Limitations in writing. This means that if the debtor fails to pay, he must wait another Statute of Limitation period before the creditor is prevented from successfully suing.

Suspending the Statute of Limitations: In a few situations, the Statute of Limitations is suspended for a period of time (lawyers say "tolled"). This occurs if the person sued is in prison, living out of the state, insane or a minor. If the Statute of Limitations is suspended ("tolled") by one of these events, it starts up again when the event causing the tolling ends.

Example: Jack borrows money from Tim under a written (e.g., four-year Statute of Limitation in California) contract. Jack fails to pay the money back on the day required. Six months later, Jack is sentenced to a year in jail. The four-year Statute of Limitations would be tolled (suspended) during this period and Tim would still have three-and-one-half years after Jack gets out of jail to collect.

C. Telling the Judge that the Statute of Limitations Has Run Out

What should a defendant do if he believes that the Statute of Limitations period has run out? Tell the judge.[4] Sometimes a judge will figure this out without a reminder, but sometimes he won't. If you are a defendant, don't ever assume that because the clerk has filed the papers and you have been properly served, this means that the plaintiff has started her suit on time. The clerk never gets involved in Statute of Limitations questions. They will cheerfully file a suit brought on a breach of contract occurring in 1917.

---

[4]If your state is one of the few that requires a defendant to file a written request prior to the hearing date (see Appendix), you should also mention any State of Limitations problem in that response.

CHAPTER 6

How to Settle Your Dispute

Litigation should be a last, not a first, resort. Suing is not as bad as shooting, but neither is it as much fun as a good back rub. In addition to being time-consuming and emotionally draining, lawsuits tend to polarize disagreements into win-all or lose-all propositions where face (and pocketbook) saving compromise is difficult. Most of us are terrified of making fools of ourselves in front of strangers. When forced to defend our actions in a public forum, we tend rather regularly to adopt a self-righteous view of our own conduct, and to attribute the vilest of motives to our opponents. Many of us are willing to admit that we have been a bit of a fool in private—especially if the other person does too—but in public, we will stonewall, even when it would be to our advantage to appear a little more fallible.

I have witnessed dozens of otherwise sensible people litigate the most appalling trivia including one case in which the parties effectively tied up over $2,000 of each other's property (and had a fist fight) over a fishing pole worth $15. This doesn't mean that I don't think you should take your case to court if necessary. What I am suggesting is this: before you file, ask yourself whether you have done everything reasonably possible (and then a little more) to try to settle with the other party.

A. Try to Talk Your Dispute Out

Trying to settle your case isn't a waste of time. Indeed, you are often required to make the attempt. The law in many states requires that a "demand" for payment be made prior to filing a court action. A number of states require this "demand" to be in writing.[1]

But first things first. Before you reach for pen and paper, try to talk to the person with whom you are having the dispute. I can't count how many times people have consulted me about supposedly insurmountable disputes in situations where they had never once tried to talk it out with the other person.[2] Apparently many of us have a strong psychological barrier to talking to people we are upset with, especially if we have already exchanged heated words. Sometimes we seem to think that a willingness to compromise shows weakness. But wasn't it Winston Churchill who said, "I would rather jaw, jaw, jaw than war, war, war"?

---

[1] In Massachusetts, for example, under the Consumer Protection Act (Mass. Gen.Law, Ch. 93A), a person can sue a business for triple damages, but only if a written demand for what is owed is made at least 30 days prior to filing suit.

[2] I sat as judge pro tem in one case where a man sued another man for $500 resulting from a car accident. Instead of putting on a defense, the defendant said he was "willing to pay." Why haven't you paid before, then?" I asked. "No one asked me to," he replied.

Important: An offer of compromise, made either orally or in writing, does not bind the person making the offer to that amount if the compromise is not accepted. Thus, you could make an original demand for $500, then offer to compromise for $350, and, if your compromise offer is turned down, still sue for $500.

If you take my advice and are able to talk things out with your opponent, write down your agreement. Oral understandings, especially between people who have small confidence in one another, are often not worth the breath used to express them. Here are two sample compromise agreements that you may be able to adopt to your uses.

SAMPLE AGREEMENT 1

Dusty Rider and Bigshot Owner agree as follows:

1. Dusty was to exercise Bigshot's horses every morning for two weeks from October 1 to October 15 at Churchill Downs Racetrack in Louisville, Kentucky, and was to be paid $15 per horse exercised each morning;

2. Bigshot's horses got sick on September 29 and there was no need for Dusty's services;

3. Dusty gave up other employment to make herself available to ride Bigshot's horses, and she couldn't find another riding job at short notice;

4. Dusty and Bigshot agree that $600 is fair compensation for her loss of work and Dusty agrees to accept this amount as a complete settlement of all of her claims.

---------------------------   ---------------------------
Date   Dusty Rider

---------------------------   ---------------------------
Date   Bigshot Owner

SAMPLE AGREEMENT 2

Walter Spottedhound and Nellie Neighbor agree that Walter's "mixed breed" black dog Clem sneaked onto Nellie's patio and bit her behind the right knee. After taking into consideration Nellie's medical bills, the fact that she had to miss two hours' work while at the doctor's office, and the pain and discomfort she has suffered, it is agreed that Walter will pay Nellie $250 in full settlement of all her claims. The money will be paid in five equal monthly installments. The first installment is hereby paid this date and the next four will be paid on the first day of February, March , April and May, 19__.

It is also agreed that Walter will commence at once to construct a six-foot high cyclone fence to keep Clem out of Nellie's yard.

_____	_____
Date	Walter Spottedhound
_____	_____
Date	Nellie Neighbor

A number of fill-in-the-blank, tear-out release forms that may be used to settle the types of disputes which commonly end up in Small Claims Court are contained in *Make Your Own Contract*, Elias (Nolo Press).

B. Write a "Demand" Letter

If your efforts to talk your problems out fail (or despite my urging you refuse to try), your next step is to send your adversary a letter. As noted above, many courts require that a "demand" letter be sent. But even if there is no such requirement, it is almost essential that you send one. Why? Simple—the "demand" letter is not only useful in trying to settle your dispute, it is also an excellent opportunity to lay your case before the judge in a carefully organized way. In a sense, it allows you to "manufacture" evidence that you will be permitted to use in court if the case isn't settled. Either way, you can't lose, so take the time to write a good letter.

Your letter should be reasonably short, directly to the point, and, above all, polite (you catch more flies with honey than by hitting them over the head with a mallet). Use a typewriter and keep a carbon, or photocopy. Limit your remarks to a page, or at most, a page and a half. Remember, if the case doesn't settle, you will want to show the letter to the judge—and what's more important, you will want the judge to read it. It's my experience that aside from letters of the heart, no one ever reads much more than the first page of any letter with attention.

Remember, the judge doesn't know anything about how your problem started and developed. This means that you will want to write the letter so that it briefly reviews the entire dispute. It may seem a little odd, to write all the facts and send them to your opponent who well knows them, and it may result in a formal sounding letter. So what? You want to state your position in a way the judge can understand.

Let's consider a case I watched one morning. The facts (with a little editorial license) were simple. Jennifer moved into Peter's house in August, agreeing to pay $450 per month rent. The house had four bedrooms, each occupied by one person. The kitchen and other common areas were shared. Things went well enough until one chilly evening in October when Jennifer turned on the heat. Peter was right behind her to turn it off, explaining that heat inflamed his allergies.

As the days passed and fall deepened, heat became more and more of an issue until one cold, late November night when Jennifer returned home from her waitress job to find her room "about the same temperature as the inside of an icicle." After a short cry, she started packing and moved out the next morning. She refused to pay Peter any additional rent, claiming that she was within her rights to terminate her month-to-month tenancy without giving notice because the house was uninhabitable.[3] It took Peter one month to find a suitable tenant and to have that person move in. Therefore, he lost rent in the amount of $450.

After calling Jennifer several times and asking her to make good the $450 only to have her slam down the phone in disgust, Peter wrote her the following letter:

---

[3]In many states tenants do have the right to simply leave, or in the alternative, to stay and cease paying rent, if conditions in their rented home become uninhabitable due to lack of heat, water, electricity, etc.

61 Spring St.
Detroit, MI.
January 1, 19___

Jennifer Tenant
111 Lake St.
Detroit, MI

Dear Jennifer:

   You are a real idiot. Actually, you're worse than that: you're malicious— walking out on me before Christmas and leaving me with no tenant when you knew that I needed the money to pay my child support. You know that I promised to get you an electric room heater. Don't think I don't know that the *real* reason you moved out was to live with your boyfriend.

   Please send me the $450 I lost because it took me a month to re-rent the place. If you don't, I will sue you.

In aggravation,

Peter Landperson

To which Jennifer replied:

111 Lake St.
Detroit, MI
January 4, 19__

Peter Landperson
61 Spring St.
Detroit, MI

Dear Mr. Landperson:

You nearly froze me to death, you cheap bastard. I am surprised it only took a month to rent that iceberg of a room—you must have found a rich polar bear (ha ha). People like you should be locked up.

I hope you choke on an ice cube.

Jennifer Tenant

As you have no doubt guessed, both Peter and Jennifer made similar mistakes. Instead of being business-like, each deliberately set out to annoy the other, reducing any possible chance of compromise. In addition, they each assumed that they were writing only to the other, forgetting that the judge would be privy to their sentiments. Thus, both lost a valuable chance to present the judge with a coherent summary of the facts as they saw them. As evidence in a subsequent court proceeding, both letters were worthless.

Now let's interrupt these proceedings and give Peter and Jennifer another chance to write sensible letters.

61 Spring St.
Detroit, MI.
January 1, 19__

Jennifer Tenant
111 Lake St.
Detroit, MI

Dear Jennifer:

As you will recall, you moved into my house at 61 Spring St.,
Detroit, Michigan, on August 1, 19__, agreeing to pay me $450
per month rent on the first of each month. On November 29, you
suddenly moved out, having given me no advance notice
whatsoever.

I realize that you were unhappy about the fact that the house
was a little on the cool side, but I don't believe that this was a
serious problem, as the temperature was at all times over 60
degrees and I had agreed to get you an electric heater for your
room by December.

I was unable to get a tenant to replace you (although I tried
every way I could and asked you for help) until January 1, 19__.
This means that I am short $450 rent for the room you occupied.
If necessary, I will take this dispute to court because, as you
know, I am on a very tight budget. I hope that this isn't
necessary and that we can arrive at a sensible compromise. I
have tried to call you with no success. Perhaps you can give me a
call in the next week to talk this over.

Sincerely,

Peter Landperson

To which our now enlightened Jennifer promptly replied:

---

111 Lake St.
Detroit, MI
January 4, 19__

Peter Landperson
61 Spring St.
Detroit, MI

Dear Peter:

I just received your letter concerning the rent at 61 Spring St. and am sorry to say that I don't agree either with the facts as you have presented them, or with your demand for back rent.

When I moved in August 1, 19__, you never told me that you had an allergy and that there would be a problem keeping the house at a normal temperature. I would not have moved in had you informed me of this.

From early October, when we had the first cool evenings, all through November (almost two months), I asked that you provide heat. You didn't. Finally, it became unbearable to return from work in the middle of the night to a cold house, which was often below 60 degrees. It is true that I moved out suddenly, but I felt that I was within my rights under Michigan law. In fact, you are lucky that I am not suing you for damages for constructive eviction.[4]

Since you mentioned the non-existent electric heater in your letter, let me respond to that. You first promised to get the heater over a month before I moved out and never did. Also, as I pointed out to you on several occasions, the heater was not a complete solution to the problem, as it would have heated only my room and not the kitchen, living room, dining area, etc. You repeatedly told me that it would be impossible to heat these areas.

---

[4]Michigan and many other states have laws allowing tenants to sue landlords for constructive eviction when the landlord fails to provide a necessity such as heat, hot water, electricity, gas, etc.

Peter, I sincerely regret the fact that you feel wronged, but I believe that I have been very fair with you. I am sure that you would have been able to rerent the room promptly if the house had been warm. I regret that I don't believe that any compromise is possible and that you will just have to go to court if that's what you wish to do.

Sincerely,

Jennifer Tenant

As you can see, while the second two letters are less fun to read, they are far more informative. Both Peter and Jennifer have clearly set forth their positions. In this instance, the goal of reaching an acceptable compromise was not met, but both have prepared a good outline of their positions for the judge. In court, both Peter and Jennifer will testify, present witnesses, etc. in addition to their letters. However, court proceedings are often rushed and confused and it's nice to have a written statement for the judge to fall back on. Be sure to bring a carbon or photocopy of your demand letter to court when your case is to be heard. Be sure, too, that the judge is given the copy as part of your case. The judge won't be able to guess that you have it; you will have to let her know and hand it to the clerk. (For more about how to conduct yourself in court, see Chapters 13-15).

Important: If you compromise your case after you have filed it in court, but before the court hearing, be sure to do so in writing. Also let the court know that you won't be appearing. Some courts will ask that the plaintiff sign a "Request for Dismissal" form. Never do this unless your compromise agreement has already been reduced to writing. Also, it is not wise to have a case dismissed unless you have been paid in full. If the compromise settlement involves installment payments, it is wise to go to court and present your agreement to the judge. She can then enter a judgment in the same terms as the compromise. If this is done and then the judgment is not paid, it can be collected using the techniques discussed in Chapter 24.

C. Settlement at Court

Sometimes cases are settled while you are waiting for your case to be heard. It is perfectly proper to ask the other person if he or she wishes to step into the hall for a moment to talk the matter over. If you can agree on a compromise, wait until the case is called and tell the judge the amount you have agreed upon and whether the amount is to be paid all at once, or over time. The judge can either order the case dismissed if one person pays the other on the spot, or can enter a judgment for the amount that you have compromised upon, if payment is to be made later.

D. Mediation as an Alternative

There is a strong national trend towards encouraging people to settle their own disputes without going to court. Mediation, a procedure in which the disputants meet with a neutral third party who helps them arrive at their own solution, is available in many areas. Trained mediators may be available free or at low cost right at your courthouse or via a referral to an outside mediation service. In other Small Claims Courts, mediators are merely volunteer attorneys who try and help people arrive at a compromise settlement. In either case, the meetings with the mediator are very informal, with the goal being to reach a solution acceptable to all rather than to win. If the dispute cannot be settled through mediation, you can still go before the regular judge to present your case.

E.   Arbitration

A few states, particularly New York, strongly encourage informal arbitration before a lawyer who is volunteering his or her time as an arbitrator. The lawyer and the parties involved just sit down at a table and talk things over. It's often faster to see an arbitrator right away than it is to wait your turn to have your case heard in the regular Small Claims Court. Some states provide arbitration as an option (you don't have to do it) but, like New York, make the parties agree that the arbitrator's decision will be final without a right of appeal by anyone. Other states require, or make available, nonbinding arbitration before going to court, but if the parties still can't agree on a settlement, the Small Claims judge will hear the case.

CHAPTER 7

Who Can Sue?

In most situations, asking who can sue in Small Claims Court is an easy question. *You* can, as long as you are of legal age in your state (18 in most) and have not been declared mentally incompetent in a judicial proceeding.[1] Sometimes, however, listing yourself as the party bringing suit isn't quite so easy.

Here are the general rules in force in all states. Your state's rules may vary slightly, however, and you will wish to check the Appendix and your local rules:

1. If you are suing for yourself alone, simply list your full name as plaintiff.

2. If more than one person is bringing suit, list all the names as plaintiffs.

---

[1]Some states do not let unlicensed contractors and other business people who work without regular licenses to bring suit. Some states *do* allow emancipated minors to sue (and be sued) and allow prisoners to sue, by allowing another person to appear for them.

3. If you are filing a claim on behalf of your individually-owned business, you (the owner of the business) must do the suing. You should list your name and the business name as plaintiffs, e.g., "Jane Poe doing business as ABC Printing." Also, if the business uses a fictitious name (e.g., Tasty Donut Shop) as opposed to the owner's name, a form stating that the fictitious business name has been properly registered must be completed in many states.

4. If you are a partner filing a claim on behalf of a partnership, list the partnership name as plaintiff. Only one of the partners need sign. If the partnership uses a fictitious name, list it and the partners' real names, e.g., ABC Printing, a partnership, and Jane Poe and Phil Roe individually.

5. If you are filing a claim on behalf of a corporation, whether profit or non-profit, list the corporation as plaintiff. The form must be signed by either:

a. an officer of the corporation, or

b. a person authorized to file claims on behalf of the corporation by the Board of Directors of the corporation who is not employed for the sole purpose of representing the corporation in Small Claims Court.[2] If a non-officer of a corporation is involved, the court clerk may want to see some documentation that the person suing is properly authorized.

6. If you are filing on behalf of an unincorporated association, do so by listing the name of the association and the name of the officer by whom it is being represented (e.g., ABC Society, by Philip Dog, President).

---

[2]Local rules differ as to requirements for filing on behalf of a corporation. Some courts no longer require an authorization adopted by the Board of Directors. Call your Small Claims Court clerk.

7. When a claim arises out of damage to a motor vehicle, the registered owner(s) of the vehicle must file in Small Claims Court. This means that, if you are driving someone else's car and get hit by a third party, you can't sue for damage done to the car. The registered owner must do the suing.

8. If you are suing on behalf of a public entity such as a public library, city tax assessor's office or county hospital, you must show the court clerk proper authorization to sue.

Other Pre-Suit Requirements: In certain situations, to qualify to sue in Small Claims Court, other legal requirements must be met. For example, in some states, contractors must be licensed, and car repair dealers, structural pest control operators, and TV repair people must be registered with the relevant state agency as a condition of using Small Claims Court. And, as noted, anyone doing business under a fictitious name must file and maintain a fictitious business name statement in most states. If you are being sued by anyone who you feel may not meet these requirements, make sure you tell the judge of your concern.

A. Participation by Attorneys and Bill Collectors

Attorneys, or other people acting as representatives, cannot normally appear in Small Claims Court in Arkansas (except in rural areas), California, Colorado, Idaho, Kansas, Michigan, Minnesota, Montana (unless all parties have attorneys), Nebraska, Oregon, and Washington.[3] In the majority of states, however, attorneys are permitted. (See Appendix.)[4] Even in states such as California, Colorado and Michigan, in which attorneys are not allowed to represent others, they are allowed to sue or defend their own claims. Getting the advice of a lawyer before going to Small Claims Court is perfectly legal in all states, however.

Many states, including California, Michigan, Missouri, Nebraska, New Jersey (except by corporations), New York, and Ohio (except by authorized employee or officer of the state to recover taxes), forbid the use of Small Claims Court by "assignees" (a fancy term that usually refers to collection agencies). The majority of states, including Pennsylvania, Massachusetts, Maine, and Oregon, still allow suits by collection agencies. Texas and Kentucky seem to be unique in barring lenders of money at interest for using Small Claims Court. New York, on the other hand, bars corporations from suing in Small Claims Court, and in most counties, also bars partnerships. See the Appendix under "Note" for information about your state.

---

[3]Minnesota, Oregon and Washington allow attorneys if the judge consents.

[4]Allowing attorneys to represent people in Small Claims Court is, in my opinion, a serious mistake. The whole idea of Small Claims Court is to allow people to settle small claims themselves without a lot of legal mumbo jumbo and expense.

B. Suits By Minors

If you are an unemancipated (in all states) minor, or an emancipated minor (in some states) your parent or legal guardian must sue for you. To do this, a form must be filled out and signed by the judge appointing the person in question as your "Guardian Ad Litem." This simply means guardian for the purposes of the lawsuit. Ask the court clerk.

C   Class Actions

In Small Claims Court there is no such thing as a true class action lawsuit where a number of people in a similar situation join together in one lawsuit. However, a number of community groups have discovered that if a large number of people with a particular grievance (pollution, noise, etc.) sue the same defendant at the same time, something remarkably like a class action suit is created. This technique was pioneered by a stubborn group of homeowners near the San Francisco Airport who several times won over 100 Small Claims Court judgments on the same day. They hired expert witnesses, did research, ran training workshops and paid for legal advice when needed as part of a coordinated effort while all arguing their own cases. The City of San Francisco maintained that they were in effect involved in a class action law suit and such suits are not permitted in Small Claims Court. A California Court of Appeals disagreed, saying that, "Numerous 'mass' actions against the City alleging that noise from the City airport constituted continuing nuisance were neither too 'complex' nor had such 'broad social policy import' that they were outside the jurisdiction of Small Claims Court...."[5]

A similar strategy has been widely used in California cities to shut down crack houses. Neighbors organize to sue landlords who rent to tenants who sell drugs, claiming the legal theory of nuisance (use of property so as to interfere with the rights of others—in this case to be free of emotional and mental distress). Each neighbor sues for $5,000 (the California Small Claims maximum). Thus, 30 neighbors who coordinate their Small Claims filings can together bring what amounts to a $150,000 case.

In a number of instances, cases such as these have resulted in large judgments against landlords who rent to dealers, with the further effect that the problem was quickly cleaned up.

Suits like these are exciting; they show that people can change their environment for the better, even in the face of overwhelming power on the other side. However, these suits also carry a negative message. They indicate that normal channels for change have broken down. For example, in the airport case, the residents only sued after prolonged inaction by officials. And in the crack house cases, residents had repeatedly informed police of illegal activities and housing code violations,

[5]*City and County of San Francisco v. Small Claims Div.*, San Mateo Co. (1983) 190 Cal. Rptr. 340.

but to no avail. Although Small Claims Court is a good way to get action on local problems when all else fails, more flexible and effective solutions are needed. One possibility is the creation of a system for community dispute resolution, one that could hear grievances, bring together all interested parties, and if necessary, impose and enforce solutions other than money awards. Such tribunals could be operated in the spirit of Small Claims Court—accessible, inexpensive, quick—with the power to fashion wide-ranging solutions to community problems. For more information on how to use Small Claims Court to close down drug houses, contact Safe Streets, U.S.A., 1221 Broadway (Suite 13), Oakland, CA 94612.

D. Special Rules for Prisoners and Military Personnel Transferred Out of State

Some states have special procedures for prisoners who wish to sue in Small Claims Court. In California, for example, a prisoner can sue in Small Claims Court by filing her papers by mail and then by either waiving personal appearance and submitting testimony in the form of written declarations *or* by having another person (other than a lawyer) appear on her behalf in court [CCP 116.540(g).]

In some states, military personnel may have problems suing in Small Claims Court once they have been transferred out of state. Check your state rules (the index of your state code) to see what to do.

E. Business Owners Do Not Always Have to Go to Court

It used to be that the owners of small unincorporated busi-nesses were discouraged from using Small Claims Court in the great majority of states. This was because there was a legal requirement that stated that the owner of the business both had to file the papers and show up in court. For example, a dentist who wished to sue on an overdue bill would have to be in court personally. But today a number of states are more understanding of business time pressures. If a business (incorporated or unincorporated) wishes to sue on an unpaid bill, it can send an employee to court to testify about the debt as it is reflected in the written records of the business. For instance, in many states a landlord suing for unpaid rent can send his or her property manager to court to establish the fact that the rent was unpaid (but see caution about bringing eviction cases in Small Claims Court in Chapter 20). For a business owner to invoke this time-saving procedure, the employee sent to court must be actually familiar with the company's books and able to testify about how this specific debt was entered in them.

This method is only recommended when the fact that the money is owed is cut and dried. If there is likely to be any dispute about how the debt arose or the amount at issue, the presence of the business owner and the testimony of someone who knows about the facts of the dispute will be necessary. For example, if a TV repair business brings suit to collect an unpaid bill and sends a bookkeeper who knows nothing about what goes on in the repair shop to court, the suit will probably be lost if the defendant shows up and says the TV was not fixed properly. In this situation, some judges may postpone (continue) the case for a few days to allow the business owner to show up and present testimony about the quality of the repair, but don't count on it.

CHAPTER 8

Who Can Be Sued?

You can sue just about anybody (person, partnership, corporation, state and local government, etc.) in Small Claims Court in most states. Indeed, it is more often the "Where can I sue" problem (see Chapter 9), not the "Who can I sue" problem that causes difficulties. For example, you can sue the First National Bank of Vermont, but you will find it very difficult to have the case heard in Billings, Montana, or Emporia, Kansas unless you can show that the bank does business there, or entered into or agreed to carry out a contract with you there. This doesn't mean that you have a problem with suing the bank—you don't. The problem is only with suing in Billings or Emporia. If you go to Vermont, where the bank is located, you can bring your suit with no problem.

Here are some hints that may prove helpful when it comes to filling out your papers. Again, the information I give here is general, but it does not differ much from state to state. See the Appendix and your local rules. Also, look at the forms in Chapter 10 for general information.

A. Suing One Person

If you are suing an individual, simply name him or her, using the most complete name that you have for that person. If the person calls himself J.R. Smith and you don't know what the J.R. stands for, simply sue him as J.R. Smith.

B. Suing Two or More People

If you are suing more than one person on a claim arising from the same incident or contract, you must list and serve (see Chapter 11) each to bring them properly before the court. This is also required with a husband and wife.[1]

Example: J. R. and June Smith, who are married, borrow $1,200 from you to start an avocado pit polishing business. Unfortunately, in the middle of the polishing, the seeds begin to sprout. J. R. and June get so furious that they refuse to repay you. If you wish to sue them and get a judgment, you should list them as J. R. Smith and June Smith—not Mr. and Mrs. Smith. But now suppose that J. R. borrowed $1,200 for the avocado pit business in January, June borrowed $1,000 to fix her motorcycle a month later, and neither loan was repaid. In this situation, you would sue each in separate Small Claims Court actions.

---

[1]A problem may arise in some states where you can sue a person only in the county or district where he or she lives. What happens when you sue two people who live in different counties or districts? In most states, including California, this type of situation is handled by allowing the person suing to sue in either place. But a few states don't make even this exception, so that it might actually be impossible to sue both these people in the same court. This possibility is noted in the Appendix where applicable.

C. Suing an Individually-Owned Business

Here you list the name of the owner and the name of the business (i.e., J. R. Smith—doing business as [d.b.a.] Smith's Texaco). Don't assume that the name of the business is in fact the same as the name of the owner. Often it is not. Jim's Garage may be owned by Pablo Garcia Motors, Inc. (see Section E, "Suing a Corporation," below). If you get a judgment against Jim's Garage and there is no Jim, you will find that it's worthless in many states—you can't collect from a nonexistent person. Take the trouble to be sure you know who the owner of the business is before you sue.

Fortunately New York, California and a few other states have liberalized their rules and do not penalize plaintiffs who incorrectly state the business defendant's name. New York allows a plaintiff to sue a defendant under any name used in conducting business if it is impossible to find out the defendant's true name. California allows a plaintiff to correct a defendant's name at the time of the hearing and in some cases, after judgment when the defendant is a business person using a fictitious name.

California requires that all people doing business in a name other than their own file a Fictitious Business Name Statement with the county clerk in the county or counties in which the business operates.[2] This is public information and you can get it

---

[2]All states have similar requirements. Call your Small Claims Court clerk or city or county offices for more information.

from the court clerk. Another way to figure out who owns a business is to check with the Business Tax and License Office in the city in which the business is located. If the business is not in an incorporated area, try the county. The tax and license office will have a list of the owners of all businesses paying taxes. They should be able to tell you, for example, that the Garden of Exotic Delights is owned by Rufus Clod. Once you find this out, you sue Rufus Clod, d.b.a. The Garden of Exotic Delights.

If for some reason the tax and license office and the county clerk can't help, you may want to check with the state. Millions of people, from exterminators to embalmers, must register with one or another state office. So, if your beef is with a teacher, architect, smog control device installer, holder of a beer or wine license, etc., you will very likely be able to learn who and where he is with a letter or phone call. Check the phone book for the capital city of your state (usually available at public libraries or the telephone company) under the listings of state offices. When you find an agency that looks like they should have jurisdiction over the type of business you wish to sue, call their public information number and explain your problem. It may take a little persistence, but eventually you should get the help you need.

D. Suing Partnerships

All partners in a business are individually liable for all the acts of the business. List the names of all the business partners, even if your dispute is only with one (Patricia Sun and Farah Moon d.b.a. Sacramento Gardens). See Section C just above for information on how to learn just who owns a particular business.

Example: You go to a local cleaners with your new, sky blue suit. They put too much cleaning fluid on it, with the result that a small grey cloud settles on the right rear shoulder. After unsuccessfully trying to get the cleaners to take responsibility for improving the weather on the back of your suit, you start thinking about a different kind of suit. When you start filling out your court papers (see Chapter 10), you realize that you know only that the stores says "Perfection Cleaners" on the front, and that the guy who has been so unpleasant to you is named Bob. You call the city business tax and license people and they tell you that Perfection Cleaners is owned by Robert Johnson and Sal De Benno. You should sue both and also list the name of the business.

Note: It is wise to get a judgment against more than one person if possible. When it comes to trying to collect, it's always nice to have someone in reserve if one defendant turns out to be an artful dodger.

E. Suing a Corporation

Corporations are legal people. This means that you can sue, and enforce a judgment against, a corporation itself. You should not sue the owners of the corporation or its officers or managers as individuals unless you have a personal claim against them that is separate from their role as part of the corporation. In most situations the real people who own or operate the corporation aren't themselves liable to pay the corporation's debts. This concept is called "limited liability" and is one reason why many people choose to incorporate.

Be sure to list the full name of the corporation when you file suit (John's Liquors, Inc., a Corporation). Here again, the name on the door or on the stationery may not be the real name.

Corporations, too, sometimes do business using fictitious names. Check with city or county business license people where the corporation does business. Information is also available from either the Secretary of State or the Corporations Commissioner's office, which you will find located in your state capital. You may sue a corporation in your state even if their headquarters are in another state, as long as they do business here.

F. Suing on a Motor Vehicle Accident

Here there are some special rules. In most states, if your claim arises from an accident with an automobile, motorcycle, truck or R.V., you should name both the driver of the vehicle and the registered owner as part of your suit. Most times you will have obtained this information at the time of the accident. If a police accident report was made, it will also contain this information. You can get a copy of any police report from the police department for a modest fee. If there was no police report, contact the Department of Motor Vehicles. In most states, for a small fee, they will tell you who owns any vehicle for which you have a license number.[3]

---

[3] In a number of other states, the Department of Motor Vehicles will ask you why you want this information. Simply tell them "to file a lawsuit based on a motor vehicle accident that occurred in (name of city or

Remember, when you sue more than one person (in this case the driver and the owner if they are different), serve papers on both. When a business owns a vehicle, sue both the driver and the owners of the business.

G. Special Procedures for Suits Against Minors

It is very difficult to successfully sue a minor for breach of contract in most states because minors can disavow (back out of) any contract they sign as long as they do it before they become adults, unless the contract was for a necessity of life, e.g., food, in which case the parents are responsible.[4] You can sue minors for damage to your person or property. If you wish to do so, you must also list a parent or legal guardian on the court papers. Do it like this:

"John Jefferey, a minor, and William Jefferey, his father."

It is very difficult to collect from minors themselves as most don't have money or income. Of course, there are exceptions to this rule, but most minors are, almost by definition, broke. Thus, it often doesn't pay to bother with suits against minors unless you can collect from the minor's parents. Normally a parent is not legally responsible to pay for damages by his or her children, but there are some exceptions to this rule. In virtually all states, if a child is guilty of "malicious or willful misconduct," a parent

---

county) on (date) at (time), involving myself and a car with a license number _____." This is a legitimate reason in most states, and you will get the information you need. However, in many states, the owner of the car will be notified of your request.

[4] Some states now let minors become emancipated before eighteen. Normally, emancipated minors can be sued under "adult" rules if they live separately form their parents and have obtained court consent or if they are married or on active duty in the military. Ask your court clerk for local rules.

may be liable up to a certain amount ($10,000 in some states) per act (often a lot more if a gun is involved) for all property damage and sometimes for personal injuries. Parents may also be liable for damage done by their minor children in auto accidents when they authorized the child to drive.[5]

Example 1: John Johnson, age 17, trips over his shoelace while delivering your newspaper and crashes through your glass door. Can you recover from John's parents? Probably not, as John is not guilty of "malicious or willful misconduct."

Example 2: John shoots out the same glass door with a slingshot after you have repeatedly asked his parents to disarm him. Can you recover from the parents? Probably.

H. Special Rules for Suits Against Government Agencies

Many states have special rules and procedures that must be followed before a suit can be brought against a state or local government entity. Often, you have to act very quickly or you lose your right to sue. The Small Claims Court clerk will be able to advise you as to the procedures you must follow and time limits you must meet.

---

[5]Check the index to your state's laws under "Minors" or "Children" or "Parent and Child" for your rules.

Let's look at the rules of a state we will call "typical." Before you can sue a city because your car was illegally towed away or a city employee caused you damage, or for any other reason involving personal injury or property damage, you must first file a claim with the city and have it denied. Get a claim form from the city clerk. Your claim must be filed within six months from the date of the incident. The city attorney will review your claim and make a recommendation to the City Council. Sometimes the recommendation will be to pay you—most often it will be to deny your claim no matter how meritorious. Once the City Council acts, you will receive a letter. If it's a denial, take it with you when you file your Small Claims action. The clerk will want to see it.

Typical rules for suits against counties and districts (e.g., school districts) are basically the same. Get your complaint form from the clerk of the governing legislative body for the county (e.g., County Commissions, Board of Supervisors, etc.). Complete and file it within six months of the incident. Within a month or so after filing, you will be told whether your claim is approved or denied. If your claim is denied, you can then proceed to file in Small Claims Court. Claims against the state must also be filed within six months for personal injury and property damage.

Suits against the federal government, a federal agency, or even against a federal employee for actions relating to his or her employment should not be brought in Small Claims Court, as the federal government may not be sued in this court without its consent. Suits against the federal government normally must be filed in Federal District Court. Unfortunately, there are no federal Small Claims procedures available except in Federal Tax Court.

I. Special Procedures for Suits Against the Estates of Deceased People

Death does not prevent lawsuits from being brought and judgments collected against the deceased. However, it does present a number of technical legal hurdles that vary somewhat from one state to the next.

Assuming the defendant made a will (or died without a will or other estate planning device such as a living trust), a probate proceeding will be held. All claims against the estate (and if necessary, law suits), should be promptly made in writing to the personal representative (called an executor or administrator in some states) of the deceased person's estate and directly to the court. If you don't know who the personal representative is (usually it's a surviving spouse, adult child or other chose relative), check filing records with the court that handles probate proceedings in the county where the defendant died. If the personal representative doesn't honor your claim, you will need to promptly check your state's rules as to where and how to sue.

These days many people use living trusts and other devices to completely avoid probate. If this is the case, there will be no personal representative and no probate court proceeding; instead, the deceased property is transferred directly to its inheritors. In this situation, you have the right to proceed against these people directly. In most states, you can do this in Small Claims Court.

CHAPTER 9

Where Can You Sue?

Small Claims Courts are local. This makes sense because the amounts involved aren't large enough to make it worthwhile to require people to travel great distances. A Small Claims Court judicial district covers part of a city, an entire city, several cities, or a county. The next city or county will have its own similar, but separate, Small Claims Court. Normally, your dispute will be with a person or business located nearby. You can sue in the judicial district in which the defendant resides or, if a corporation is involved, where its main place of business is located. Sometimes though, it is not so easy to understand where to file your suit. This might be the case if the person you wish to sue lives 100 (or 500) miles away, or has moved since the dispute arose.

Of all the aspects of Small Claims Court that differ from state to state, the rule on where to sue seems to be the most variable. Some states let you sue another person only in the district or county where he or she resides. Others also allow you to choose the place in which an accident occurred, a contract was broken or originally signed, merchandise was purchased, a corporation does business, and so on. If the person you want to sue has no contracts with your state, however, you almost surely can't sue there, but must sue in the state where the defendant is located.

On the first page of the first chapter we asked you to get a copy of the rules for your local Small Claims Court.[1] Refer to them and to the listing for your state in the Appendix under "Where to Sue." The first thing you will wish to understand are the types of political subdivisions (judicial districts, precincts, cities, counties, etc.; for brevity we will refer to them as "judicial districts") that your state uses to separate the territory of one Small Claims Court from another. Next, you will want to carefully study your local rules in order to understand the geographical boundaries of the Small Claims Court judicial district or districts that are relevant to you. If this information is not set out in the information sheet, call the clerk of the court and ask. You may be able to sue in more than one judicial district. If this is the case, choose the one that is most convenient to you. In a few states, this can be very important, because suits can be brought for different amounts in different parts of each of these states. (The rules for all states are set out in the Appendix.)

---

[1] If your dispute arose at an area some distance from your home and the person you wish to sue also lives there, you will want the rules for that district.

Summary of General Rules as to Where You Can Sue

Depending on the specific rules of your state, you can generally sue in any one of the following counties:

1. In all states, you can sue in the county in which defendant resides or has a place of business at the commencement of the action.

2. In about half of the states, you can also sue in the county in which the obligation on which the suit is based was contracted to be performed.

3. In about half of the states, you can also sue in the county in which an injury to persons or personal property occurred.

4. In a very few states, including California, you can also sue in the county in which the defendant resided or did business at the time a contract was entered into in some circumstances.

Note: As a general rule, it is not possible to bring into court a person who lives outside of the state in which you bring suit, unless that person shows up voluntarily. However, if you are suing a business, and they conduct operations in your state (e.g., an airline sells tickets, a multi-national corporation has an office, store or authorized dealership), you can sue them in your state even if they are incorporated elsewhere.

Now let's consider in more detail the rules concerning where you can sue.

A. You Can Sue a Person Where He Resides/or a Corporation Where It Does Business[2]

This rule makes good sense, doesn't it? If a suit is brought where the defendant is located, he or she can't complain that it is unduly burdensome to appear. Books have been written about the technical definition of residence. Indeed, I remember with horror trying to sort out a law school exam in which the professor had given a person with numerous homes and businesses "contact" with six different judicial districts. The point of the examination was for us students to figure out where he could be sued. Thankfully, you don't have to worry about this sort of nonsense. If you believe a business or individual to be sufficiently present within a particular judicial district so that it would not be a hardship for the business owner to appear in court there, go ahead and file your suit. The worst that can happen—and this is highly unlikely—is that the judge or clerk will tell you to start over someplace else or transfer your case to another judicial district.

Example: Downhill Skier lives in the city, but also owns a mountain cabin at which he spends several months a year. Late one snowy afternoon, Downhill drives his new Porsche from the ski slopes to his ultra-modern, rustic cabin. Turning into his driveway, he skids and does a bad slalom turn right into Woodsey Carpenter's 1957 International Harvester Pickup. Where can Woodsey sue? He can sue in the city where Downhill has his permanent address. He can probably also sue in the county where the cabin is located, on the theory that Downhill also lives there. But read on—as you will see below, it might not be necessary for Woodsey to even get into the residence question

---

[2]This rule can sometimes cause problems if you wish to sue a corporation or other business that operates in your area but has its headquarters elsewhere. Most states solve the problem by allowing you to sue in any judicial district in which the business operates and/or where the act or omission that gave rise to your lawsuit occurred. See Appendix and your state rules.

because many states would allow Woodsey to sue in the mountain county on the theory that the damage occurred there.

Note: In California, Illinois, Minnesota, New Jersey, and the great majority of states, you can sue multiple defendants in any judicial district in which one resides, even though the other(s) live in another part of the state. But in a few states, including New York and Massachusetts, you can sue only in the place in which the defendant resides or does business and thus can't bring one lawsuit against defendants who reside in different judicial districts. (See Appendix; if the listing says that you must sue where "a defendant resides," you can sue them all in one place, but if it says that you must sue where "the defendant resides," you can't sue them all in the same place unless you can find another valid reason to do so (such as where the act or omission occurred).

B. The Contract Which Is the Basis of Your Suit Was Entered Into in a Particular Judicial District

Most states assume that where a written contract is signed is the place where it will be carried out. Thus they assume that the place where the contract was signed is the place in which "the act or omission occurred" if a problem develops.

Arizona, California, Indiana, and a few other states are more thorough. (See Appendix.) In these states, a suit can be brought either where the contract was signed or where the contract was to be performed. This is good common sense, as the law assumes that, if people enter into a contract to perform something at a certain location, it is probably reasonably convenient to both. If, for example, Downhill gets a telephone installed in his cabin, or has a cesspool put in, or agrees to sit for a portrait in the mountain county, he can be sued there if he fails to keep his part of the bargain because the contract was (or was to be) performed in the mountain county. Of course, as we learned above, Downhill might also be sued in the city (judicial district) where he resides permanently, or where the contract was entered into.

Example: John Gravenstein lives in Sonoma County, California, where he owns an apple orchard. He signs a contract with Acme Mechanical Apple Picker Co., an international corporation with offices in San Francisco, New York, Paris and Guatemala City. John signs the contract in Sonoma County. The parts are sent to John from San Francisco via U.P.S. They turn out to be defective. After trying and failing to reach a settlement with Acme, John wants to know if he can sue them in Sonoma County. Yes. Even though Acme doesn't have a business office in Sonoma County and they performed no action there in connection with their agreement to sell John the spare parts, the contract was signed there. But what if John was from Bergen County, New Jersey and signed the contract in New York City (with the goods going through New York City?) Could John sue in Bergen County? No. Acme doesn't reside in Bergen County, and performed no action there in connection with their agreement to sell John the spare parts.[3]

John would have to bring his claim in New York City. But now let's assume that John dealt with Acme's Bergen County representative, who came to his orchard to take the order and who later installed the defective machinery. In this case John can

---

[3]The fact that John spoke to Acme while John was on the phone at his home in Bergen County makes no difference. Acme "accepted the offer to make a contract" while in its office elsewhere.

sue locally because the contract was to be performed in Bergen County.

Reminder: You should realize by now that there may be several reasons why it can be okay to bring a suit in a particular place. You only need one, but it never hurts to have more. Also, as you should now understand, there may be two, three or more judicial districts in which you can file your case. In this situation, simply choose the one most convenient to you, or at least the one in which it's permissible to bring all the defendants (if there are more than one) into court. But check the Appendix and your local rules to make sure which places are appropriate in your case. If you choose the wrong one, your action will either be transferred or dismissed. If it is dismissed, you can refile in the correct district.

Contract Note: It isn't always easy to know where a contract has been "entered into" in a situation where the people making the contract are at different locations. If you enter a contract over the phone, for example, there could be an argument that the contract was entered into either where you are or where the other party is.[4] Rather than trying to learn all the intricacies of contract law, your best bet is probably to sue in the place most convenient to you. On the other hand, if someone sues you at the wrong end of the state and you believe they have not met any of the requirements set out in the Summary above, write the court as soon as you have been served and ask that the case be transferred to a court closer to you. Either way, if in doubt, let the judge decide.

---

[4]To vastly oversimplify, a contract needs both an offer and an acceptance to exist. If I call you and order two widgets and you say okay, you might argue that the contract was entered into at your location. If you write me and order the widgets and I fill the order, however, I might argue that the contract was entered into where I am.

C. In Most (But Not All) States, You Can Sue Where the Injury to a Person or to His/Her Property Occurred

California, Illinois, Indiana, and many other states allow you to sue in the district in which the "act or omission occurred" (see Appendix). "Act or omission" is a shorthand way of purpose together things like automobile accidents, warranty disputes, and landlord-tenant disputes for the purpose of deciding where you're allowed to sue. This means that if you are in a car accident, a dog bites you, a tree falls on your noggin, or a neighbor floods your cactus garden, etc., you can sue in the judicial district where the "act" or injury occurred, even if this is a different district from the one in which the defendant resides.

Example: Addison is returning to his home in Indianapolis from Bloomington, Indiana following an Indiana University basketball game. At the same time, Lenore is rushing to Bloomington from her home in Brown County, Indiana, more than 40 miles west of Bloomington. Lenore jumps a red light and crumples Addison's Toyota near the Indiana University gym in downtown Bloomington, which is in Monroe County. After parking his car and taking a bus home, Addison tries to figure out where he can sue if he can't work out a fair settlement with Lenore. Unfortunately for him, he can't sue in Indianapolis, as Lenore doesn't reside there and the accident occurred in Bloomington. Addison would have to sue either in Monroe County, where his property was damaged, or in Brown County, where Lenore lives. Luckily for Addison, Monroe County is just an hour from Indianapolis. Had the accident occurred in Gary, Indiana, however, which is much further away, Addison would have been put to a lot more trouble if he wished to sue. (Presumably he would have chosen Brown County, which is much closer to his home than is Gary.)

CHAPTER 10

Plaintiffs' and Defendants' Filing Fees, Court Papers and Court Dates

A. How Much Does It Cost?

Fees for filing a case in Small Claims Court are very moderate. It's rare to find a state that charges as much as twenty five dollars, and many charge less than ten.[1] Normally, a defendant is not charged at all unless he or she files an independent claim. There is usually an additional fee for serving papers on the opposing party, unless you are in a state that allows personal service to be carried out by a nonprofessional process server and you have a friend who will do it for you without charge (see Chapter 11).

---

[1]People with very low incomes can often get court filing fees waived. Inquire at your Small Claims clerk's office for more information.

Most states allow service by certified or registered mail, so service costs are usually low. In a few situations you may have to hire a professional process server. This will normally cost less than twenty dollars, but may be higher if the person you are suing is a pro at evading service. You can get your filing fees and service costs added to the court judgment if you win (see Chapter 15).

B. Filling Out Your Court Papers and Getting Your Court Date

Now let's look at the initial court papers themselves to be sure that you don't trip over a detail. Again, I refer specifically to forms in use in California and also include some New York forms, but you will find that your local forms will require similar information. You should have little trouble filling out your papers by following the examples printed here but, if you do, simply ask the clerk for help. Small Claims Court clerks are required by law in most states to give you as much help as possible short of practicing law (whatever that is). A friendly, courteous approach to the clerk can often result in securing much helpful information and advice. In a very few Small Claims Courts, such as those in New York City, trained legal assistants will be available to help you.

Step 1. The Plaintiff's Statement

(In some states, slightly different terminology, such as "General Claim" or "Plaintiff's Claim," is used.)

To start your case in Small Claims Court, go to the Small Claims Court clerk's office and fill out the form entitled "Plaintiff's Statement." If you have carefully read the first nine chapters of this book, this should be easy. Be particularly careful that you are suing in the right judicial district (Chapter 9) and that you are naming the defendant properly (Chapter 8).

Step 2. The Claim of Plaintiff

When you have completed your "Plaintiff's Statement," give it to the county clerk. In some states, the clerk will file your form, but often, he or she will retype it and then assign you a case number. You will be asked to sign this second form under penalty of perjury. A copy of the "Claim of Plaintiff" will go to the judge, and another must be served on the defendant (see Chapter 11).

Step 3. Supplying Documentary Evidence

In most Small Claims Courts, no written evidence need be provided until you get to court, but others, such as Washington D.C., require that certain types of evidence (e.g., copies of unpaid bills, contracts, or other written instruments on which the claim is based) be provided at the time that you file your first papers.

Whether your local rules require written documentation of certain types of claims or not, it is wise to spend a little time thinking about how you will prove your case. We discuss this in detail in the later chapters of this book. You should read ahead and figure out exactly what proof you will need and how you will present it, before you file your first court papers. Being right is one thing—proving it is another.

PLAINTIFF'S STATEMENT

1. State your name and residence address, and the name and address of any other person joining with you in this action. If this claim arises from a business transaction, give the name and address of your business and complete a fictitious business name declaration on back of this form if applicable.

   a. Name Andrew Printer
      Address 1800 Marilee St.   Phone No. 827-7000
                        Street
               Fremont,   CA   94536
                City   State   Zip

   b. Name _____
      Address _____ Phone No. _____
                        Street
               _____ _____ _____
                City   State   Zip

2. State the name and address of each person or business firm you are suing. See "Information to Plaintiff".
   If you are suing one or more individuals, give full name of each.
   If you are suing a business owned by an individual, give the name of the owner and the name of the business he/she owns. You must state if you want to sue the individual as well as the business.
   If you are suing a partnership, give the name of the partners and the name of the partnership.
   If you are suing a corporation, give the corporations full name, and the name and title of an officer.
   If your claim arises out of a vehicle accident, the driver and the registered owner of the other vehicle must be named.

   a. Name Acme Illusions, Inc.
      Address 100 Primrose Road   Phone No. 654-1201
                        Street
               Oakland   CA   94602
                City   State   Zip

   b. Name _____
      Address _____ Phone No. _____
                        Street
               _____ _____ _____
                City   State   Zip

   c. Name _____
      Address _____ Phone No. _____
                        Street
               _____ _____ _____
                City   State   Zip

3. State the amount you are claiming. $950.00

4. Describe briefly the nature of your claim and date it happened:
   Failure to pay for printing and typesetting
   which was completed on April 15, 19__.

5. ☒ I have asked defendant to pay this money, but it has not been paid.

   ☐ I have NOT asked defendant to pay this money because (explain): _____

6. From venue table on reverse side select the reason why this is the proper court for your case.

   [A] Place appropriate letter in box.

   If you select D, E, or F, specify additional facts in this space.
   _____

7. Give address below where obligation was entered into or was to be performed or where injury was incurred, IF NOT A VEHICLE ACCIDENT. See #8 for vehicle accident claims.
   1800 Marilee St., Fremont, California
        (Street address)   (City or locality)

8. If your claim DOES arise out of a vehicle accident, fill out this section:
   a. Date on which accident occurred: _____, 19 _____.
   b. Street or intersection and city or locality where accident occurred:

   c. If you are claiming damages to a vehicle, were you on the date of the accident the registered owner of that vehicle?
      ☐ Yes   ☐ No (Place X in one box)

9. I have received and read the form entitled "Information to Plaintiff".

Date April 27, 19   Signature Andrew Printer

Form No. 214-127 (REV. 3/93)   **PLAINTIFF'S STATEMENT SMALL CLAIMS**
                                     (SEE REVERSE)

CIVIL COURT OF THE CITY OF NEW YORK
SMALL CLAIMS PART
REQUEST FOR INFORMATION

MAXIMUM: $1,500.00

TIME OF TRIAL: 6:30 P.M.

FILING FEE: —NO CHECKS

NAME AND ADDRESS OF PARTY BEING SUED: {See Ch.8}

Lester Landlord

127 E. 89th St.

New York, New York

NAME AND ADDRESS OF PARTY SUING: {See Ch.7}

Theresa Tenant

1234 Park Avenue

New York, New York

AMOUNT: $ 200.00   {See Ch.4}

STATE YOUR CLAIM HERE: Failure of landlord to return
residential rental security deposit after
I moved out of apartment.

{See Ch.2}

Name and Address of Court:
Alameda County Municipal
Oakland-Piedmont
600 Washington St.
Oakland, CA

SMALL CLAIMS CASE NO.

— NOTICE TO DEFENDANT — YOU ARE BEING SUED BY PLAINTIFF To protect your rights, you must appear in this court on the trial date shown in the table below. You may lose the case if you do not appear. The court may award the plaintiff the amount of the claim and the costs. Your wages, money, and property may be taken without further warning from the court.	— AVISO AL DEMANDADO — A USTED LO ESTAN DEMANDANDO *Para proteger sus derechos, usted debe presentarse ante esta corte en la fecha del juicio indicada en el cuadro que aparece a continuación. Si no se presenta, puede perder el caso. La corte puede decidir en favor del demandante por la cantidad del reclamo y los costos. A usted le pueden quitar su salario, su dinero, y otras cosas de su propiedad, sin aviso adicional por parte de esta corte.*

PLAINTIFF/DEMANDANTE *(Name, address, and telephone number of each)*:

Andrew Printer
1800 Marilee St.
Fremont, California 94536

Telephone No.:

Telephone No.:

Fict. Bus. Name Stmt. No.   Expires:

DEFENDANT/DEMANDADO *(Name, address, and telephone number of each)*:

Acme Illusions, Inc.
100 Primose Path
Oakland, California 94602

Telephone No.:

Telephone No.:

☐ See attached sheet for additional plaintiffs and defendants.

PLAINTIFF'S CLAIM

1. Defendant owes me the sum of $ 950.00   , not including court costs, because *(describe claim and date)*:
   He failed to pay for a printing and typesetting job which was completed on April 15, 19__ .

2. a. ☒ I have asked defendant to pay this money, but it has not been paid.
   b. ☐ I have NOT asked defendant to pay this money because *(explain)*:

3. This court is the proper court for the trial because ☐ A *(In the box at the left, insert one of the letters from the list marked "Venue Table" on the back of this sheet. If you select D, E, or F, specify additional facts in this space.)*

4. I ☐ have ☒ have not   filed more than one other small claims action anywhere in California during this calendar year in which the amount demanded is more than $2,500.

5. I ☐ have ☒ have not   filed more than 12 small claims, including this claim, during the previous 12 months.

6. I understand that
   a. I may talk to an attorney about this claim, but I cannot be represented by an attorney at the trial in the small claims court.
   b. I must appear at the time and place of trial and bring all witnesses, books, receipts, and other papers or things to prove my case.
   c. I have no right of appeal on my claim, but I may appeal a claim filed by the defendant in this case.
   d. If I cannot afford to pay the fees for filing or service by a sheriff, marshal, or constable, I may ask that the fees be waived.

7. I have received and read the information sheet explaining some important rights of plaintiffs in the small claims court.
   I declare under penalty of perjury under the laws of the State of California that the foregoing is true and correct.

Date: (fill in date)

Andrew Printer
(TYPE OR PRINT NAME)

▶ *Andrew Printer*
(SIGNATURE OF PLAINTIFF)

ORDER TO DEFENDANT

You must appear in this court on the trial date and at the time LAST SHOWN IN THE BOX BELOW if you do not agree with the plaintiff's claim. Bring all witnesses, books, receipts, and other papers or things with you to support your case.

TRIAL DATE FECHA DEL JUICIO		DATE	DAY	TIME	PLACE	COURT USE
	1.					
	2.					
	3.					
	4.					

Filed on *(date)*:   Clerk, by_____, Deputy

— The county provides small claims advisor services free of charge. Read the information on the reverse. —

Form Adopted by the
Judicial Council of California
SC-100 (Rev. January 1, 1993)

PLAINTIFF'S CLAIM AND ORDER TO DEFENDANT
(Small Claims)

Rule 982.7

Step 4: Getting a Hearing Date

One of the great advantages of Small Claims Court is that disputes are settled quickly. This is important. Many people avoid lawyers and the regular courts primarily because they take forever to get a dispute settled. Business people, for example, increasingly rely on private arbitration, caring more that a dispute be resolved promptly than that they win a complete victory. Anyone who has had to wait for four years for a case to be heard in some constipated state trial court knows through bitter experience that the old cliche, "justice delayed is justice denied," is all too true.

In New York and many other states, an "early" hearing is required, but no maximum number of days is set. Other states require that the case be set for trial within a certain number of days.

When you file your papers, you should also arrange with the clerk for a court date. Get a date that is convenient for you. You need not take the first date the clerk suggests. Be sure to leave yourself enough time to get a copy of the "Claim of Plaintiff" or "Notice of Claim" form served on the defendant(s). (See Chapter 11 for service information.) If you fail to properly serve your papers on the defendant in time, there is no big hassle—just notify the clerk, get a new court date, and try again.

Small Claims Courts are most often held at 9:00 A.M. on working days. Some judicial districts are beginning to hold evening and Saturday sessions. (New York City's sessions are held in the evenings.) Ask the clerk for a schedule. If evening and Saturday sessions aren't available, ask why not.

C. The Defendant's Forms

In most states, no papers need be filed to defend a case in Small Claims Court.[2] You must show up on the date and at the time indicated, ready to tell your side of the story. If you need to get the hearing delayed, see "Changing a Court Date" below. It is proper, and advisable, for a defendant to call or write the plaintiff and see if a fair settlement can be reached without going to court (see Chapter 6).

Sometimes, someone you were planning to sue sues you (i.e., over a traffic accident in which you each believe the other is at fault). As long as your grievance stems from the same incident, you can file a written "Claim of Defendant" or "Counterclaim" for up to the Small Claims Court maximum and have it heard by a judge at the same time that the plaintiff's claim against you is considered.[3] However, if you believe that the plaintiff owes you

---

[2]In a few states, including Alabama, Arkansas, Iowa, and Oregon, a defendant must respond in writing. This is unusual—see Appendix.

[3]Many states call a "Claim of Defendant" either a "cross-complaint" or a "counterclaim." Many states have rules stating that any defendant's claim (counterclaim) must be filed in writing within a certain time period. When you file a Claim of Defendant, you become a plaintiff as far as this claim is concerned. In a few states, such as California, where only the defendant can appeal, this means that, if you lose on your Claim of Defendant, you can't appeal. Of course, even in these states, if you lose on the original plaintiff's claim, you can normally appeal that portion of the judgment. Appeal rules vary a great deal form state to state and can be complicated. See Chapter 23 and the Appendix.

money as the result of a different injury or breach of contract, you may have to file your own separate case.

But what happens if you wish to make a claim against the plaintiff (on facts arising out of the same incident) for more than the Small Claims Court maximum? First reread Chapter 4 and decide whether you want to scale down your claim to fit into Small Claims. If you don't, you can have the whole case transferred to a formal court in most states.[4] The defendant does this either by initiating an action in formal court prior to the Small Claims Court hearing date and notifying the Small Claims Court that this has been done, or by filing the over-the-limit claim in Small Claims Court. In California, the defendant must file an affidavit with the Small Claims Court clerk notifying the court that she has filed in formal court. This paper must be served on the plaintiff by personal service prior to the Small Claims Court hearing. The judge will approve the transfer only if "the ends of justice would be served."

Important: In some states, a judge will check to see if a counterclaim is filed in bad faith (i.e., if there is no reasonable chance that it will succeed) and won't transfer the case if this is so.

Note: If you have a claim against a plaintiff for an amount less than the Small Claims Court maximum that arises out of the same transaction or situation that forms the basis of his suit against you, you are required in many states to file it prior to the time when the plaintiff's case is to be heard. If you fail to file and let the case be decided, you may find that you will not be permitted to file at a later time.

---

[4]In several states, including California, transfer is possible only if the defendant's claim is over the Small Claims Court dollar limit. In a few other states, such as Hawaii, a defendant's claim over the small claims dollar limit won't cause a transfer unless the amount exceeds a higher limit ($5,000 in Hawaii).

Name and Address of Court:
Alameda County Municipal
Oakland-Piedmont
600 Washington St.
Oakland, CA

SMALL CLAIMS CASE NO.

| — NOTICE TO PLAINTIFF —
YOU ARE BEING SUED BY DEFENDANT
To protect your rights, you must appear in this court on the trial date shown in the table below. You may lose the case if you do not appear. The court may award the defendant the amount of the claim and the costs. Your wages, money, and property may be taken without further warning from the court. | — AVISO AL DEMANDANTE —
A USTED LO ESTA DEMANDANDO EL DEMANDADO
Para proteger sus derechos, usted debe presentarse ante esta corte en la fecha del juicio indicada en el cuadro que aparece a continuacion. Si no se presenta, puede perder el caso. La corte puede decidir en favor del demandado por la cantidad del reclamo y los costos. A usted le pueden quitar su salario, su dinero, y otras cosas de su propiedad, sin aviso adicional por parte de esta corte. |

PLAINTIFF/DEMANDANTE (Name, address, and telephone number of each):

Andrew Printer
1800 Marilee St.
Fremont, California 94536

Telephone No.:

DEFENDANT/DEMANDADO (Name, address, and telephone number of each):

Acme Illusions, Inc.
100 Primrose Path
Oakland, California 94602

Telephone No.:

Telephone No.:

☐ See attached sheet for additional plaintiffs and defendants.

Telephone No.:

Fict. Bus. Name Stmt. No.   Expires:

DEFENDANT'S CLAIM

1. Plaintiff owes me the sum of $300.00 , not including court costs, because (describe claim and date):
   of delays and poor workmanship in a printing job he performed for me in April of 19___ .

2. a. ☐ I have asked plaintiff to pay this money, but it has not been paid.
   b. ☐ I have NOT asked plaintiff to pay this money because (explain):

3. I ☐ have ☐ have not filed more than one other small claims action anywhere in California during this calendar year in which the amount demanded is more than $2,500.

4. I understand that
   a. I may talk to an attorney about this claim, but I cannot be represented by an attorney at the trial in the small claims court.
   b. I must appear at the time and place of trial and bring all witnesses, books, receipts, and other papers or things to prove my case.
   c. I have no right of appeal on my claim, but I may appeal a claim filed by the plaintiff in this case.
   d. If I cannot afford to pay the fees for filing or service by a sheriff, marshal, or constable, I may ask that the fees be waived.

5. I have received and read the information sheet explaining some important rights of defendants in the small claims court.

I declare under penalty of perjury under the laws of the State of California that the foregoing is true and correct.

Date: (fill in date)

Waldo Fergus
(TYPE OR PRINT NAME)

Waldo Fergus President
(SIGNATURE OF DEFENDANT)

ORDER TO PLAINTIFF

You must appear in this court on the trial date and at the time LAST SHOWN IN THE BOX BELOW if you do not agree with the plaintiff's claim. Bring all witnesses, books, receipts, and other papers or things with you to support your case.

	DATE	DAY	TIME	PLACE	COURT USE
TRIAL DATE FECHA DEL JUICIO	1.				
	2.				
	3.				
	4.				

Filed on (date):   Clerk, by _____ , Deputy

— The county provides small claims advisor services free of charge. (Advisor phone no:)—

Form Approved by the
Judicial Council of California
SC-120 (Rev. January 1, 1992)

DEFENDANT'S CLAIM AND ORDER TO PLAINTIFF
(Small Claims)

Rule 982.7

D. Jury Trials

Jury trials are not available in Small Claims Court in the great majority of states, including California, Colorado, and Michigan. Some states allow a defendant to transfer a case to a formal court in order to be eligible for a jury trial, no matter how small her claim, while the majority, including California and Ohio, allow transfer when the "Claim of Defendant" is over the Small Claims Court maximum. Normally, a jury trial must be requested as soon as notice of the case is received, and "jury fees" (that often range from $100 to $500) must be paid in advance. Fees are normally recoverable if you win. Asking for a jury trial tends to delay proceedings, and some people will make the request for this reason. The trend across the country is to eliminate jury trials in Small Claims Court. I believe that this is a good idea—it is simply too expensive to round up a large group of people to decide a small claim.[5]

---

[5]In Massachusetts, North Carolina, Virginia and a few other states, especially those which allow new trials on appeal, jury trials are allowed at the appeal stage.

E. Changing a Court Date

It is sometimes impossible for a defendant to be present on the day ordered by the court for the hearing. It can also happen that the plaintiff will pick a court date and get the defendant served only to find that an unexpected emergency makes it impossible for the plaintiff to be present.

It is normally not difficult to get a case postponed. To arrange this, call the other party and see if you can agree on a mutually convenient date. Don't call the clerk first—he doesn't know what days the other party has free. Sometimes it is difficult to face talking to someone with whom you are involved in a lawsuit, but you will just have to swallow your pride. Once all parties have agreed to a new date, send the court clerk a notice in writing signed by both parties.[6] Here is a sample:

---

11 South Street
Denver, CO
January 10, 19__

Clerk of the Small Claims Court
Denver, CO

Re: SC 4117 Rodriguez v. McNally

Mr. Rodriguez and I agree to request that you postpone this case to a date after March 1, 19__.

_____

JOHN MCNALLY

_____

JOHN RODRIGUEZ

---

[6]Check your local Small Claims Court rules and contact the court clerk if you have any questions.

If you speak to the other party and find that he is completely uncooperative, put your request for a delay (continuance) in writing, along with the circumstances that make it impossible for you to keep the first date. Send your letter to the clerk of the Small Claims Court.

Here is a sample:

---

37 Birdwalk Blvd.
Trenton, NJ
January 10, 19__

Clerk
Small Claims Court
Trenton, NJ

Re: Small Claims No. 374-628

Dear Clerk:

I have been served with a complaint (No. 374-628) by John's Laundry, Inc. The date set for a hearing, February 15, falls on the day of my son's graduation from Nursing School in Oscaloosa, Oklahoma, which my husband and I plan to attend.

I called John's Laundry and asked to have the case delayed one week. They just laughed and said that they would not give me any cooperation.

I feel that I have a good defense to this suit. Please delay this case until any date after February 22, except March 13, which is my day for a medical check-up.

Thank you,

Sally Wren

F. If One Party Doesn't Show Up

If one party to a case doesn't appear in court on the proper day at the proper time, the case is normally decided in favor of the other. Depending on whether it is the plaintiff or defendant who fails to show up, the terms used by the judge to make her decision are different. If the plaintiff appears, but the defendant doesn't, a "default judgment" is normally entered in favor of the plaintiff (see Chapters 12 and 15 for more information on defaults). Occasionally, although it happens far less frequently, it is the plaintiff who fails to show up. In this situation, the judge may normally either dismiss the case or decide it on the basis of the defendant's evidence. The defendant will usually prefer this second result, especially if a Claim of Defendant has been made. If the judge dismisses the case, depending on how it is done and the rules of the particular state, the plaintiff may or may not have the right to begin the case again. Ask about this if it affects you.

In some states, if neither party appears, a judge may simply take the case "off calendar," meaning that the plaintiff will get another chance to schedule it for a hearing.

If you are the person who failed to show up (whether defendant or plaintiff) and you still want a chance to argue the case on its merits, you must act immediately or forever hold your peace.

1. Setting Aside a Default (Defendant's Remedy)

Courts are not very sympathetic to setting aside or vacating a default judgment to allow a defense to be made unless you can show that the original papers weren't properly served on you and that you didn't know about the hearing. In some states this can happen if someone signs your name for a certified letter and then doesn't give it to you. In all states it can occur because a dishonest process server doesn't serve you, but tells the court he did. As soon as you find out that a default judgment has been entered against you, call the court clerk. It doesn't make any difference if the hearing you missed was months before as long as you move to set it aside immediately upon learning about it.

If you have had a default judgment entered against you after you were properly served, you will face an uphill struggle to get it set aside. Some judges will accept excuses such as "I forgot," "I was sick," "I got called out of town," etc., and some will not. Generally, judges assume that you could have at least called, or had a friend call, no matter what the emergency. However, if you act promptly and if you have a good excuse, you stand a reasonable chance of getting the judge to set the default aside

Note: In most states, you can't appeal a default judgment even if you have a great case. You must try to get the default set aside or the judgment will be final. To try to set aside a default, go to the Small Claims Court clerk's office and ask for the proper form, titled something like "Notice of Motion to Vacate Judgment."

Writ of Execution Note: If a motion to vacate a default judgment is filed in a situation where a "writ of execution" to collect a Small Claims judgment has already been issued by the court, in most states, the writ of execution must be recalled by the court until a decision on the motion to vacate the default judgment is made. In these states, if the writ of execution has already been served on the judgment debtor, this person must file a motion so that the writ of execution is suspended,[7] pending the decision on the motion to vacate the default judgment. For more information on how to do this, or to find out the exact rules for your state, consult your Small Claims Court clerk.

---

[7]This type of motion is called a motion to stay or a motion to quash.

Name and Address of Court:

SMALL CLAIMS CASE NO.

PLAINTIFF DEMANDANTE (Name, address, and telephone number of each):

DEFENDANT DEMANDADO (Name, address, and telephone number of each):

Telephone No.:

Telephone No.:

Telephone No.:

Telephone No.:

☐ See attached sheet for additional plaintiffs and defendants.

NOTICE TO (Name):

One of the parties has asked the court to CANCEL the small claims judgment in your case. If you disagree with this request, you should appear in this court on the hearing date shown below. If the request is granted, ANOTHER TRIAL may immediately be held. Bring all witnesses, books, receipts, and other papers or things with you to support your case.	*Una de las partes en el caso le ha solicitado a la corte que DEJE SIN EFECTO la decisión tomada en su caso por la corte para reclamos judiciales menores. Si usted está en desacuerdo con esta solicitud, debe presentarse en esta corte en la fecha de la audiencia indicada a continuación. Si se concede esta solicitud, es posible que se efectúe otro juicio inmediatamente. Traiga a todos sus testigos, libros, recibos, y otros documentos o cosas para presentarlos en apoyo de su caso.*

NOTICE OF MOTION TO VACATE JUDGMENT

1. A hearing will be held in this court at which I will ask the court to **cancel** the judgment entered against me in this case.
   If you wish to oppose the motion you should appear at the court on

HEARING DATE FECHA DEL JUICIO		DATE	DAY	TIME	PLACE	COURT USE
	1.					
	2.					
	3.					

2. I am asking the court to cancel the judgment for the reasons stated in item 5 below. My request is based on this notice of motion and declaration, the records on file with the court, and any evidence that may be presented at the hearing.

DECLARATION FOR MOTION TO VACATE (CANCEL) JUDGMENT

3. Judgment was entered against me in this case on (date):
4. I first learned of the entry of judgment against me on (date):
5. I am asking the court to cancel the judgment for the following reason:
   a. ☐ I did not appear at the trial of this claim because (specify facts):

   b. ☐ Other (specify facts):

6. I understand that I must bring with me to the hearing on this motion all witnesses, books, receipts, and other papers or things to support my case.
   I declare under penalty of perjury under the laws of the State of California that the foregoing is true and correct.

Date: ▶

. . . .
(TYPE OR PRINT NAME)   (SIGNATURE)

CLERK'S CERTIFICATE OF MAILING

I certify that I am not a party to this action. This Notice of Motion to Vacate Judgment was mailed first class, postage prepaid, in a sealed envelope to the responding party at the address shown above. The mailing and this certification occurred
at (place):   , California,
on (date):

Clerk, by _____ , Deputy

— The county provides small claims advisor services free of charge. —

Form Approved by the
Judicial Council of California
SC-135 (Rev. January 1, 1992)

**NOTICE OF MOTION TO VACATE
JUDGMENT AND DECLARATION**
(Small Claims)

Rule 982.7

2. Vacating a Judgment of Dismissal (Plaintiff's Remedy)

The plaintiff who fails to show up in court at the appointed time and then requests that the judge vacate his decision to dismiss the case will encounter even more difficulty than a no-show defendant who tries to persuade the judge to set aside a default. Why? Because the plaintiff is the one who started the case and arranged for the court date. The judge assumes that the plaintiff should be able to show up for his or her own case, or at least call the court clerk prior to the court date and explain why not.

However, now and then emergencies happen, or someone simply makes a mistake about the day. Judges can, and do, vacate dismissals if both of the following circumstances exist. One, the plaintiff moves to have the judgment vacated "immediately" upon learning of his mistake. "Immediately" is never interpreted to be more than a few weeks, at most, after the day the dismissal was entered, and is thought by most judges to be a much shorter time. Two, the plaintiff has a good explanation as to why he or she was unable to be present or call on the day the case was regularly scheduled. A judge might accept something like this: "I had a flu with a high fever and simply lost track of a couple of days. As soon as I felt better, which was two days after my case was dismissed, I came to the clerk's office to try to get the case rescheduled."

To get a dismissal vacated (when allowed), you must fill out a form similar to the one shown above.

CHAPTER 11

Serving Your Papers

After you have filed your "Claim of Plaintiff" form with the clerk, following the instructions in Chapter 10 under "Filling Out Your Court Papers and Getting Your Court Date," a copy must be served on the person, persons, or corporation you are suing. This is called "service of process." Your lawsuit is not complete without it. The reason that you must serve the other side is simple—the person(s) you are suing are entitled to be notified of the general nature of your claim and the day, time and place of the hearing so that they can show up to defend themselves. The general rules of all states are similar, but details do differ. Refer to your local rules and to the Appendix of this book.

A. Who Must Be Served

All defendants that you list on your "Claim of Plaintiff" or "Notice of Claim" should be served. It is not enough to serve one defendant and assume that he will tell the other(s). This is true even if the defendants are married or living together. If you don't serve a particular defendant, the court can't enter a judgment against that person. If you sue more than one person and can serve only one, a judge can only enter a judgment against the person served, in effect dismissing your action against the other defendant(s). Depending on the state, you may be able to refile against these defendants if you wish.

B. Where Can Papers Be Served?

Normally papers must be served within the state in which your action is brought. Thus, you can't sue someone in a Massachusetts court and serve papers on them in Oklahoma. The one exception involves suits having to do with motor vehicle accidents. Many states have a procedure for out-of-state service on this type of claim. Your Small Claims Court clerk will show you how this is handled in your state.

Now let's assume that the person you want to sue resides or does business in your state. In most states, papers can be served anyplace in the sate as long as the suit is brought in the correct judicial district. (See Chapter 9, "Where Can I Sue?") But a few states, including New York, require with some exceptions that a defendant be served in the same county or judicial district where the suit was filed. (See the Appendix.)

C. How to Serve Your Papers

There are several approved ways to serve papers. All depend on your knowing where the defendant is. If you can't find the defendant and do not know where she lives or works, you can't serve her and it makes little sense to file a lawsuit.

Method 1:   Personal Service

Sheriff, Marshal, or Constable: All states allow personal service to be made by law officers. This is often good for its sobering effect, but can cost a few dollars. Twenty to thirty dollars is the average fee, but you can get it added to your judgment if you win. Many states also allow service by private process servers. whom you will find listed in the Yellow Pages. (See Appendix for other states which allow professional process servers.)

Service by Disinterested Adult: California, Colorado, Ohio, and a number of other states (but by no means all—see Appendix) allow service by any person who is eighteen years of age or older, except the person bringing a suit. Any person means just that—a relative or a friend is fine.

The "Claim of Plaintiff" or "Notice of Claim" must be handed to the defendant personally. You can't simply leave the paper at her job, or home, or in the mailbox. A person making a service who doesn't know the person involved should make sure that he is serving the right person. If a defendant refuses to take the paper, acts hostile or attempts to run away, the process server should simply put the paper down and leave. Valid service has been accomplished. The process server should never try to use force to get a defendant to take any papers.

Method 2: By Certified or Registered Mail

In California, New York, and the majority of states, you can also serve papers by certified mail. In some states service by certified (or registered) mail is an option of the plaintiff, while others require that it be tried before any other method of service is attempted (see Appendix). Normally, the court clerk does the mailing for you and charges a small fee. This is recoverable if you win (see Chapter 15). The mail method is both cheap and easy, but depends for its success on the defendant signing for the letter. Most businesses and many individuals routinely sign to accept their mail. However, some people never do, knowing instinctively, or perhaps from past experience, that nothing good ever comes by certified mail.[1] I have asked several court clerks for an estimate as to the percentage of certified mail services that are accepted. The consensus is 50%. If you try using the mail to serve your papers and fail, simply get a process server. Chances are the defendant will end up paying for it.

Note: Never assume that your certified mail service has been accomplished and show up in court on the day of the court hearing. If the defendant didn't sign for the paper, you will be wasting your time in all but a few states. Call the clerk a couple of days in advance and find out if the service of process has been completed. This means the certified letter has been signed for by the defendant, not by someone else at the address.

Method 3: By Regular First-Class Mail

A minority of states, including New York and Connecticut, allow papers to be served by first-class mail. The states differ, however, on what you must do if the defendant doesn't answer your complaint within the time limit. New York, for example, presumes that the defendant received the papers unless the envelope comes back as "undeliverable." Connecticut, on the

---

[1]In a few states, including Alaska and Arkansas, service is accomplished even though a certified letter is rejected by the defendant.

other hand, requires you to back up unanswered regular mail service with personal service by the sheriff. Check with your court clerk to see if this method is available where you are.

Method 4:   Substituted Service
(or "Nail and Mail")

Often it is hard to serve particular individuals. Some people have developed their skill at avoiding process servers into a high (but silly) art. In some states, this no longer works, as there is now a procedure which allows "substituted service" if you try to serve a defendant and fail." Often the slang for this type of service is "Nail and Mail," because in several states, if you are unable to serve the defendant personally, you do not have to leave the claim with a live person, but can simply tack one copy to the defendant's door and mail the second copy.

In a typical state, substituted service works like this. If a person can't be served with "reasonable diligence," the papers may be served by leaving a copy at the person's dwelling place in the presence of a competent member of the household who is at least 18 years of age and who must be told what the papers are about *and* thereafter mailing a copy by first-class mail to the person served. Service is complete ten days after mailing. Be sure that all steps are carried out by an adult who is not named in the lawsuit. Because some Small Claims Court clerks interpret the requirement for "reasonable diligence" differently, you will wish to run through the substituted service procedure with your local clerk before trying it. If your suit is against a corporation, the substituted service procedure is easier, as there is no "diligence" requirement before using it. Papers may be served by leaving them at the defendant's office with a person apparently in charge of the office during normal business hours, and then mailing another copy to the person to be served at the same address. Service is accomplished ten days after mailing.

After service is accomplished, you must return a "Proof of Service" form to the court clerk stating that all proper "service" steps have been completed.(See "Serving a Business" below).

Method 5:   For Serving Subpoenas Only

In Chapter 14 we discuss subpoenaing witnesses and documents. Subpoenas can't be served by mail. They must be served by personal service. The rules as to who can do the serving, etc., are the same as those set forth above in Method 1, with one important difference: any person, including the person bringing the suit, can serve the subpoena. In addition, in many states, the person making the service must be ready to pay the person subpoenaed a witness fee on the spot if it is requested.[2] If you hire a sheriff or marshal to do the service, he or she will ask you to pay this fee, plus the service fee, in advance. In many states, if the witness doesn't ask for the fee, it will be returned to you.

D. Costs of Personal Service

Professional process servers commonly charge from $20-$50 per service, depending on time and mileage involved.[3] You can usually get your costs of service added to your judgment if you win, but be sure to remind the judge to do this when you con-

---

[2]This is usually a flat fee (normally $40-$100), plus a mileage fee based on the distance from the courthouse.

[3]County officials such as sheriffs and marshals will only serve papers in the county in which they are located. Call them to ask about fees. Be sure to authorize them to serve papers by either personal or substituted service if the latter exists in your state. If you don't arrange for substituted service in advance, they may not be able to use it.

clude your court presentation. However, a few courts, will not give the successful party an award of costs for a process server unless he or she first tried to have the papers served by the cheaper certified mail approach (Method 2 above). Other judicial districts prefer that you don't use the mail approach at all because they feel that, too often, the mail isn't accepted. Ask the Small Claims Court clerk in your district how she prefers that you accomplish service and how much the judge will allow as a service of process fee.

E. Time Limits in Which Papers Must Be Served

All states have a rule that the defendant is entitled to receive service of the "Claim of Plaintiff" or "Notice of Claim" form before the date of the court hearing. Rules as to how many days in advance of the hearing papers must be served vary considerably, with some states requiring as little as five and others requiring as many as 30. Check your local rules for details.

If the defendant is served fewer than the required number of days before the trial date, he can either go ahead with the trial anyway, or request that the case be delayed (continued). If a delay is granted, it is normally in the range of two weeks to a month. If it is impossible to show up in person to ask for a delay, call the court clerk (telegraph if you can't call) and point out that you weren't served in the proper time and that you want the case put over. The clerk will see that a default judgment is not entered against you (see Chapter 10, "Changing a Court Date.") But just to be sure, get the clerk's name.

To count the days to see if service has been accomplished in the correct time, in most states you do not count the day the service is accomplished, but do count the day of the court appearance (check your local rules). Also count weekends and holidays. Thus, if Jack served Julie on July 12 in Los Angeles County (where the limit is five days), with a "Declaration and Order" listing a July 17 court date in the same county, service would be proper. This is true even if Saturday and Sunday fell on July 14 and 15. To determine the number of days you would not count July 12, the day of service, but you would count July 13, 14, 15, 16, and 17 for a total of five days. If you are unable to serve the defendant(s) within the proper time, simply ask the court clerk for a new court date and try again.

Defendant's Note: If you are improperly served either because you are not given adequate time, or the papers weren't handed to your personally, or a certified letter wasn't signed for by you, it is still wise for you to call the court clerk or show up in court on the day in question. Why should you have to do this if service was improper? Because the plaintiff may succeed in getting the case heard as a default if you fail to show up. While this is improper, the fact remains that it is often more trouble to get an improper default judgment set aside than to protect yourself from the start. But isn't this a Catch-22? You are entitled to proper service, but if you don't get it, you have to show up in court anyway? Perhaps, but as Catch-22's go, this one is mild. You can call the clerk or show up in court and request that the judge grant you a continuance to prepare your case. If the original service was in fact improper, your request will be honored. Of course, if you were improperly served and simply want to get the hearing out of the way, you can show up and go ahead with your case.

F. Serving a Business

If you are suing someone who is the sole proprietor of a business, or is a partner in a business, you must serve the person individually, using the rules set out above. However, if you are suing a corporation, the rules are a little different.

Although a corporation is a legal person for purposes of lawsuits, you will still need to have your papers served on someone who lives and breathes. This is true whether you have the papers served personally, or use certified mail. The flesh-and-blood person should be an officer of the corporation (president, vice-president, secretary or treasurer). Simply call the corporation and ask who, and where, they are. If they won't tell you, the city or county business tax and license people should be able to, at least for local corporations (see Chapter 8). If you have trouble getting someone at a large national corporation to accept service, call or write your Secretary of State or Commissioner of Corporations. Their office will be located in your state capital. They will be able to tell you who is authorized to accept service for the company in your state. Try calling information for a phone number before writing for the information. If you are suing a corporation in a situation where you know that the officers (or general manager) of the corporation work out of a local office, in most states it is easy to use substituted service, as set out in Method 3 above.

G. Serving a Public Agency

As discussed in Chapter 8, before you can sue a city, county or other government body, you often must first file a claim against that agency within a specified number of days of the incident that gives rise to your claim. Once your claim is denied, you can sue in Small Claims Court. To serve your papers, call the governmental body in question and ask them who should be served. Then proceed following the rules set out in Method 1 or 2 above.

H. Notifying the Court that Service Has Been Accomplished ("Proof of Service")

Where certified or registered mail is involved, you need do nothing. The court clerk sends out the certified mail for you, and the signed post office receipt comes back directly to the clerk if service is accomplished. It's as simple as that.

However, a court has no way of knowing whether or not papers have been successfully served by personal service unless you tell them. This is done by filing a piece of paper known as a "Proof of Service" with the court clerk after the service has been made. The "Proof of Service" is often a small, perforated, tear-off form, or a separate form which you get from the court clerk, and which must be signed by the person actually making the service. A "Proof of Service" is used both by the plaintiff and by the defendant if he files a "Claim of Defendant." It must be returned to the clerk's office before the trial. A "Proof of Service" is used when any legal documents are served by personal service.

We will refer back to this example several times in future chapters. Frequently there isn't time after a defendant is served for her to properly complete service of a Claim of Defendant. In this situation, the defendant should simply file her Claim of Defendant and bring up the service problem in court. The plaintiff may well waive the time of service requirement and agree to proceed. Or, the plaintiff may request that the judge continue the case to a later date. The judge will normally grant the continuance if there is a good reason. If the papers are served by a law enforcement officer, he or she will prepare and file the "Proof of Service" automatically. Check your local rules for specific filing requirements.

ATTORNEY OR PARTY WITHOUT ATTORNEY *(Name and Address)*

TELEPHONE NO.:

FOR COURT USE ONLY

Ref. No. or File No.

ATTORNEY FOR *(Name)*:

Insert name of court and name of judicial district and branch court, if any:

SHORT TITLE OF CASE:

PROOF OF SERVICE (Summons)	DATE:	TIME:	DEPT./DIV.:	CASE NUMBER:

1. At the time of service I was at least 18 years of age and not a party to this action, and I **served copies** of the *(specify documents)*:

2. a. Party served *(specify name of party as shown on the documents served)*:

   b. Person served: ☐ party in item 2a ☐ other *(specify name and title or relationship to the party named in item 2a)*:

   c. Address:

3. I served the party named in item 2
   a. ☐ **by personally delivering the copies** (1) on *(date)*:   (2) at *(time)*:
   b. ☐ **by leaving the copies** with or in the presence of *(name and title or relationship to person indicated in item 2b)*:

      (1) ☐ **(business)** a person at least 18 years of age apparently in charge at the office or usual place of business of the person served. I informed him or her of the general nature of the papers.
      (2) ☐ **(home)** a competent member of the household (at least 18 years of age) at the dwelling house or usual place of abode of the person served. I informed him or her of the general nature of the papers.
      (3) on *(date)*:   (4) at *(time)*:
      (5) ☐ A declaration of diligence is attached. *(Substituted service on natural person, minor, conservatee, or candidate.)*
   c. ☐ **by mailing** the copies to the person served, addressed as shown in item 2c, by first-class mail, postage prepaid,
      (1) on *(date)*:   (2) from *(city)*:
      (3) ☐ with two copies of the Notice and Acknowledgment of Receipt and a postage-paid return envelope addressed to me.
      (4) ☐ to an address outside California with return receipt requested.   ◄ *(Attach completed form.)* ◄
   d. ☐ by causing copies to be mailed. A declaration of mailing is attached.
   e. ☐ other *(specify other manner of service and authorizing code section)*:
4. The "Notice to the Person Served" (on the summons) was completed as follows:
   a. ☐ as an individual defendant.
   b. ☐ as the person sued under the fictitious name of *(specify)*:
   c. ☐ on behalf of *(specify)*:
      under: ☐ CCP 416.10 (corporation)   ☐ CCP 416.60 (minor)   ☐ other:
             ☐ CCP 416.20 (defunct corporation)   ☐ CCP 416.70 (conservatee)
             ☐ CCP 416.40 (association or partnership)   ☐ CCP 416.90 (individual)
5. **Person serving** *(name, address, and telephone No.)*:
   a. Fee for service: $
   b. ☐ Not a registered California process server.
   c. ☐ Exempt from registration under B&P § 22350(b).
   d. ☐ Registered California process server.
      (1) ☐ Employee or independent contractor.
      (2) Registration No.:
      (3) County:
6. ☐ I declare under penalty of perjury under the laws of the State of California that the foregoing is true and correct.
7. ☐ I am a California sheriff, marshal, or constable and I certify that the foregoing is true and correct.

Date:

►

(SIGNATURE)

Form Adopted by Rule 982
Judicial Council of California
982(a)(23) (New July 1, 1987)

PROOF OF SERVICE
(Summons)

Code Civ. Proc. § 417.10(f)

I. Serving A Claim of Defendant

As you will remember from our discussion in Chapter 9, a Claim of Defendant is the form that the defendant files when he wishes to sue the plaintiff for money damages arising out of the same incident that forms the basis for the plaintiff's suit. A Claim of Defendant must be filed with the Small Claims Court clerk and served on the plaintiff. Time limits vary from state to state, as do the technical requirements for service. In California, a Claim of Defendant should be filed and served at least five days prior to the date that the court has set for the hearing on the plaintiff's claim. In New York, the time limit is seven days. Check your local rules. If you file a Claim of Defendant and can't find the plaintiff to serve the papers, all is not lost. Explain your problem to the court clerk. In most states, the clerk will either arrange to have the hearing date delayed or will tell you to show up for the first hearing with your papers. You can serve them on the plaintiff in the hallway (not the courtroom). Then explain to the judge why it was impossible to locate the plaintiff earlier. The judge will either put the whole case over for a few days or allow you to proceed with your claim that day. Either way, she will accept your Claim of Defendant as validly served.

J. Serving Someone In the Military— Declaration of Non-Military Service

It is proper to serve someone who is on active duty in the armed forces. If she shows up, fine. If she doesn't, you have a problem. We learned in Chapter 10 that as a general rule, if a properly served defendant doesn't show up, you can get a "default judgment" against her. This is not true if the person you are suing is in the military (the reserves don't count).

Default judgments cannot normally be taken against people on active duty in the armed forces because Congress has given our military personnel special protections. To get a default judgment, a statement normally must be filed under penalty of perjury that he or she is not in the military. This declaration is available from the clerk. Clerks almost always accept Declaration of Non-Military Service signed by the plaintiff, as long as the plaintiff reasonably believes that the defendant is not on active duty. This constitutes a lenient interpretation of the law by clerks, but no one seems to be complaining.

CHAPTER 12

The Defendant's Options

This chapter is devoted to a review of the concerns of the defendant. Most of this material has already been discussed in the first eleven chapters, but it will be helpful to pull it all together in one place. Let's start by assuming that you are the person being sued. How do you approach what's happening to you? First, when you receive the plaintiff's papers, you will have to make one of several decisions. There is no one correct course of action—it all depends on your circumstances.

A. Improper Service

You may conclude that the service was not proper (see Chapter 11). Perhaps the "Claim of Plaintiff" was left with your neighbors, or maybe you didn't have the correct number of days in which to respond. You may be tempted not to show up in court, figuring that since you weren't served properly, the case can't be heard. As noted, this is not smart if you wish to defend the case. The judge can easily be unaware of, or overlook, the service problem and issue a default judgment against you. If this happens, you will have to go to the trouble of requesting that the default be set aside. You are better off to contact the clerk, explain the problem with the service, and ask that the case be continued to a date that is convenient. If the clerk can't help, write the judge or show up on the day in question and request a continuance.

B. No Defense

Now let's assume that the service was okay, but you have no real defense, or don't have the time to defend yourself, or for some other reason don't feel like going to court.[1] A decision not to show up will very likely result in a default judgment being entered against you. It will most probably be for the dollar amount demanded by the plaintiff, plus his or her filing fee and costs to serve you. We discuss default judgments and how you can try to set them aside if you take action immediately in Chapters 10 and 15.

If you do not dispute the plaintiff's claim, but cannot afford to pay it all at once and want to make payments in installments, your best bet is to show up in court and explain your situation to the judge. If you can't be present, write a letter to the court prior to the court hearing (be sure to properly identify the case, using the number from the Claim of Plaintiff form) explaining why it

---

[1]Many people are tempted not to show up and defend a case in Small Claims Court because they have no money and figure that even if they lose, the plaintiff can't collect. This is "grasshopper thinking." The sun may be shining today and the judgment may cause you no immediate problem, but remember, judgments are good for ten to twenty years, depending on the state, and can usually be renewed for a longer period of time, if necessary. You may put a few nickels together sometime in the future and you probably won't want them taken away by an industrious little ant holding a Small Claims judgment in his mouth. So wake up and defend yourself while you can.

would be difficult or impossible to pay any judgment all at once.
For example, if you are on a fixed income, have recently been
unemployed and have a lot of debts, or have a low or moderate
income and a large family, explain this to the judge. Just state the
facts; there is no need to tell a long sob story. When the judge
enters a judgment against you, she will very likely order you to
pay in reasonable monthly installments.

C. Try to Compromise

If you feel that perhaps the plaintiff has some right on his
side, but that you are being sued for too much, contact the
plaintiff and try to work out a compromise settlement. Any
settlement you make should be set down in writing along the
lines outlined in Chapter 6. It should also include a specific
statement that the plaintiff will forever drop his pending lawsuit.
Simply add a clause like the following to the sample agreement
outlined in Chapter 6:

"As part of this settlement, __(name of plaintiff)__ hereby
agrees to drop the lawsuit, number __(insert number)__ filed in
Small Claims Court in the __(insert judicial district or county)__
court on __(date)__ against __(name of defendant)__ and
that no further court action(s) will be filed regarding the subject
matter of this agreement."

As a practical matter, any lawsuit that is not actively prose-
cuted will be dropped by the clerk. The reason that you want to
have a settlement agreement written out is to cover the unlikely

possibility that the other party will accept money from you and then try to go ahead with his suit. If this happens, you need only show your written settlement agreement to the judge.

A few states prefer that both parties prepare and file a written settlement agreement with the Small Claims Court clerk. There is a sample form in use in New York on the next page.

D. Fight Back

Now we get to those of you who feel that you don't owe the plaintiff a dime. You will want to actively fight. This means that you must show up in court on the date stated in the papers served on you, unless you get the case continued (see Chapter 10). In the great majority of states, a defendant need not file any papers with the court clerk; showing up ready to defend yourself is enough.[2] The strategies to argue a case properly, including the presentation of witnesses, estimates, diagrams, etc. are discussed in Chapters 13-21 and apply both to defendants and plaintiffs. You will wish to study this information carefully and develop a strategy for your case. You will also want to see whether the plaintiff has brought the case within the time allowed by the Statute of Limitations (Chapter 5) and whether he has asked for a reasonable amount of money (Chapter 4). If you simply show up without thinking out a coherent presentation, you are likely to lose.

---

[2]This is not true in a few states, where a written response must be filed. States where a response is necessary include Alabama, Alaska, Oregon, South Carolina (oral is okay), Vermont (oral is okay), Virginia, and West Virginia.

Civil Court of the City of New York   Index No. _____

COUNTY OF _____
                    Part
_____

                                                      STIPULATION OF SETTLEMENT
              _____   and
                  Claimant(s), Plaintiff(s),   AFFIDAVIT UPON DEFAULT
          against
              _____
                       Defendant(s),

STIPULATION OF SETTLEMENT

   It is hereby agreed by and between the parties that this claim is settled for the sum of $_____.
                                                                              (Amount)
to be paid on or before _____, to _____ at:
                              (Date)   (Creditor)
_____ or as follows:
                              (Address)

   Upon such payment all parties shall be released from liability to each other concerning the matters in this dispute.

   In the event _____ fails to make payment within _____ days,
                          (Debtor)
Creditor, upon completing the Affidavit below setting forth such default, shall be entitled to: *(SELECT ONE OPTION)*
      ☐ a) enter Judgment, without further notice to the Debtor, for the amount (originally sued for/agreed to above)
             less any payments made, together with interest and disbursements.   (Cross out inapplicable choice)

      ☐ b) restore the case to the calendar for trial.

_____   _____
Signature   Date   Signature   Date

_____   _____
Signature   Date   Signature   Date

AFFIDAVIT UPON DEFAULT OF STIPULATION

State of New York, County of _____ ss:

_____, being duly sworn, deposes and says:
                         (Creditor)
   This case was settled as indicated above. The Debtor has failed to comply with the terms of the settlement. I,
therefore, request, in accordance with the settlement, that:

_____
                  (Specify your request)

Sworn to before me this

_____ day of _____, 19____

_____   _____
     Notary Public or Court Employee and Title   Signature of Deponent

CIV-GP-31 (5/92) (Replaces CIV-SC-91 and 43-2031)

E. File a "Claim of Defendant"

Finally, there are those of you who not only want to dispute the plaintiff's claim, but also want to sue him. This involves either promptly filing a "Claim of Defendant" (often called a cross-complaint or counterclaim) in Small Claims Court for up to the Small Claims Court maximum, or having the case transferred to a formal court where you can sue for more. See Chapter 10 under "How to Serve Your Papers" and Chapter 11 under "Notifying the Court that Service Has Been Accomplished" for more details.[3]

---

[3]In most states, filing a Claim of Defendant, Counterclaim, or Cross-Complaint results in your case staying in Small Claims Court, unless your claim is over the Small Claims limit, in which case it will usually be transferred to a formal court. In a few states, a defendant has the right to have a case transferred to a formal court even without filing a claim in excess of the Small Claims Court limit, although this often can be done only by demanding a jury trial, which is almost always silly if the claim is small. A few states, such as California, will not automatically allow transfer by reason of an over-the-limit counterclaim (see Appendix). In some states, such as Colorado, if the court finds you filed an over-the-limit counterclaim just to get transferred out of Small Claims jurisdiction, it may penalize you by making you pay some of the plaintiff's increased costs.

CHAPTER 13

Getting Ready for Court

Once you have your papers on file and the defendant(s) served, the preliminaries are over and you are ready for the main event—your day in court. Movies, and especially TV, have done much to make court proceedings false. Ask yourself, what was a trial like *before* every lawyer fancied himself Raymond Burr or Charles Laughton and judges acted "fatherly," or "stern," or "indignantly outraged" in the fashion of Judge Wopner of "People's Court"?

There are people whose lives revolve around courthouses, and who have been playing movie parts for so long that they have become caricatures of one screen star or another. Lawyers are particularly susceptible to this virus. All too often they substitute posturing and theatrics for good, hard preparation. Thankfully though, most people who work in our courts quickly recover from movieitis and realize that the majestic courtroom is, in truth, a large, drafty hall with a raised platform at one end: His honor is only a lawyer dressed in a black shroud, who knew the right politician, and that they themselves are not bit players in "Witness For The Prosecution," "L.A. Law" or "The Verdict."

I mention movieitis because it's a common ailment in Small Claims Court. Cases that should be won easily are often lost because somebody goes marching around the courtroom antagonizing everyone with comic opera imitations of E. G. Marshall. And don't assume that you are immune. Movieitis is a subtle disease, because people often don't realize they have it. Ask yourself a few self-diagnostic questions:

• Have you watched courtroom scenes on TV or in the movies?

• Have you ever imagined that you were one of the actor-lawyers?

• How many times have you been in a real courtroom in comparison to watching movie-set courtrooms?

My purpose here is not to lecture you on how to present yourself in court. But perhaps I can get you to remember something that you already know—you don't need to be false to yourself to succeed in Small Claims Court. You don't need to put on fancy clothes or airs, or try to appear more polished, intelligent or sophisticated than you are. Be yourself and you will do just fine. If you have a chance, go to the court a few days before your case is heard and watch for an hour or two. You may not learn a great deal that will be helpful in your case, but you will be a lot more relaxed and comfortable when your turn comes. Watching a few cases is a particularly good thing to do if you feel anxious about your court appearance. For those of you who love to act, who simply can't pass up an opportunity to perform, at least act real. That's right, go ahead and act if you must; but make your performance that of a person—not a personality.

Movieitis aside, most people I have watched in Small Claims Court have done extremely well. Many mornings I have been inspired, feeling that for the first time in years I have seen honesty and truth put in an appearance before the Bar of Justice. When I first witnessed this phenomenon as part of doing research for this book, I was surprised. I had stopped taking on clients several years ago, in part because I hated the dishonest sham that goes on in the courtroom—hated the endless natterings between lawyers about logic-chopping technicalities while clients paid and paid and paid. It was wonderful to see that once the lawyers were removed and people began communicating directly, there was much about our court system that made sense.

Commonly a judge must decide a case, at least in part, on the basis of who seems to be the most believable. This happens when there isn't enough hard evidence to be conclusive either way. Different judges have varying prejudices, hunches, feelings, etc., about who is, or isn't, telling the truth. Often, they themselves can't explain the many intangibles that go into making this sort of decision, but most agree that a person who presents herself in a simple, straightforward way is more likely to be believed than is a person who puts on airs. For example, a house painter who shows up in his overalls and puts his lunchbox under the chair will probably be much more convincing (and comfortable) than he would be if he came painfully squeezed into his blue wedding and funeral suit. As one judge told me, "A pimp being a pimp has as good a chance as anyone else in my courtroom, but a pimp who tries to act like Saint Paul better watch out."

Before we get into a discussion of how to prepare and present different types of cases, here are a few general suggestions:

A. Interpreter Services

In several states, Small Claims Courts are required to make an effort to have interpreter services available for those who need them. Notify the court clerk well in advance if you or one of your witnesses will need an interpreter. In most areas, interpreters are not routinely made available by the court. It is normally permissible to bring your own, however. Many ethnic and cultural organizations offer interpreter services to low-income persons free of charge.

B. Court Times

Small Claims courts can schedule cases any time they wish on business days. Most commonly, court is held at 9:00 a.m. In larger judicial districts, Saturday or evening sessions may also be held. If it is not convenient for you to go to court during business hours, request that your case be scheduled at one of these other sessions.

C. Legal Advisors

A few Small Claims Courts are experimenting with legal advisor programs. In some areas of New York and California, free legal advisor programs have met with success. While there is no set approach, most court-sponsored legal advisor programs make it possible for people involved in Small Claims Court actions, either as plaintiffs or defendants, to meet with a lawyer or a person with paralegal training before going to court. The idea is that the legal advisor will help the person using Small Claims Court to understand and prepare his or her case properly. You may wish to inquire if a legal advisor program is available in your area, but don't be disappointed if you don't find one. For most people, most of the time, it is not difficult to prepare a case properly for Small Claims Court without professional help. Indeed, a study prepared for the National Center for State Courts concluded that people whose education stopped before eleventh grade did just as well as those who had completed graduate school.[1]

---

[1]Small Claims Court, A National Examination, Ruhnka *et al.*, National Center for State Courts.

D. Lawyers

As noted several times, a number of states have quite sensibly banned lawyers from appearing in Small Claims Court on behalf of either plaintiff or defendant. Unfortunately, however, most states still allow representation by an attorney. (See Appendix.) This is a mistake—it is past time that the lawyers that we have elected to our state legislatures pass laws to ban their brethren in private practice from appearing in what should be the people's court.

Let's suppose that you live in a state that allows lawyers to appear in Small Claims Court, and that your case is against a lawyer, or someone represented by one. Should you hire one too? No! I think that, ordinarily, you will be better off to handle the case yourself. As you will have gathered from this book, Small Claims Court rules and procedures are quite simple—with a little study, you should be able to do a fine job of presenting your case. And you may actually have a psychological advantage—as a person without legal training, you can play David to the lawyer's Goliath. You may also be reassured to know that the National Center for State Courts found that, broadly speaking, having an attorney represent (or advise) a person in Small Claims Court did not statistically enhance that person's chances of winning. Or, put another way, people who spoke for themselves did just as well as those who hired a mouthpiece.

If you are worried about some aspect of the law that applies to your case, it is sensible to get legal advice on that particular point. This should not be expensive as long as you don't hire the attorney to handle the entire case. If no legal advisor program is available through your Small Claims Court and you are not a low-income person eligible for free legal assistance through a federally-sponsored "legal aid" (often called "legal services") program, simply hire a lawyer for a short consultation. For $75 or so, you should be able to find one who will review your entire case and advise you on any tricky points. Also, you may wish to spend a few hours doing some of your own research in your local law library. If you don't understand how law materials are catalogued and organized, see *Legal Research: How to Find and Understand the Law*, Elias & Levinkind (Nolo Press).

E. Mediation and Arbitration

Some states, most notably New York, have set up optional arbitration procedures. Arbitration usually involves a volunteer attorney who hears a dispute and makes a binding decision. Although the typical arbitration proceeding is even less formal and intimidating than the normal Small Claims Court, the ability of the arbitrator to impose a decision also means it's very different from mediation (see below), where there is no resolution unless both parties agree.

In most states that offer arbitration as an alternative, you can still elect to have your case heard in a regular Small Claims Court. However, in New York at least, it's much quicker to have your case go to an arbitrator, and as a result, many people choose this route even though there is no appeal from an arbitrator's decision.

Many other states, including Maine, utilize mediation techniques. In mediation, the parties sit down with a third person, whose job it is to help them arrive at their own solution. In Maine, the mediator is a person trained by the state in the art of helping disputing people arrive at their own negotiated settlement. In other states, however, the mediator may be a local volunteer attorney with no formal training. A mediator doesn't render a "decision." Rather, the parties either settle their own dispute consensually or the case is referred to Small Claims Court. In Maine, where mediators stand by in every courthouse and judges have the power to refer appropriate cases to them, over 50% of cases that go to mediation are settled. California is another state where mediation is growing in popularity. In that state, many judges routinely use their legal power to postpone hearings and refer the parties to mediation if they think the case will settle.

If a good mediation program is available in your area, I recommend that you give it a try, especially if the other party is a neighbor, local business person or anyone else where it's important to preserve or restore a decent personal relationship. In mediation, not only can parties often get their dispute resolved more quickly, but the fact that a solution is agreed to, not imposed by a judge, commonly results in everyone supporting it. An additional advantage of this is there will normally be no need to call on the sheriff to enforce the agreement.

Warning: Although arbitration and mediation are very different procedures in theory, they are sometimes combined in Small Claims Court in an effort to save time. For example, in a few areas, a hybrid process—non-binding arbitration—is used, which allows an arbitrator to suggest a solution, but does not require the parties to accept it. The point is that the terms mediation and arbitration are often used so loosely, you can't always be sure what they mean. So if anyone suggests either of these programs (sometimes called Alternative Dispute Resolution or ADR), check your local court rules to be sure what's involved before agreeing to participate.

F. Getting to The Courthouse

Before you get to the right courtroom, you have to get to the right building. Small Claims Courts are often not in the main courthouse, but like a half-forgotten stepsister, are housed wherever there's an empty room. The point is, don't assume that you know where to go if you haven't been there before. Plaintiffs have already had to find the clerk's office to file their papers, so they probably know where the courtroom is, but defendants should check this out. Be sure too, that your witnesses know exactly where and when to show up. And do plan to be a few minutes early—people who rush in flustered and late start with a strike against them.

Note: Courts in many areas of the country use a "hurry-up-and-wait" technique that would make the Army blush. San Francisco, California, is a typical example of a county using this

day (9:00, 10:00, 11:00, etc.) results in far less public inconvenience. But wherever you are, be warned —courts almost never start before 9:00 a.m.; if the clerk tells you to appear earlier, call up and ask what time the judge *really* gets there.

G. Understanding The Courtroom

Most Small Claims proceedings are conducted in standard courthouses that are also used for other purposes. Indeed, sometimes you will have to sit through a few minutes of some other type of court proceeding before the Small Claims calendar is called.

Most judges still sit on high in their little wooden throne boxes and most still wear those depressing judicial robes that trace their history back over a thousand years to England, at a time when courts were largely controlled by king, nobility and clergy. There are court rules requiring these out-of-date traditions, although a few judges conduct their court more informally anyway. In addition to the judge, a clerk and a bailiff will normally be present. They sit at tables immediately in front of the judge. The clerk's job is to keep the judge supplied with necessary files and papers, and to make sure that proceedings flow smoothly. A clerk is not the same as a court reporter, who keeps a word-by-word record of proceedings. No such record is kept in Small Claims Court, and no court reporter is present.[2]

Courtrooms are divided about two-thirds of the way toward the front by a little fence. This fence is known to initiates as the "bar." The public must stay on the opposite side of the bar from the judge, clerk, bailiff, attorneys, etc., unless invited to cross. This invitation occurs when your case is called by the clerk. At this point you come forward and sit at the long table (known as the "counsel table") just inside the fence.[3] You and your witnesses sit facing the judge with your backs to the rest of the courtroom. In Small Claims Courts, you will have been sworn (or affirmed, if you wish) to tell the truth before the judge arrives. If this has not already been done, the oath will be administered at this time. In the great majority of Small Claims Courts you, your opponent and your witnesses will present the entire case from the long table. This means that you do not sit in the witness box next to the judge. Many people (and judges) feel that it is polite to stand when addressing the judge, but you should do what feels most comfortable to you.

When your case is called and you come forward to take your turn at the counsel table, have all your papers with you ready to present to the judge. This can include bills, receipts, estimates, photographs, contracts, letters to or from your opponent, etc. When the time comes to show these to the judge, simply hand them to the clerk, who will pass them to the judge. As I have said before, documentation is a great aid to your case, but don't go overboard. Judges are a little like donkeys—load them too heavily and they are likely to lie down and go to sleep.

---

[2]This is the rule in the vast majority of states, but there are exceptions.

[3]In a few courtrooms judges try to hurry things by asking everyone to stand in front of the judge's bench. The idea seems to be if people can't sit down they will present their cases faster. This might be okay if the judge would stand too. As it is, I feel it's insulting.

H. Dealing With Your Opponent

Before you get to the courtroom, you should do a little thinking about your opponent. Perhaps you can guess what sort of presentation she will make. If so, ask yourself how you can best deal with these arguments. This is a good way to take the negative energy you may feel (frustration, annoyance, anger) and turn it into creative planning and preparation. In court, always be polite. You will gain nothing, and may lose the respect of the judge, if you are obviously hostile or sarcastic. Don't interrupt your opponent when she is speaking—you will get your chance. When you present your case, lay out the facts to the judge; don't conduct an argument with the other side.

I. Dealing With the Judge

It is hard to generalize about judges—each is an individual. I have seen more good than bad, but that doesn't help if your case comes up before an idiot. Unlike higher courts, no great intellectual ability is required to be a good Small Claims Court judge. Indeed, most of the judges sitting on the United States Supreme Court would probably be lousy at it.[4] What is required is a liking for people, open-mindedness and, above all, patience.

---

[4]Many people act as if I am nuts when I suggest nonlawyer judges. But why not? Vermont has used them with success in parts of its court system for generations.

Everyone who comes to Small Claims Court should have the feeling that they got a fair chance to have their say.

Most Small Claims Court judges are judges in the formal, lawyer-dominated courts who also hear the Small Claims calendar. This is a mistake. The last thing that is needed in Small Claims Court is the "me judge, you peasant" philosophy of our formal court system. Hopefully as Small Claims Court expands in the future, it will be staffed by people (not necessarily lawyers) specifically trained to meet its needs (see Chapter 25).

In many states, lawyers are often appointed as temporary judges when a judge is ill or on vacation. The legal slang for a temporary judge is "Judge, pro tem." If your case comes up on a day when there is a "Judge, pro tem," you normally have the option of refusing to accept that judge and asking that your case be heard by a regular judge. If your case is contested and you feel it involves fairly complicated legal issues, I recommend you do this. Pro tem judges are not paid, not trained and often do not have much practical experience in the legal areas that are commonly heard in Small Claims Court. While some are excellent, a fair number are seriously substandard and, as a general rule, they are best avoided.

What if it's a regular judge—or commissioner— you don't like after having seen a few cases before yours? Little-known laws present in nearly all states allow you to "disqualify" a judge simply on your honest belief that he is "prejudiced" against you. No one will ask you to prove it. To disqualify a judge, you can simply say, when your case is called (after you've been "sworn in"), something like this: "Your Honor, I believe you are prejudiced against my interest, and I request a trial before another judge." You must find out ahead of time whether this procedure is available in your state. If it isn't, and you attempt to disqualify the judge, she may truly be prejudiced against you, even if she wasn't before.

When thinking about presenting your case to a judge, there is one constructive thing that you can do. Imagine yourself in the judge's shoes. What would you value most from the people appearing before you? Before I ever sat as a judge, my answer was politeness, good organization of the material to be presented, and reasonable brevity. After experiencing Small Claims Court from the judge's chair, I would only add— documented evidence. By this, I mean testimony that consists of more than the word of the person bringing, or defending, the case. Witnesses, written statements, police accident reports, photographs—all these give the judge a chance to make a decision based on something more than who tells the better story. And one final thing. Remember, the judge has heard thousands of stories very much like yours, and will either cease paying attention or get annoyed if you repeat yourself three times.

J.   Organizing Your Testimony and Evidence

It's essential that you organize what you have to say and the physical evidence you wish to show the judge. I recommend that you divide your testimony into a list of the main points you want to make. Under each heading, list any items of physical evidence you wish to show the judge. If your evidence consists of a number of items, make sure that you have put them in order and can find each quickly when you need it.

Example: In cases based on a hotel's failure to return your deposit when you cancelled a wedding reception three months before the event was to be held, your list might look like this:

• General Explanation of Lawsuit: "Hotel refused to return my $500 deposit when I cancelled the wedding."

• This was true even though I cancelled 83 days before the event.

• The contract I signed with the hotel allowed full refund if cancellation occurred more than 60 days before the event.

• Show contract to the judge.

• When I cancelled the hotel told me (and then sent me a letter) stating that their cancellation policy had been changed a month ago to require 90 days in order to get a refund.

• This was the first time I was notified of this policy change.

• The change should not affect my contract, and anyway, 90 days in advance is an unreasonably long cancellation policy.

• In any event, the hotel has a duty to try and rerent the banquet room to minimize damages (mitigation of damages) and they had plenty of time to do so.

• Present the judge with a list of short cancellation policies of five other hotels in the area, all of which allow a full refund on much shorter notice than 83 days.

Note: In Chapter 2, I discuss the mitigation of damages point mentioned above. In Chapters 14-22, you will find extensive discussion about how to prepare for court and what to do once you get there.

CHAPTER 14

Witnesses

It is often helpful to have someone in court with you who has a firsthand knowledge of the facts of your case and who can support your point of view. In many types of cases, such as car accidents, or disputes concerning whether or not a tenant left an apartment clean, witnesses are particularly valuable. In other fact situations, they aren't as necessary. For example, if a friend borrowed $500 and didn't pay it back, you don't need a witness to prove that your friend's (ex-friend's?) signature on the promissory note is genuine unless you expect him to base his defense on the theory that his signature was forged.

A good witness should have firsthand knowledge of the facts in the dispute. This means that either she saw something that helps establish your case (e.g., the car accident, dog bite, or dirty apartment, etc) or is an expert you have consulted about an important aspect of your case (e.g., a car mechanic who testifies your engine wasn't fixed properly). The judge will not be interested in the testimony of a person who is repeating secondhand or generalized information such as "I know Joe is a good, safe driver and would never have done anything reckless," or "I didn't see Joe's apartment before he moved out, but both Joe and his mother, who couldn't be here today, told me that they worked for two days cleaning it up."

A good witness is believable. This isn't always an easy quality to define. For example, a police officer may be a symbol of honesty to some people, while others will automatically react to him with hostility and fear. But remember, it's the judge you are trying to convince and judges tend to be fairly establishment folk. They make comfortable salaries, own their own homes and generally tend to like the existing order of things. Most judges I know would tend to believe a police officer.

In many types of cases such as a car accident, you won't have much choice as to witnesses. You will be lucky to have one. But in other disputes (was the house properly painted, or the work on the car engine competently completed?), you have an opportunity to plan ahead. When you do, try to get an expert witness who is particularly knowledgeable about the dispute in question. Thus, in a dispute over whether car repairs were properly done, it's preferable to bring a working car mechanic rather than your neighbor "who knows a lot about cars."

Unfortunately, in some types of disputes, close friends and family are often your only witnesses. There is no rule that says that you can't have these people testify for you. Indeed, I have often seen a person's spouse, or the friend that she lives with, give very convincing testimony. But, given a choice, it is usually better to have a witness who is neither friend nor kin. A judge may discount testimony of people to whom you are close on the theory that they would naturally be biased in your favor. One little trick to dispel this judicial cynicism is to have a closely-related witness bend over backwards to treat the other party as fairly as possible. Thus, if your brother is your only witness to the fact that ABC Painting splashed paint on your boat, he might point out to the judge not only that he saw them to do it, but that it was a very windy day and they were having a hard time painting the breakwater.

I will talk more about witnesses as I go through the various case examples (Chapters 16-21), but let's outline a few basic rules here:

• Prepare your witness thoroughly as to what your position is, what your opponent is likely to say and what you want the witness to say. In court, the witness will be on her own and you want to be sure that the story comes out right. It is completely legal to thoroughly discuss the case with your witness beforehand;

• Never bring a witness to court who is hostile to you or hostile to the idea of testifying;

• Do not ask a witness to testify unless you know exactly what he will say. This sounds basic, but I have seen people lose cases because their witnesses got mixed up, and in one instance, where the witness actually supported the other side;

• It's not illegal to pay an expert witness a reasonable fee (say a car mechanic who has examined your engine). In addition, a subpoenaed witness is entitled to a small witness fee (see A below), but no other money;[1]

---

[1]Traditionally, it has been legal to pay expert witnesses. These are not people who personally witnessed anything to do with your case. They are likely to be scientists, physicians, mechanics or others who have specific technical information about some point in the dispute. Expert witnesses are rarely used in Small Claims Court. If you wish to hire one, check with the court clerk, or, better yet, the judge in advance, to see if it is okay to do so. You will not be able to recover expert witness fees if you win.

• Never use a subpoena form to require a witness to be present unless you have made sure that it is okay with the witness (more in A below).

Important: In court a witness will be pretty much on her own when it comes to giving testimony. The witness will normally sit with you at the table facing the judge and talk to the judge from there.[2] I generally recommend that you stand when it's your turn to speak. It is fairly rare for a witness to take the witness stand in Small Claims Court. Most judges prefer that you don't pretend to be a lawyer and ask your witness a lot of questions. Simply let the witness explain what happened as he saw it. The judge is likely to ask the witness questions. If you feel that the witness has left something out, ask a question designed to produce the information you want.

A. Subpoenaing Witnesses

In most states, you can require that a witness be present if that person resides within a certain distance from the courthouse (the distance varies from state to state, but it is often about 150 miles).[3] To do this, go to the clerk's office and get a "Subpoena" form. Fill it out and have it served on the person who you wish to have present. But remember, you never want to subpoena a person unless you have talked to her first and gotten an okay. The very act of dragging someone into court who doesn't want to come may set her against you. A subpoenaed witness is normally entitled to a fee upon demand.[4] The person serving the subpoena

---

[2]In a few courtrooms, the judge may ask all parties and witnesses to approach the judge's bench and stand there in a little group, and in others, small claims proceedings are conducted informally with all parties and the judge seated at a table.

[3]In some states, subpoenas reach only within county boundaries.

[4]This is often a fixed amount (often $30-$100 plus mileage to the courthouse).

must have this money ready to pay if it is requested. If you win your case, you will probably be able to recover your witness fees from the other side. The judge has discretion as to whether to grant you your witness fees. Some judges are strict about this, making the loser pay the winner's witness fees only if he finds that the subpoenaed witness was essential to the presentation of the case. This means that if your case is so strong that you don't need a witness but you subpoena one anyway, you may well have to pay the witness even though you win.

Here is the standard California subpoena form. You will need to prepare an original and two copies. Once prepared, take the subpoena form to the clerk who will issue it. Service must be made personally, and the "Proof of Service," which is probably on the back of the subpoena, returned to the clerk's office. Rules for service are discussed in Chapter 11.

B.   Subpoenaing Police Officers

You have probably already noticed that on the California subpoena form there is a special box to use if you wish to subpoena a police officer. The box is easy to fill out, but expensive to pay for in most states. The deposit to subpoena a police officer is at least $125. This money must be paid to the clerk at the time the subpoena is issued. Depending on the amount of the officer's time that is used, you may eventually get a refund of some of your $125. Be sure to check your local rules.

ATTORNEY OR PARTY WITHOUT ATTORNEY *(Name and Address)*:	TELEPHONE NO.	FOR COURT USE ONLY

ATTORNEY OR PARTY WITHOUT ATTORNEY *(Name and Address)*:   TELEPHONE NO.

   John O'Gara
   15 Scenic St.
   Albany, CA

ATTORNEY FOR *(Name)*: In Pro Per

NAME OF COURT: Municipal Court, County of Alameda
STREET ADDRESS: 2000 Center St.
MAILING ADDRESS:
CITY AND ZIP CODE: Berkeley, CA 94704
BRANCH NAME: Berkeley-Albany Judicial District

PLAINTIFF/PETITIONER: Public Library

DEFENDANT/RESPONDENT: John O'Gara

FOR COURT USE ONLY

CIVIL SUBPENA

☐ Duces Tecum

CASE NUMBER:

(fill in number)

THE PEOPLE OF THE STATE OF CALIFORNIA, TO (NAME): Jane Doe

1. **YOU ARE ORDERED TO APPEAR AS A WITNESS** in this action at the date, time, and place shown in the box below UNLESS you make a special agreement with the person named in item 3:

a. Date:	Time:	☐ Dept.:	☐ Div.:	☐ Room:
b. Address:				

2. **AND YOU ARE**
   a. ☒ ordered to appear in person.
   b. ☐ not required to appear in person if you produce the records described in the accompanying affidavit and a completed declaration of custodian of records in compliance with Evidence Code sections 1560, 1561, 1562, and 1271. (1) Place a copy of the records in an envelope (or other wrapper). Enclose your original declaration with the records. Seal them. (2) Attach a copy of this subpena to the envelope or write on the envelope the case name and number, your name and date, time, and place from item 1 (the box above). (3) Place this first envelope in an outer envelope, seal it, and mail it to the clerk of the court at the address in item 1. (4) Mail a copy of your declaration to the attorney or party shown at the top of this form.
   c. ☐ ordered to appear in person and to produce the records described in the accompanying affidavit. The **personal attendance** of the custodian or other qualified witness and the production of the original records **is required** by this subpena. The procedure authorized by subdivision (b) of section 1560, and sections 1561 and 1562, of the Evidence Code will not be deemed suffficient compliance with this subpena.

3. **IF YOU HAVE ANY QUESTIONS ABOUT THE TIME OR DATE FOR YOU TO APPEAR, OR IF YOU WANT TO BE CERTAIN THAT YOUR PRESENCE IS REQUIRED, CONTACT THE FOLLOWING PERSON BEFORE THE DATE ON WHICH YOU ARE TO APPEAR:**
   a. Name: John O'Gara
   b. Telephone number: (510)555-1212

4. **Witness Fees:** You are entitled to witness fees and mileage actually traveled both ways, as provided by law, if you request them at the time of service. You may request them before your scheduled appearance from the person named in item 3.

> DISOBEDIENCE OF THIS SUBPENA MAY BE PUNISHED AS CONTEMPT BY THIS COURT. YOU WILL ALSO BE LIABLE FOR THE SUM OF FIVE HUNDRED DOLLARS AND ALL DAMAGES RESULTING FROM YOUR FAILURE TO OBEY.

Date issued:

....
(TYPE OR PRINT NAME)

▶

_____
(SIGNATURE OF PERSON ISSUING SUBPENA)

(TITLE)

(See reverse for proof of service)

Form Adopted by Rule 982	**CIVIL SUBPENA**	Code of Civil Procedure, §§ 1985, 1986, 1987
Judicial Council of California		
982(a)(15) [Rev. January 1, 1991]		

C. Subpoenaing Documents

In addition to witnesses, you can also subpoena documents. It is rare that this is done in Small Claims Court, but it may occasionally be helpful. Someone (police department, phone company, hospital, corporation) may have certain books, ledgers, papers or other documents that can help your case. To get them in many states, you must prepare a form entitled "Subpoena Duces Tecum." This is very similar to the standard subpoena form, except that there is a space to describe the papers or other documents that you want brought to court. To get a "Subpoena Duces Tecum" issued, you must normally follow a procedure along the following lines. Attach an affidavit stating why you need the written material. Prepare three copies of all papers and, after you get the clerk to issue the subpoena, serve it on the witness using personal service as described in Chapter 11. As with a regular subpoena, the witness is entitled to ask for the regular fee. The "Proof of Service" is on the back of the subpoena form and must be filled out and returned to the clerk.[5]

A Subpoena Duces Tecum must be directed to the person who is in charge of the documents, books or records that you want. It may take a few phone calls to find out who this is. Be sure you get this information accurately. If you list someone on the "Subpoena Duces Tecum" who has nothing to do with the documents, you won't get them. When dealing with a large corporation, public utility, municipal government, etc., it is wise to list the person who is in overall charge of the department where the records are kept. Thus, if you want records from a public library having to do with library fines, or from the city tax

---

[5]Technical rules on filing and serving papers, as well as paying witness fees, vary from state to state. Before subpoenaing documents, be sure to ask if the other side will bring them voluntarily or give you photocopies.

and license department having to do with business license fees, you should not list the city manager or the mayor, but should list the head librarian or the director of the tax and license office.

Example: Let's take a hypothetical case. You are being sued by the city on behalf of the public library for $300 for eight rare books which they state you failed to return. You know that you did return the books, but can't seem to get that across to the library, which insists on treating you like a thief. You learn that each April the library takes a yearly inventory of all books on their shelves. You believe that if you can get access to that inventory, you may be able to figure out where the library misplaced the books, or at least show that a significant percentage of the library's other books are not accounted for, raising the implication that they lost the books, not you.

Your first step is to ask the library officials to voluntarily open the inventory to you. If they refuse, you may well want to subpoena it. Here's how:

1. Check the "Duces Tecum" box on the Subpoena form.

2. Prepare an affidavit using a form available from the court. It should be brief. Describe the documents you need and why they are necessary to prove issues involved in the case. If you want the custodian of the records to show up in person, give a reason. Don't argue the merits of your case.

3. Have the subpoena issued by the Small Claims clerk. Then have the subpoena served, being sure that the "Proof of Service" (see Chapter 11) is properly filled out and returned to the clerk.

Name and Address of Court: Municipal Court, County of Alameda
Berkeley-Albany Judicial District
2000 Center Street
Berkeley, CA 94704

SMALL CLAIMS CASE NO. (fill in number)

PLAINTIFF-DEMANDANTE *(Name, address, and telephone number of each):*

Public Library
100 Allston Way
Berkeley, CA 94704

Telephone No.:

DEFENDANT DEMANDADO *(Name, address, and telephone number of each):*

John O'Gara
100 Scenic Drive
Berkeley, CA 94702

Telephone No.:

Telephone No.:

Telephone No.:

☐ See attached sheet for additional plaintiffs and defendants.

DECLARATION FOR SUBPENA DUCES TECUM

1. I, the undersigned, declare I am the ☐ plaintiff ☒ defendant ☐ judgment creditor ☐ other *(specify)*:
   in the above entitled action.
2. This action has been set for hearing on *(date):* (fill in date) at *(time):* (fill in time) in the above named court.
3. *(Name)*: Robert Riwyle   has in his or her possession or under his or her control
   the following documents relating to *(name of party)*:
   a. ☐ Payroll receipts, stubs, and other records concerning employment of the party. Receipts, invoices, documents, and other papers or records concerning any and all accounts receivable of the party.
   b. ☐ Bank account statements, cancelled checks, and check registers from any and all bank accounts in which the party has an interest.
   c. ☐ Savings account passbooks and statements, savings and loan account passbooks and statements, and credit union share account passbooks and statements of the party.
   d. ☐ Stock certificates, bonds, money market certificates, and any other records, documents, or papers concerning all investments of the party.
   e. ☐ California registration certificates and ownership certificates for all vehicles registered to the party.
   f. ☐ Deeds to any and all real property owned or being purchased by the party.
   g. ☒ Other *(specify)*:
      Book inventory information collected by the main branch of the public library during the calendar year 19__.

These documents are material to the issues involved in this case for the following reasons *(specify)*:
My contention is that I returned the books for which the library is suing me. The inventory should back me up on this.

I declare under penalty of perjury under the laws of the State of California that the foregoing is true and correct.

Date: (fill in)

John O'Gara
(TYPE OR PRINT NAME)

▶ *John O'Gara*
(SIGNATURE OF JUDGMENT CREDITOR)

Form Approved by the
Judicial Council of California
SC-107 (New January 1, 1992)

DECLARATION FOR SUBPENA DUCES TECUM
(Small Claims)

Code of Civil Procedure, §§ 1985–1987.5

Note: On the day of the hearing, the person you have subpoenaed will show up with the documents in question. The documents will be presented to the court—not to you. If you need an opportunity to examine the documents, request it from the judge. He may well let you do your examining right there in the courtroom while other cases go ahead, or, if necessary, he may continue the case for a few days and arrange to have you make your examination at the place of business of the owner of the records.

D. Written Evidence

In most Small Claims Courts, there are no formal rules of evidence requiring that a witness testify in person. While it is best to have a witness appear in court, this isn't always possible and a judge will accept written statements from both eye witnesses ("I was there and saw the filthy apartment") and expert witnesses ("I examined the transmission and found that it was not the original one, but a rebuilt part installed improperly"). If you do present the written statement of a witness, make sure the witness states the following facts:

• The date of the event.

• If she is an eye witness, what she saw and where she saw it from.

• If he is an expert witness, the credentials that make him an expert ("I am a state certified TV repairperson and have run my own repair business for 12 years"), as well as his relevant opinion.

• Any other facts that have a bearing on the dispute.

A letter that accomplishes this, written by an eye witness to an automobile accident, would look like this (see Chapter 17 for a written statement by an expert witness):

37 Ogden Court
Kansas City, Kansas
September 30, 19___

Presiding Judge
Small Claims Court
Kansas City, Kansas

Re: John Swift vs. Peter Petrakos

Small Claims Case No. 11478

Your Honor:

On September 15, 19___, I witnessed an auto accident a little after 7:30 a.m., involving John Swift and Peter Petrakos. I clearly saw Mr. Petrakos' Toyota, which was heading north on South Dora, go through a red light and hit Mr. Swift's blue van, which was proceeding south on West 7th, well inside the 25 MPH speed limit. I noticed that the traffic light facing Mr. Petrakos did not turn to green for ten seconds or so after the accident, so it is clear to me that this was not a case of Mr. Petrakos just being a little early or late getting through an intersection at a light change.

Sincerely,

Victor Van Cleve

E. Judges as Witnesses

Using a judge as a witness is a valuable technique in many situations. This is done routinely in many types of disputes, such as clothing cases in which you bring the damaged garment into court for the judge's examination. Always bring into the court any physical evidence that meets these two criteria:

• Showing it to the judge will help your case;

• It will fit through the door.

But what if your evidence is impossible to bring into the courtroom (a car with a poor paint job or a supposedly pedigreed puppy that grew up looking as if Lassie were the mother and Rin Tin Tin the father)? Why not ask the judge to accompany you outside the building to examine the car, or the dog, or whatever else is important to your case? Many (but not all) judges are willing to do so if they feel that it is necessary to better understand the dispute and won't take too long. But never ask a judge to take time to leave her court to view evidence if you can prove your case just as well by other means, such as witnesses and pictures. A good approach is to do as much as you can in court, and to ask the judge to view evidence outside of court only if it is essential. Sometimes it clearly is. For example, one excellent judge I know was disturbed one morning when two eye witnesses gave seriously contradictory testimony about a traffic accident. He questioned both in detail and then took the case under submission. That evening, he drove over to the relevant corner. Once there, it was clear that one of the witnesses couldn't possibly have seen the accident from the spot on which she claimed to be standing (in front of a particular restaurant). The judge decided the case in favor of the other.

F.   Testimony by Telephone

A surprising number of Small Claims Court judges will take testimony over the phone if a witness cannot be present because he or she is ill, disabled, out-of-state, or can't take time off from work. While procedures vary, some courts will set up conference calls so that the opposing party has the opportunity to hear what is being said and to respond.

Don't just assume that your local court will allow telephone testimony. Ask the clerk. If you get a negative response, don't give up—ask the judge when you get into the courtroom. It is also an extremely good idea to have a letter from the witness who you want to reach by phone, explaining what he or she will testify to (e.g., your opponent's car ran a red light and broadsided you) and explaining why it is impossible for him to be in court. Such a letter might look like the one above, except the witness should add:

"Mr. Swift has asked me to testify on his behalf, and normally I would be happy to do so. However, I will be in New York City on business during the months of October, November and December 19__ and cannot be present.

"I have asked Mr. Swift to let me know the day and approximate time of the court hearing and have told him that I will give him a phone number where I can be reached. If you think it desirable, I will be pleased to give my testimony by phone."

CHAPTER 15

Presenting Your Case to the Judge

A. Uncontested Cases—Getting a Judgment by Default

Surprisingly often, presenting your case will be easy—your opponent simply will not show up.[1] If this occurs in most states, you will be asked to briefly state your case. There is no need to present extensive arguments or lots of evidence. The judge may check to see that your opponent was properly served and may ask you a question or two to make sure that there is no obvious flaw in your case, such as the Statute of Limitations having run out two years ago. A defendant who doesn't show up to argue

---

[1]In the few states that require an answer to be filed (see Appendix), you should know before the court date whether the other side will appear. Check with the court clerk to see what, if anything, you must do to get your default judgment.

his or her case usually can't appeal to a formal court (see Chapter 23) unless the default is first set aside.

Note: In some Small Claims Courts, such as those in Washington, D.C., a court clerk will enter the default if the case is for unpaid bills or some other amount of money and the person bringing suit has good documentation, such as statements, ledgers, etc. This means that you will not appear before a judge at all. If you are a plaintiff and you know that the defendant will not show up, you still must bring the evidence necessary to establish your case.

On rare occasions, a person who has defaulted will show up in court a few days later with a super excuse. The judge does have the discretion to reopen the case by "setting aside the default judgment." If the defaulting party makes a motion to set aside the default within a relatively short time (almost always under a month), the judge in many states may—but does not have to—set it aside. The defaulting party has the burden of convincing the judge that the reason she didn't show up or phone earlier is good enough to justify setting aside the default. As you might guess, not many people can lift a burden this heavy. (We discuss the mechanics of setting aside a default in Chapter 10, "If One Party Doesn't Show Up.")

B. Contested Cases

Assuming now that both sides show up and step forward when the case is called by the clerk, what happens next? First, the judge will establish everyone's identity.[2] Next, he will ask the plaintiff to briefly state his case.

---

[2]In a few states, including California, when a suit is brought by or against an unincorporated business, it is permissible for someone other than the business owner to appear in court. Thus a dentist or store owner could send a bookkeeper to establish that a bill wasn't paid. As noted in Chapter 7, corporations can routinely appoint representatives. And some states require corporations to appear through an attorney. See Appendix.

The plaintiff should tell the judge what is in dispute and then briefly outline his position. It is critical that the judge know what the case is about before you start arguing it. For example, if your case involves a car accident, you might start by saying, "This case involves a car accident at Cedar and Rose Streets in which my car suffered $372 worth of damage," not "It all started when I was driving down Rose Street after having two eggs and a danish for breakfast." Only occasionally have I seen a case where the plaintiff's initial presentation should take longer than five minutes. As part of his statement the plaintiff should present any relevant papers, photos or other documentary evidence. These should be handed to the clerk and explained. If the plaintiff has done any legal research and believes that a statute or court decision supports his position, he should call it to the attention of the judge. One good way to do this is to write the statute and the name of the court decision, along with its citation (the book it is found in, the volume number and the page number), on a piece of paper and hand it to the judge.

Example: Assume you live in Ukiah, California and are slightly injured when a portion of the ceiling in your rented apartment falls. You miss a couple of days work (you are out $200 per day) and have doctor's bills of $200. You decide to sue for $1,200 to include the pain and discomfort you experienced. However, you are worried about one thing—was the defendant negligent (the ceiling looked fine before it fell). You go to the law library and find that there is a California Supreme Court case which states that landlords are "strictly liable" to tenants for injuries caused by defective rental premises, whether negligence can be shown or not (see Chapter 2 for more on strict liability). To tell the judge about this case, prepare a memo like this:

John Tenant, Plaintiff v. Tillie Landlord, Defendant

Small Claims Case #123456

Memorandum of Legal Authority
Supporting Plaintiffs' Position

A main issue of my case is whether I need to prove that defendant was negligent. I contended that the law only requires me to show that a defect in defendant's building caused me to be injured. I base this assertion that the doctrine of "strict liability" applies on the decision in the case of *Becker v. I.R.M.* 38 Cal.3d 454 (1985).

Respectfully Submitted,

John Tenant

4/7/____

The plaintiff should also be sure to indicate the presence of any witnesses to the judge.

When the plaintiff is finished, the judge may wish to ask questions. He may or may not wish to hear from the plaintiff's witnesses before the defendant speaks. Each judge will control the flow of evidence differently. It's best to go with the judge's energy, not against it. Just be sure that, at one time or another, you have made all of your points. If you feel rushed, say so. The judge will normally slow things down a little. If you appear before a lawyer-arbitrator, in a system such as that of New York City, you can expect that the arbitrator will take a very active role in questioning the parties and witnesses.

Sooner or later the defendant will get his chance. Defendants often get so angry at something the plaintiff has said ("Lies! Lies!") that when their turn comes, they immediately attack. This is silly and usually counter-productive. The defendant should calmly and clearly present his side of the dispute to the judge. If the plaintiff has made false or misleading statements, these should be answered, but at the end of the presentation, not at the beginning. Tell your story first, then deal with the plaintiff's testimony if this seems necessary.

Here are a few tips that you may find helpful. These are not rules written on golden tablets, but only suggestions. You may want to follow some and ignore others.

• Stand when you make your initial presentation to the judge. Standing gives most people a sense of presence and confidence at a time when they may be a little nervous. But this doesn't mean that you have to jump to your feet every time the judge asks you a question.

• Don't read your statement. Reading in court is almost always a bore. Some people find it helpful to make a few notes on a card to serve as a reminder if they get nervous or forget something. If you decide to do this, list the headings of the various points you want to make in an outline form. Be sure your list is easy to read at a glance and that the topics are in the correct order. (I give a sample list in Chapter 13.)

• Be as brief as you can and still explain and document your case thoroughly.

• Never interrupt your opponent or any of the witnesses no matter how outrageous their "lies." You will get your chance to respond.

• Be prepared to present any section of your case that is difficult to get across in words in another way. This means bringing your used car parts, damaged clothing or other exhibits, such as photographs or cancelled checks with you, and having them organized for easy presentation.

• There will be a blackboard in court. If drawings will be helpful, as is almost always true in cases involving car accidents, be sure to make one. You will want to draw clearly and legibly the first time, so it's wise to have practiced in advance. If you wish to make a drawing and the judge doesn't ask you to, simply request permission to do so.

A SAMPLE CONTESTED CASE

Now let's take a typical case and pretend that someone has made a written record of it (usually, no transcript is made in Small Claims Court).

Clerk: "The next case is *John Andrews v. Robertson Realty.* Will everyone please come forward?" (Four people come forward and sit at the table facing the judge.)

Judge: "Good morning. Which one of you is Mr. Andrews? Okay, will you begin, Mr. Andrews?"

John Andrews: (stands) "This is a case about my failure to get a $400 cleaning deposit returned, your Honor. I rented a house from Robertson Realty at 1611 Spruce St. in Rockford in March of 19_ on a month-to-month tenancy. On January 10, 19_, I sent Mr. Robertson a written notice that I was planning to move on March 10. In fact, I moved out on March 8 and left the place extremely clean. All of my rent was properly paid. A few days after I moved out, I asked Mr. Robertson to return my $400 deposit. He wrote me a letter stating that the place was dirty and he was keeping my deposit.

I have with me a copy of a letter I wrote to Mr. Robertson on March 15 setting out my position in more detail. I also have some photographs that my friend Carol Spann, who is here as a witness, took on the day I moved out. I believe the pictures show pretty clearly that I did a thorough clean-up. (John Andrews hands the letter and pictures to the clerk who hands them to the judge.)

Your Honor, I am asking not only for the $400 deposit, but also for $200 in punitive damages plus 2% monthly interest that the law allows a tenant when a landlord improperly refuses to return a deposit."[3]

Judge: "Mr. Andrews, will you introduce your witness."

Andrews: "Yes, this is Carol Spann. She helped me clean up and move on March 7 and 8."

Judge: (looking at the pictures) "Ms. Spann, were you in the apartment the day John Andrews moved out?"

Carol Spann: (standing) "Yes, I was and the day before too. I helped clean up and I can say that we did a good job. Not only did we do the normal washing and scrubbing, but we waxed the kitchen floor and shampooed the rugs."

Judge: (turning to Mr. Robertson) "Okay, now it's your turn to tell me why the deposit wasn't returned."

Harry Robertson: (standing) "I don't know how they could have cleaned the place up, your Honor, because it was filthy

---

[3]Many states make some provision for "punitive damages" if a landlord retains a tenant's deposit in "bad faith." You should check to see if you are entitled to punitive damages before you file your suit. If you are entitled to them, the judge will not award them if you don't ask for them in your claim.

when I inspected it on March 9. Let me give you a few specifics. There was mildew and mold around the bathtub, the windows were filthy, the refrigerator hadn't been defrosted and there was dog—how shall I say it—dog manure in the basement. Your Honor, I have brought along Clem Houndstooth as a witness. Mr. Houndstooth is the tenant who moved in three days after Mr. Andrews moved out. Incidentally, your Honor, the place was so dirty that I only charged Mr. Houndstooth a $200 cleaning deposit, because he agreed to clean it up himself."

Judge: (looking at Clem Houndstooth) "Do you wish to say something?"

Clem Houndstooth: (standing) "Yes, I do. Mr. Robertson asked me to come down and back him up and I am glad to do it because I put in two full days cleaning that place up. I like a clean house, your Honor, not a halfway clean, halfway dirty house. I just don't think that a house is clean if the oven is full of gunk, there is mold in the bathroom, and the insides of the cupboards are grimy. All these conditions existed at 1611 Spruce St. when I moved in. I just don't believe that anyone could think that that place was clean."

Judge: "Mr. Andrews, do you have anything to add?"

John Andrews: (standing up) "Yes, I sure do. First, as to the mildew problem. The house is forty years old and there is some dampness in the wall of the bathroom. Maybe there is a leaky pipe someplace behind the tile. I cleaned it a number of times, but it always came back. I talked to Mr. Fisk in Mr. Robertson's office about the problem about a month after I moved in and he told me that I would have to do the best I could because they couldn't afford to tear the wall apart. As to the cupboards and stove, they are both old. The cabinets haven't been painted in ten years, so, of course, they aren't perfect, and that old stove was a lot dirtier when I moved in than it is now."

Judge: "What about the refrigerator, Mr. Andrews? Was that defrosted?"

John Andrews: "No, your Honor, it wasn't, but it had been defrosted about three weeks before I moved out and I thought that it was good enough the way it was."

Judge: "Okay, if no one else has anything to add, I want to return your pictures and letters. You will receive my decision by mail in a few days."

Now, I have a little surprise for you. This was a real case. As they used to say on *Dragnet,* "Only the names have been changed to protect the innocent." And I have another surprise for you. I spoke to the judge after the court session and I know how the case came out. The judge explained his reasoning to me as follows.

"This is a typical case in which both sides have some right on their side. What is clean to one person may be dirty to another. Based on what I heard, I would have to guess that the old tenant made a fairly conscientious effort to clean up and probably left the place about as clean as it was when he moved in, but that the new tenant, Houndstooth, had much higher standards and convinced the landlord that it was filthy. The landlord may not have needed too much convincing since he probably would just as well keep the deposit. But I did hear enough to convince me that Andrews, the old tenant, didn't do a perfect job cleaning up. My decision will be that Andrews gets a judgment for the return of $250 of the $400 deposit, with no punitive damages. I believe that $150 is more than enough to compensate the landlord for any damages he suffered as a result of the apartment "being a little dirty."

I then asked the judge if he felt that the case was well presented. He replied substantially as follows:

"Better than average. I think I got a pretty good idea of what the problems were. The witnesses were helpful and the pictures gave me an idea that the place wasn't a total mess. Both sides could have done better, however. Andrews could have had a witness to talk about the condition when he moved in if it was truly dirtier than when he left. Another witness to testify to the apartment's cleanliness when he moved out would have been good too. His friend, Carol Spann, seemed to be a very close friend and I wasn't sure that she was objective when it came to judging whether the place was clean. The landlord, Robertson, could also have done better. He could have presented a more disinterested witness, although I must say that Houndstooth's testimony was pretty convincing. Also he could have had pictures documenting the dirty conditions and an estimate from a cleaning company for how much they would have charged to clean the place up. Without going to too much trouble, I think that either side could have probably done somewhat better with more thorough preparation."

C. Don't Forget to Ask for Your Costs

When you finish your presentation to the judge, you should be sure he realizes that you have incurred certain court costs. These can be added to the judgment amount. As I have mentioned, you can't recover for such personal expenses as taking time off from work to prepare for or attend court, paying a babysitter, or photocopy charges. In most states you can recover for:

• Your court filing fee.

• Service of process costs. (In some districts, you must try and fail to serve papers by certified mail as a condition of the court awarding you the fees of a process server—see Chapter 11.)

• Subpoenaed witness fees (which often must be approved by the judge ahead of time. Fees for subpoenaing witnesses and documents are only likely to be approved if absolutely necessary).

• The cost of obtaining necessary documents, such as verification of car ownership by the D.M.V.

For information on recovering costs incurred after judgment when your opponent won't voluntarily pay the judgment, see Chapter 24, "Recovering Collection Costs and Interests."

CHAPTER 16

Motor Vehicle Repair Cases

Most Small Claims Court cases fall into a dozen or so broad categories with perhaps another dozen subcategories. In the next six chapters, we look at the most common types of cases and discuss strategies to handle each. Even if your fact situation doesn't fit neatly in one of these categories, read them all. By picking up a few hints here and a little information there, you should be able to piece together a good plan of action. For example, many of the suggestions I make to handle motor vehicle repair disputes can be applied to cases involving major appliances such as televisions, washers, and expensive stereos.

Let's start by imagining that you go to the auto repair shop to pick up your trusty, but slightly greying, steed after a complete engine overhaul. The bill, as agreed to by you in advance, is $1,225. This always seemed a little steep, but the mechanic had talked you into it based on his claim that he will do a great job and that the engine should last another 50,000 miles. At any rate, you write out a check and drive out of the garage in something approaching a cheerful mood. One of life's not so little hassles has been taken care of, at least temporarily.

You're right—temporarily can sometimes be a very short time. In this case, it lasts only until you head up the first hill. What's that funny noise, you think? Why don't I have more power? "Oh shit," you say (you never swear, but there are some extreme provocations where nothing else will do). You turn around and drive back to the garage. Not only are you out $1,225, but your car runs worse than it did when you brought it in.

Funny, no one seems as pleasant as they did before. Funny, no one seems to have time to listen to you. Finally, after several explanations and a bit of foot stomping, you get someone to say that they will look the car over. You take a bus home, trying not to be paranoid. The next day you call the garage. Nothing has been done. You yell at the garage owner and then call your bank to stop payment on the check. You are told that it has already been cashed. The next day the garage owner tells you that the problem is in a part of the engine that they didn't work on. You only paid for a "short block job" they tell you. "Give us another $500 and we can surely solve this new problem," they add.

In disgust, you go down and pick up your handicapped friend and drive it home—slowly. You are furious and decide to pursue every legal remedy, no matter what the trouble. How do you start?

First, park your car, take a shower and have a glass of wine. Nothing gets decided well when you're mad. Now, going back to the reasoning we used at the beginning of this book, ask yourself some basic questions:

A. Have I Suffered a Loss?

That's easy. Your car doesn't work properly, you paid out a lot of money and the garage wants more to fix it. Clearly, you have suffered a loss.

B. Did the Negligence of the Garage Cause My Loss?

Ah ha, now we get to the nitty gritty. In this type of case you can almost always expect the garage to claim that they did their work properly and that the car simply needs more work. Maybe the garage is right—it's your job to prove that they aren't. Doing so will make your case; failing to do so will break it. You better get to work.

Step 1. Collect Available Evidence

First, get all evidence together where time is of the essence. In this situation, this means getting your used parts (it's a good idea to do this anytime you have major work done.)[1] If the garage will not give them to you, make your request by letter, keeping a copy for your file. If you get the parts, fine—if you don't, you have evidence that the garage is badly run or has something to hide.

Step 2. Have the Car Checked

Before you drive many miles, have your car checked by an established local mechanic or mechanics. Sometimes it is possible to get a free estimate from a repair shop if the shop thinks it will get the job of fixing your car. In this situation, however, you may be better off paying for someone to look at the engine thoroughly, as you want to be sure that at least one of the people who looks the car over is willing to come with you to Small Claims Court if the need arises, or at the very least, write a convincing letter stating what's wrong with the engine. One way to try and accomplish this is to take your car to a garage that

---

[1]In many states you are legally entitled by law to get your parts back, just as you are entitled to a written estimate before repairs are made.

someone you know already has a good personal relationship with. A few states require that you present three written estimates in Small Claims Court. Whether this is required or not, it's a good idea to have them.

Step 3. Try to Settle Your Case

By now you should have a pretty good idea as to what the first garage did wrong. Call them and ask that either the job be redone, or that they give you a refund of part or all of your money. Often the repair shop will agree to do some, or all, of the work over to avoid a further hassle. If they agree to take the car back, insist on a written agreement detailing what they will do and how long it will take. Also, talk to the mechanic who will actually work on the car to be sure he understands what needs to be done. Naturally, you may be a little paranoid about giving your car back to the garage that screwed it up, but unless they have been outrageously incompetent, this is probably your best approach at this stage. If you sue and the garage owner shows up in court and says he offered to work on the car again but you refused, it may weaken your case.

Step 4. Write a Demand Letter

If the garage isn't cooperative, it's time to write them a formal demand letter. Remember our discussion in Chapter 6. Your letter should be short, polite and written with an eye to a judge reading it. In this situation you could write something like the one below.

Jorge Sotomayor
15 Orange St.
Hamden, CT

Happy Days Motors
100 Speedway
New Haven, CT

Dear People:

On August 13, 19_, I brought my 1988 Dodge to your garage. You agreed to do a complete engine rebuild job for $1,225. You told me, "Your car will be running like a watch when we're through with it." The car worked well when I brought it in, but was a little short on power. Two days later, when I picked up my car, it barely moved at all. The engine made such a clanging noise that I have been afraid to drive it.

I have repeatedly asked you to fix the car or to refund my money. You have refused. Shortly after the work was done, I asked for my used parts to be returned. You refused to give them to me, even though it is a violation of state law.

I have had several mechanics look my car over since you worked on it. They all agree that you did your job improperly and even installed some used parts instead of new ones. The work you did on the engine rings was particularly badly done.

After receiving no response from you, I had the work redone at a cost of $900.[2] My car now works well. Please refund my $1,225. Should you fail to do so, I will exhaust all my legal remedies, including complaining to interested state and local agencies and taking this dispute to Small Claims Court. I hope to hear from you promptly.

Jorge Sotomayor

cc: Connecticut Dept. of Consumer Affairs
Bureau of Automotive Repair
Hartford, CT

---

[2]Most Small Claims Courts do not require that you actually have the work redone before going to court, but a few, such as New York City, require a repair bill marked "Paid."

Note: Most small independent garages don't make any written warranty or guaranty of their work. However, if you were given any promises in writing, mention them here in your letter. Also, if you were told things orally about the quality of the work the garage planned to do and you relied on these statements as part of your decision to have the work done, you should call attention to this express verbal warranty (see Chapter 2).

Step 5. File Your Court Papers

If you still get no satisfactory response from the garage, file your papers at the Small Claims clerk's office of your local Small Claims Court. Reread Chapters 7-10.

Step 6. Prepare for Court

If you want a third person (a judge) to understand your case, you must understand it yourself. Sounds simple, doesn't it? It does to me too until I get involved with machinery. My opinion of cars (and most other mechanical devices) is low—they are supposed to work without trouble, but most of us know better.

For me to argue a case in Small Claims such as the one we are talking about here could be a disaster unless I did some homework. This sort of disaster is repeated often in Small Claims. I have seen many, many people argue cases about their cars knowing no more than "the car was supposed to be fixed, your Honor, and it's worse than ever." On some mornings when the roses are in bloom, the peaches are sweet and the angels are in heaven, this is enough to win—usually it isn't. Why? Because the people from the garage are likely to have a terrific sounding story about the wonderful job they did. They will talk about pistons, rings, bearings, pulling the head and turning the cam shaft. It's all likely to sound so impressive that you can easily find yourself on the defensive.

This sort of thing needn't happen if you are willing to learn a little about your car (or whatever machinery is involved). Fifteen minutes' conversation with a knowledgeable mechanic may be all you need to understand what's going on. Also, your local library will have manuals about every type of car, complete with diagrams, etc.

Remember the Judge: In Chapter 13, I mentioned that it's important to pay attention to whom you are presenting your case. Most Small Claims judges don't understand the insides of cars any better than you do. People often become lawyers because they don't like to get their hands dirty. So be prepared to deal with a person who nods his head but doesn't really understand the difference between the drive shaft and the axle. Car cases are sometimes easier to present to a woman judge. Cultural changes in the last few years notwithstanding, women still don't usually have the same ego involvement with being mechanical car experts that men do. They are often more willing to say "I don't know" and to listen.

Step 7. Appearing In Court

When you appear in court, be sure that you are well organized. Bring all the letters you have written, or received, about your car problem as well as written warranties (if any), photographs if they are helpful and your used parts if they aid in making your case. If you have a witness to any oral statements (warranties) made by the garage be sure to bring that person. Also, be sure to present any written letters by independent garage people who have examined your car. Several times in cases involving machinery, I have seen people give effective testimony by presenting a large drawing illustrating the screw-up. Also, be sure that you get your witnesses to the courtroom on time. The best way to do this is to pick them up at home or work and personally escort them.

If you are well prepared, you should win the sort of case outlined here without difficulty. Judges drive cars and have to get them fixed; they tend to be sympathetic with this type of consumer complaint. Simply present your story (see Chapter 15), your documentation and your witnesses. If you feel that your opponent is snowing the judge with a lot of technical lingo, get his Honor back on the track by asking that the technical terms be explained in ordinary English. This will be a relief to everyone in the courtroom except your opponent. You will likely find that, once his case is shorn of all the magic words, it will shrink from tiger to pussycat.

Step 8:   Ask for a Continuance in the Middle of Your Presentation If It Is Essential

The best-laid plans can occasionally go haywire. Perhaps a key witness doesn't show up, or maybe, despite careful preparation, you overlook some aspect of the case that the judge feels is crucial. If this occurs, you may want to ask the judge to reschedule the case on another day so that you can prepare better. It is proper to make this sort of request. Whether or not it will be granted is up to the judge. If he or she feels that more evidence isn't likely to change the result or that you are making the request to stall, it will not be granted. If there is a good reason for a delay, however, it will usually be allowed. But if you want a delay, you have to ask for it—the judge isn't going to be able to read your mind.

CHAPTER 17

Motor Vehicle Purchase Cases

All too often someone buys a motor vehicle, drives it a short way, and watches it fall apart. And all too often the seller won't stand behind the product sold or work out some sort of fair adjustment. There are major differences in approach between buying a new vehicle from a dealer, buying a used vehicle from a dealer and buying a used vehicle from a private party. Let's look at each situation individually.

A. New Vehicles

Here, the most common problem is the lemon with major manufacturing defects. Here is an example:

Example: You trade in your rusty '74 bomb that served you well for longer than you want to remember and fork over a ridiculously large pile of money on a shiny new car. Your new carriage runs fine for a few months, but then it begins to vibrate uncontrollably whenever you drive over 50 mph. You take it back to the dealer, who tries to fix it, but it still shakes. You take it back again, but it's still not right. By now you're tired of countless repairs. You paid for a car that works and you feel you should either get a refund or get a new car that works. How can you do this?

At least 43 states have enacted some sort of "lemon law" to protect consumers in your situation. Although the laws vary from state to state, they follow the same basic structure: If your new car has a substantial defect which cannot be repaired after repeated attempts or 30 days of service, you have a right to a refund or replacement vehicle from the manufacturer if you notify them of the problem and submit to arbitration. The arbitration is free and you don't need a lawyer.

ENFORCING YOUR LEMON RIGHTS

To qualify for a refund or replacement under most lemon laws you (or your car) must meet the following conditions:

1. Substantial Defect. Your new car must have a defect within the first year. The defect must substantially impair the car's use, value, or safety (or some combination of the three). Unfortunately, many lemons have lots of little problems rather than one big one, and most of these laws don't recognize this. Massachusetts and Rhode Island, however, do allow a bunch of "little" defects to be lumped together and treated as one "substantial" one.

2. Opportunity to Repair. The dealer or manufacturer gets three or four (depending on the state) chances to fix the defect within the first year, but can't keep the car in the shop for more than a total of 30 days. If the defect can't be fixed, the car is legally a lemon. (Note that the 30 total days during the year need not be consecutive days; also some states only count "business" days.) Most states treat each defect separately, and thus allow four repair attempts or 30 days for each one. A few states, however, allow the dealer only four repairs or 30 days to cure all the defects.

3. Notice to Manufacturer. You must notify the manufacturer about the repairs as they are being done. In most states, this requirement is satisfied by simply taking the car to the dealer, since the dealer contacts the manufacturer for reimbursement for all repairs done under warranty. A few states, however, including California and Washington, additionally require that you notify the manufacturer *in writing*—merely taking it into the dealer is not enough.

Once you've given the manufacturer three or four attempts or 30 days to fix your car, you have to notify the manufacturer again, in writing, that you want a refund or replacement vehicle.

4. Arbitration. After you've made your demand, you must submit to arbitration. In most states (except Texas and Vermont), you must use the manufacturer's arbitrator if it has one (most major companies do). These arbitrators or arbitration boards must meet federal and/or state standards of impartiality. Arbitration must be free and designed to be conducted without a lawyer. You explain the problem to the arbitrator either in person or in writing, and the arbitrator rules within 60 days whether your car is a lemon and whether you're entitled to a refund, replacement or something less. The arbitrator, however, will not award consequential damages, such as the cost of a car you had to rent while your car was in the shop. For that you have to go to court.

In all likelihood, the manufacturer will try to settle before you ever get to arbitration. Manufacturers hate to buy back cars or give replacements because they get stuck with a defective car which they have to resell as a used car, at a substantial loss. (One study showed that GM settled 90% of its cases before they reached arbitration. Of the 10% who did arbitrate, 60% got more than GM's final offer.)

If the arbitrator decides you don't qualify for a refund or a replacement, you can take your case to court. If you go to Small Claims Court, you'll be limited by the maximum amount your state allows in recovery. If you go to a formal court, and hire an attorney, the attorney's fees may exceed the cost of fixing the car and your case may not be heard for several years.

Unfortunately, many disputes involving new vehicles don't fall under the lemon law. This would be the situation if the same defect didn't recur four times or if problems develop just after the warranty expires.

Sometimes it seems as though there is a little destruct switch set to flip fifteen minutes after you hit the end of the warranty period. Often too, a problem starts to surface while the car is still under warranty and a dealer makes inadequate repairs which last scarcely longer than the remainder of the warranty term. When the same problem develops again after the warranty has run out, the dealer refuses to fix it.

Not long ago I saw a case involving this sort of problem. A man—let's call him Bruno—with a new, expensive European car was suing the local dealer and the parent car company's West Coast representative. Bruno claimed that he had repeatedly brought the car into the dealer's repair shop with transmission problems while it was still under written warranty. Each time adjustments were made which seemed to eliminate the problem. But each time, after a month or so, the same problem would reappear. A few months after the written warranty ran out, the transmission died. Even though the car was only a little over a year old, and had gone less than 20,000 miles, both the dealer and the parent car company refused to repair it. Their refusals continued even though the owner repeatedly wrote them, demanding action.

How did Bruno go about dealing with his problem? First, because he needed his car, he went ahead and had the repairs made. Then, although the repairs cost slightly in excess of the Small Claims limit, he decided that because it was too expensive to hire a lawyer and sue in a formal court, he would scale down his claim and sue for the Small Claims maximum. Because the dealer was located in the same city as Bruno was, he sued locally.[1] In this situation it would have been adequate to sue only the local dealer and not the car company, but it didn't hurt to sue both following the general rule, "when in doubt, sue all possible defendants."

In court, Bruno was well prepared and had a reasonably easy time. Both he and his wife testified as to their trials and tribulations with the car. They gave the judge copies of the several letters they had written the dealer, one of which was a list of the dates they had taken the car to the dealer's shop. They also produced a letter from the owner of the independent garage which finally fixed the transmission stating that, when he took the transmission apart, he discovered a defect in its original assembly. The new car dealer simply testified that his mechanics had done their best to fix the car under the written warranty. He then contended that, once the written warranty had run out, he was no longer responsible. The dealer made no effort to challenge the car owner's story, nor did he bring his own mechanics to testify as to what they had done while the car was still under warranty. Bruno won. He presented a convincing case to the point that the defect had never been fixed when it should have been under the written warranty. The dealer did nothing to rebut it. As the judge noted to me after the hearing, an $18,000 car should come with a transmission that lasts a lot longer than this one did. Bruno would have had an even stronger case if he had brought the independent garage man to court, but the letters, along with his own testimony and that of his wife, were adequate in a situation where the dealer didn't put up much of a defense.

---

[1]In most states, only one defendant need be local to sue in a particular judicial district (see Appendix). The fact that the car company's West Coast headquarters was in a different part of the state didn't cause a problem with bringing the suit where the dealer was located (see Chapter 9).

Note: In this sort of case it is very convincing to have documentation of all the trips you have made to the dealer's repair shop. You may be able to find copies of work orders you signed, or your cancelled checks. If you don't have this sort of record, sit down with a calendar and do your best to make an accurate list. Give the list to the judge in court. He will accept it as true unless the car dealer disputes it.

Even if your car is no longer covered by a written warranty when trouble develops, you may have a case. When a relatively new car falls apart for no good reason, many Small Claims Court judges bend over backwards to give you protection over and above the actual written warranty period that comes with the vehicle. In addition, many states have warranty laws that require that a product be reasonably fit for normal use. These laws have been interpreted to give the consumer more rights than the limited warranty that comes with the car. Thus, if the engine on your properly-maintained car burns out after 25,000 miles, you will stand a good chance of recovering some money even if the written warranty has expired.

In other words, many judges will not follow the strict letter of the law when doing so would produce a clearly unfair result. You may also wish to consider other remedies in addition to Small Claims Court, such as trying to enlist the help of state regulatory agencies. One strategy of last resort if you don't have much equity in the car is to simply drive it to the dealer and leave it there, refusing to make any more payments until it is fixed.[2]

Note: Particular models of cars are prone to particular problems. After a car has been in production for awhile, a pattern develops. Manufacturers are extremely sensitive to complaints in "high problem" areas and may even have issued an internal memo telling dealers to fix certain types of problems upon request. One reason for this is that they want to avoid Federal Government-required recalls. How can knowing this benefit you? By giving you the opportunity to pressure the company where it is most vulnerable. If your car which is no

---

[2]This remedy is discussed in more detail below under Used Vehicles.

longer covered by a written warranty develops a serious problem before it should, talk to people at independent garages that specialize in repairing this type of car. If they tell you the problem is widespread and that the company has fixed it for some persistent customers, write a demand letter to the car dealer and manufacturer (see Chapter 6). Mention that if your problem is not taken care of, you will sue in Small Claims Court and you will subpoena all records having to do with this defect (see Chapter 14). This may well cause the company to settle with you. If not, do both.

B. Used Vehicle Dealers

Recovering from used vehicle dealers can be tricky for several reasons. Unlike new vehicle dealers, who are usually somewhat dependent upon their reputation in the community for honesty, used vehicle dealers commonly have no positive reputation to start with and survive by becoming experts at self-protection. Also (and don't underestimate this one), judges almost never buy used vehicles and therefore aren't normally as sympathetic to the problems used vehicle owners encounter. Chances are a judge has had a problem getting her new car fixed under a warranty, but has never bought a ten year old Plymouth in "tip-top shape," only to have it die two blocks after leaving Honest Al's.

The principal self-protection device employed by used vehicle dealers is the "as is" designation in the written sales contract.[3] The salesperson may promise the moon, but when you read the fine print of the contract, you will see it clearly stated that the seller takes absolutely no responsibility for the condition of the vehicle and that it is sold "as is."

Time and again I have sat in court and heard hard luck stories like this:

"I bought the car for $1,200 two months ago. The man at Lucky Larry's told me that it had a completely reconditioned engine and transmission. I drove the car less than 400 miles and it died. I mean really died— it didn't roll over and dig itself a hole, but it may as well have. I had it towed to an independent garage and they told me that, as far as they could see, no engine or transmission work had ever been done. They estimated that to put the car right would cost $800. I got one more estimate which was even higher, so I borrowed the $800 and had the work done. I feel I really got took by Lucky Larry. I have with me the cancelled check for the $800 in repairs, plus the mechanic who did the work who can testify as to the condition of the car when he saw it."

Unfortunately, this plaintiff will probably lose. Why? Because going back to the sort of issues we discussed in Chapter 2, he has proven only half of his case. He has shown his loss (he bought a $1,200 car that wasn't worth $1,200), but he has not dealt with the issue of the defendant's responsibility to make the loss good ("liability"). Almost surely the used car dealer will testify that he "had no way of knowing how long a ten year old Plymouth would last and that, for this very reason, sold the car 'as is.' " He will then show the judge a written contract that not only has the "as is" designation, but which will say someplace in the fine print

---

[3]A couple of states now require that used car dealers give customers a history of the car, as well as a statement as to what's wrong with it, and stand behind whatever they claim. In Massachusetts, as of July 1, 1988, used car dealers must give buyers written warranties on cars having less than 125,000 miles.

that "this written contract is the entire agreement between the parties and that no oral statements or representations made by the dealer or any salesperson are part of the contract."

How can you fight this sort of cynical semi-fraud? It's difficult to do after the fact. The time for self-protection is before you buy a vehicle when you can have it checked by an expert and can insist that any promises made by the salesperson as to the condition of the car or the availability of repairs, be put in writing. Of course, good advice such as this, after the damage has been done, "isn't worth more than a passel of warm spit" as former Vice-President John Nance Garner so graphically put it. If you have just been cheated on a used car deal, you want to know what, if anything, you can do now. Here are some suggestions.

1. If the car broke almost immediately after you took it out of the used car lot, you can file in Small Claims and argue that you were defrauded. Your theory is that, no matter what the written contract said, there was a clear implication that you purchased a car, not a junk heap. When the dealer produces the "as is" contract you signed, argue that it is no defense to fraud. I discuss fraud in more detail in Chapter 2.

2. If the dealer made any promises either in writing or orally about the good condition of the vehicle, he may be required to live up to them. Why? Because, as noted in Chapter 2, statements about a product that you rely on as part of deciding whether to purchase may constitute an express warranty. This is true even if the seller had you sign an "as is" statement which disclaims all warranties. The key to winning this sort of case is to produce a witness to the dealer's laudatory statements about the vehicle, copies of ads which state the car is in good shape, plus anything else which will back up your story. Although not every state will let you make this argument (under the theory that the written agreement is the sum total of what applies), try making it anyway It can't hurt.[4]

3. You may also want to claim an implied warranty. One kind—the implied warranty of fitness—means that the vehicle is

---

[4]The argument has succeeded in California and Oklahoma.

warranteed to work for a particular purpose (say consistency).[5] The more common implied warranty is for merchantability. Here, if the car doesn't run at all, your basic claim is you haven't gotten a car worth anything—that is, it isn't merchantable.

4. You may want to consider having the car towed back to the lot and refusing to make future payments. This is an extreme remedy and should only be considered in an extreme situation. It does have the beauty of shifting the burden of taking legal action to the other side, at which point you can defend on the basis of fraud. If you take this approach, be sure you have excellent documentation that the car was truly wretched and be sure to set forth in writing the circumstances surrounding the difficulties, sending copies to the dealer and the bank or finance company to whom you pay your loan. Of course, you will probably have made some down payment, so even in this situation you may wish to initiate action in Small Claims Court.

5. Have your car checked over by someone who knows cars and will be willing to testify if need be. If this person can find affirmative evidence that you were cheated, you will greatly improve your Small Claims case. They might, for example, find that the odometer had been tampered with in violation of federal or state law, or that a heavy grade of truck oil had been put in the crank case so that the car wouldn't belch smoke. Also, this is the sort of case where a Subpoena Duces Tecum (subpoena for documents) might be of help (see Chapter 14). You might wish to subpoena records the car dealer has pertaining to his purchase price of the car, or its condition when purchased. It might also be helpful to learn the name of the car's former owner with the idea of contacting him. With a little digging you may be able to develop information that will enable you to convince a judge that you have been defrauded.

6. Consider other remedies besides Small Claims Court. These can include checking with your state Department of Consumer Affairs, or the local Department of Motor Vehicles to see if used

---

[5]California is one state we know that expressly provides for this application; however, it is limited to a situation in which the buyer received an express warranty.

car lots are regulated. In many states, the Department of Motor Vehicles licenses used car dealers and can be very helpful in getting disputes resolved, particularly where your complaint is one of many against the same dealer for similar practices. Also, contact your local District Attorney's office. Most now have a consumer fraud division which can be of great help. If you can convince them that what happened to you smells rotten, or your complaint happens to be against someone they have already identified as a borderline criminal, they will likely call the used car dealer in for a chat. In theory, the D.A.'s only job is to bring a criminal action which will be of no direct aid in getting your money back, but in practice, negotiations often go on which can result in restitution. In plain words, this means that the car dealer may be told, "Look buddy, you're right on the edge of the law here (or maybe over the edge). If you clean up your act, which means taking care of all complaints against you and seeing that there are no more, we will close your file. If you don't, I suggest you hire a good lawyer because you are going to need one."[6]

C. Used Vehicles from Private Parties

Normally it is easier to win a case against a private party than it is a used vehicle dealer. This runs counter to both common sense and fairness, as a private party is likely to be more honest than a dealer. But fair or not, the fact is that a non-dealer is usually less sophisticated in legal self-protection than is a pro. Indeed, in most private party sales the seller does no more than sign over the title slip in exchange for the agreed upon price. No formal contract is signed that says the buyer takes the car "as is."

---

[6]If you live in New York, you've got one last remedy: New York's lemon law applies to used car purchases.

If trouble develops soon after you purchase the vehicle and you are out money for unexpected repairs, you may be able to recover. Again, the problem is usually not proving your loss, but convincing the judge that the seller of the vehicle is responsible ("liable") to make your loss good. To do this, you normally must prove that the seller represented the vehicle to be in better shape than, in fact, it was, and that you relied on these promises when you made the deal.

Recently, I watched Barbara, a twenty-year-old college student, succeed in proving just such a case. She sued John for $1,150, claiming that the BMW motorcycle she purchased from him was in far worse shape than he had advertised. In court, she ably and convincingly outlined her conversations with John around the purchase of the motorcycle, testifying that he repeatedly told her that the cycle was "hardly used." She hadn't gotten any of his promises in writing, but she did a creative job of developing and presenting what evidence she had. This included:

• A copy of her letter to John which clearly outlined her position, such as the letter below:

14 Harrison St.
Moline, IL
January 27, 19__

John Malinosky
321 Adams St.
Moline, IL

Dear Mr. Malinosky:

This letter is a follow-up to our recent phone conversation in which you refused to discuss the fact that the BMW motorcycle I purchased from you on January 15 is not in the "excellent condition" that you claimed.

To review: on January 12, I saw your ad for a motorcycle that was "almost new— hardly used—excellent condition" in the local flea market newspaper. I called you and you told me that the cycle was a terrific bargain and that you would never sell it except that you needed money for school. I told you that I didn't know much about machinery.

The next day, you took me for a ride on the cycle. You told me specifically that:

1. The cycle had just been tuned up.

2. The cycle had been driven less than 30,000 miles.

3. The cycle had never been raced or used roughly.

4. That if anything went wrong with the cycle in the next month or two, you would see that it was fixed.

I didn't have the cycle more than a week when the brakes went out. When I had them checked, the mechanic told me that the carburetor also needed work (I confirmed this with another mechanic—see attached estimate). The mechanic also told me that the cycle had been driven at least 75,000 miles (perhaps a lot more) and that it needed a tune-up. In addition, he showed me caked mud and scratches under the cycle frame which indicated to him that it had been driven extensively off the road in rough terrain and had probably been raced on dirt tracks.

The low mechanic's estimate to do the repairs was $1,150. Before having the work done, I called you to explain the situation and to give you a chance to arrange for the repairs to be made, or to make them yourself. You laughed at me and said, "Sister, do what you need to do—you're not getting dime one from me."

Again I respectfully request that you make good on the promises (express warranty) you made to me on January 15. I relied on the truth of your statements (express warranty) when I decided to buy the bike. I enclose a copy of the mechanic's bill for $1,150, along with several higher estimates that I received from other repair shops.

Sincerely,

Barbara Parker

• Copies of repair bills (and three estimates) dated within two weeks of her purchase of the cycle, the lowest of which came to $1,150.

• A copy of John's newspaper ad which she answered. It read: "BMW 500, almost new—hardly used—excellent condition—$3,500."

• Finally, Barbara presented the judge with this note from the mechanic who fixed the cycle.

To Whom It May Concern:

It's hard for me to get off work, but if you need me, please ask the judge to delay the case a few days. All I have to say is this: the BMW that Barbara Parker brought to me was in *fair* shape. It's impossible to be exact, but I guess that it had been driven at least 75,000 miles and I can say for sure that it was driven a lot of miles on dirt.

Respectfully submitted,

Al "Honker" Green

February 3, 19___

Barbara quickly outlined the whole story for the judge and emphasized that she had saved for six months to get the money to make the purchase.[7]

Next, John had his turn. He helped Barbara make her case by acting like a weasel. His testimony consisted mostly of a lot of vague philosophy about machinery. He kept asking "how could I know just when it would break?" When the judge asked him specific questions about the age, condition and previous history of the cycle, he clammed up as if he was a mafioso called to testify by a Senate anti-racketeering committee. When the judge asked him if he had, in fact, made specific guarantees about the condition of the bike, John began a long explanation about how

---

[7]This sort of testimony isn't relevant, but it never hurts. As an old appeals court judge who had seen at least 75 summers told me when I graduated from law school and was proud of my technical mastery of the law, "Son, don't worry about the law—just convince the judge that truth and virtue are on your side and he will find some legal technicality to support you." No one ever gave me better advice.

when you sell things, you "puff them up a little" and that "women shouldn't be allowed to drive motorcycles anyway." Finally, the judge asked him to please sit down.

Important: In this type of case, absent a written warranty such as an ad that states the vehicle is in great shape, it's often one person's word against another's. Any shred of tangible evidence that the seller has made an express verbal warranty as to the condition of the goods can be enough to shift the balance to that side. Of course, if you have a friend who witnessed or heard any part of the transaction, his or her testimony will be extremely valuable. Getting a mechanic to check over a vehicle and then testify for you is also a good strategy. Sometimes you can get some help from publications such as bluebooks that list wholesale and retail prices for used cars. Several times I have seen people bring bluebooks (car dealers have them) into court and show the judge that they paid above the bluebook price for a used car "because the car was represented to be in extra good shape." This doesn't constitute much in the way of real proof that you were ripped off, but it is helpful to at least show the judge that you paid a premium price for unsound goods.

CHAPTER 18

Cases in Which Money Is Owed

The most common type of Small Claims case involves the failure to pay money. Let's look at how these disputes commonly develop from both the debtor's and creditor's point of view.

A. From the Creditor's Point of View[1]

The job of the plaintiff in a case where he or she is suing for non-payment of a debt is to prove that a valid debt exists and that it has not been paid. Here are a few suggestions.

---

[1]Most states allow the person to whom money was owed to sue to collect it, whether the debt was a business or a personal one. However, many states bar assignees (collection agencies) from suing in Small Claims Court. Rules around the country vary—New York bars all corporations and insurers from regular small claims court, but has a special commercial small claims court where only corporations, partnerships and associations can sue. Texas bars money lenders from suing in Small Claims Court and so on. (Check Appendix for your state.)

1. Sue Promptly

When you are owed money, be sure to sue promptly. You will find a discussion of the Statutes of Limitations applicable to different sorts of debts in Chapter 5. But even when there is no danger that the limitation period will run out, it makes sense to proceed as soon as reasonably possible. Another reason to bring your case promptly is that judges just aren't as sympathetic to old claims. Several times when I have sat as judge, I have wondered why someone waited three years to sue for $500. Was it because she wasn't honestly convinced that her suit was valid? Perhaps the best reason to sue right away is that you will get your money faster. Indeed you may be pleasantly surprised that a considerable number of people who said they would never pay will, in fact, pay up when you demonstrate you are serious enough to go to court.

2. Written Contracts

If the debt is based on a written contract, be sure that your paperwork is in order. Bring to court the original copy of any written note proving the indebtedness so that the court can cancel it when the judgment is entered. Also bring any ledger sheets or other documentation as to any payments made, interest charged, etc. Often I have seen otherwise sensible looking business people show up with botched records and become flustered when closely questioned by the judge. The courtroom is not the place to straighten out a poor accounting system. Some courts require that a copy of an unpaid bill or other evidence of indebtedness be submitted at the same time your action is filed. Check your local rules.

Note: If you provide goods or services, it's wise to include in all letters and bills to people who owe you money a request that they notify you if the goods are defective, or the services substandard. Bring copies of these notices to court. If the debtor shows up with a story about not paying because of some problem or defect, produce your documents. The fact that you requested to be informed about any problems with the product or service long ago and that no complaints were made previous to your court hearing will pretty clearly imply that the defendant is fabricating or at least exaggerating his current complaint.

3. Oral Contracts

A debt based on an oral contract is legal as long as the contract could have been carried out in one year. However, you may face a problem proving that the debt exists if the defendant denies that he borrowed the money or bought the goods. Your best bet is to come up with some written documentation that your version of the story is true. If you have no written evidence (cancelled checks, letters or notes asking for more time to pay, etc.), your next step is to try to think of any person who knows about the debt and who is willing to testify. For example, if you asked the defendant to pay you and he said in the presence of your friend, "I'll pay you next month," or "You will never get your money back," or anything to indicate that a loan existed, bring your friend as a witness.

Of course, in many situations, no direct written or verbal evidence sufficient to prove the existence of a contract exists. If this is your situation, you will have to try and establish the existence of the contract by reference to the conduct of the parties. For example, if Richard, a professional painter, paints Tara's house, and Tara refuses to pay him, a judge will almost surely use what is known in law as the "quantum meruit doctrine"[2] to presume that an oral contact exists calling for Tara to pay Richard a reasonable amount for his work. (Judges, like everyone else, know that professional painters don't work for free.) However, it will be much harder for Richard to establish the amount and terms of the contract using this approach. Thus, if Richard says he was to be paid $20 per hour and Tara says he agreed to work for $15, Richard may have a hard time convincing the judge to award him the higher amount.

4. Proving Your Case

When it comes to establishing that money is owed, many states allow a business to send a bookkeeper to court (see Chapter 7 for details). This works well if the defendant defaults (doesn't show up) or appears in court but doesn't dispute the amount owed. Unfortunately, a bookkeeper is not competent to testify if the defendant shows up and defends on the basis that

---

[2]See Chapter 2 for a brief discussion of *"quantum meruit,"* which basically means that if a person receives goods or services in a situation where payment is normally expected, he is liable to pay for them.

the goods or services were defective, delivered late, etc. For example, if you own a TV repair business and are suing on an unpaid repair bill in a situation where you expect the defendant may show up in court and claim (whether falsely or not) that you did lousy work, you will need to have someone in court who knows the details of the particular job. This can be the employee who knows firsthand all the facts of the situation. In the context of this example, this would be the person who repaired the TV.

But what happens if you or your bookkeeper find yourself in Small Claims Court suing on what you think is a routine debt in a situation where you do not expect the defendant to show up and contest, and you are surprised by the presence of a fire-eating defendant who raises all sorts of substantive claims that you (or your bookkeeper) have no firsthand knowledge about? Your best bet is to ask the judge to delay (continue) the case for a few days to give you the opportunity to get the right witness (or at least the person's written testimony) to court. Many judges will do this if they feel you made a sincere effort to be ready in the first place.

Note: Many businesses, and especially professionals such as doctors, dentists and lawyers, don't use Small Claims Court to collect unpaid bills because they think it takes too much of their own time, or is "undignified." You will have to worry about your "dignity" yourself, but I can tell you that Small Claims Court actions can be handled with very little time and expense once you get the hang of it. This is especially true when you consider that the alternative is to turn the bill over to a collection agency or not to collect it at all. As long as the suit simply involves getting a judgment for an unpaid bill, rules in effect in many states allow you to send your bookkeeper to court. Wait until you have several cases and schedule them on the same day. You will find that once your bookkeeper understands the system, she can often be in and out of court in fifteen minutes to a half hour. Once you get your judgment, your secretarial staff should be able to handle the collection activities described in Chapter 24.

B.   From the Debtor's Point of View

While there are an increasing number of private individuals using Small Claims Court, most plaintiffs are business people or employees of government entities, such as a library, hospital or city tax office, trying to collect debts. When I first watched debt collection cases, I did so with scant attention. I assumed that individuals being pursued by large institutions were bound to .lose, especially since I guessed they mostly did owe the money. I even wondered why a lot of folks bothered to show up— knowing in advance that they had no defense and no money. I thought it unjust that our society divided its bounty so unfairly and sad that the poor had no better defense than their inability to pay.

But then a curious thing happened. Many of the "down-trodden" I had dismissed so easily refused to play their docile parts. Instead of shuffling in with heads down and nothing constructive to say, they argued back, stamped their feet and acted like the proud and dignified people they were. I realized suddenly that I was the only person in the courtroom that had dismissed them. I learned that morning, and on dozens of subsequent mornings, that there are lots of ways to constructively defend non-payment of debt cases. Here are some examples.

• A local hospital sued an unemployed man for failure to pay an emergency room bill for $478. It seemed an open and shut case—the person from the hospital had all the proper records, and the defendant hadn't paid. Then the defendant told his side of it. He was taken to the emergency room suffering from a superficial but painful gunshot wound. Because it was a busy night and he was not about to die, he was kept waiting four hours for treatment. When treatment was given, it was minimal, and he suffered later complications that might have been avoided if he had been treated more promptly and thoroughly. He said he didn't mind paying a fair amount, but that he didn't feel he got $478 worth of care in the twenty minutes the doctor spent with him. The judge agreed and gave judgment to the hospital for $150, plus court and service of process costs. After the defendant explained that he had only his unemployment check, the judge ordered that he be allowed to pay off the judgment at the rate of $10 per month.

• A large tire company sued a woman for not paying the balance on a tire bill. She had purchased eight tires for two pickup trucks and still owed $512.50. The tire company properly presented the judge with the original copy of a written contract along with the woman's payment record, and then waited for judgment. They are still waiting. The woman, who ran a small neighborhood gardening and landscaping business, produced several advertising flyers from the tire company which strongly implied that the tires would last at least 40,000 miles. She then testified and presented a witness to the fact that the tires had gone less than 25,000 miles before wearing out. The defendant also had copies of four letters written over the past year to the headquarters of the tire company in the Midwest complaining about the tires. Both in the letters, and in court, she repeatedly stated that the salesperson at the tire company told her several times that the tires were guaranteed for 40,000 miles. Putting this all together, the judge declared the tires should be pro-rated on the basis of 40,000 miles and gave the tire company a judgment for only $210, instead of the $512.50 requested. The woman wrote out a check on the spot and departed feeling vindicated.

• A rug company sued a customer for $686 and produced all the necessary documentation showing that the carpet had been installed and that no payment had been received. The defendant testified that the rug had been poorly installed with an uneven seam running down the center of the room. He had pictures that left no doubt that the rug installer was either drunk or blind. The defendant also presented drawings that illustrated that there were obviously several better ways to cut the carpet to fit the room. The rug company received nothing.

The point of these examples is not the facts of the individual situations—yours will surely differ. The point is that there are all sorts of defenses, and partial defenses, and that it makes good sense to defend yourself creatively if you feel that goods or services you received were worth less than the amount for which you are being sued (see Chapter 2 for information on warranties and fraud). It is usually not enough to tell the judge that you were dissatisfied with what you received. A little more imagination is required. If shoddy goods are involved, show them to the judge. If you received bad service, bring a witness or other supporting evidence. If, for example, you got roof repairs done that resulted in more holes than you had before, take pictures of the rain leaking in, and get an estimate from another roofer.

There is often a tactical advantage for the debtor in the fact that the person who appears in court on behalf of the creditor is not the same person with whom he had dealings. If, for example, you state that a salesperson told you X, Y and Z, that person probably won't be present to state otherwise. This may tilt a closely balanced case to you. It is not inappropriate for you to point out to the judge that your opponent has only books and ledgers, not firsthand knowledge of the situation. The judge may sometimes continue the case until another day to allow the creditor to have whatever employee(s) you dealt with present, but often this is impossible because the employee in question will have left the job, or be otherwise unavailable.

A Little More Time to Pay: In California, the District of Columbia, New York, Rhode Island and Washington, and in many other areas, the judge has considerable discretion to order that a judgment be paid in installments. Thus, a judge could find that you owe the phone company $200, but allow you to pay it off at $20 per month, instead of all at once. Time payments can be particularly helpful if you don't have the money to pay all at once, but fear a wage attachment or other collection activity by the creditor. Don't be afraid to ask the judge for time payments—he or she won't know that you want them if you don't ask for them.

CHAPTER 19

Vehicle Accident Cases

It is a rare Small Claims Court session that does not include at least one fender bender. Usually these cases are badly prepared and presented. The judge commonly makes a decision at least partially by guess. I know from personal experience when I sat as a "pro tem" judge that it sometimes wouldn't take much additional evidence for me to completely reverse a decision.

The average vehicle accident case that ends up in Small Claims Court doesn't involve personal injury, but is concerned with damage to one, or both, parties' car, cycle, RV, moped or whatever.[1] Because of some quirk of character that seems to be

---

[1] Cases involving all but small personal injuries don't belong in Small Claims Court, as they will result in settlements of more than the Small Claims maximum. And in states that have no-fault insurance, even simple property damage cases may not be allowed unless you've complied with certain requirements of your state's no-fault insurance law. In Massachusetts (one of the first states to enact no-fault), Small Claims Court is actually considered to be a sort of court of appeal from an earlier administrative determination of who gets paid what. New Jersey allows auto accident claims for property damage only, not for personal

deeply embedded in our overgrown monkey brains, it is almost impossible for most of us to admit that we are bad drivers, or were at fault in a car accident. We will cheerfully acknowledge that we aren't terrific looking or geniuses, but we all believe that we drive like angels. Out of fantasies such as these are lawsuits made.

In Chapter 2, I discuss the concept of negligence. Please re-read this material. To recover in a vehicle accident case, you have to either prove that the other person was negligent and you were not or, if both of you were negligent, that you were less so. Normally dealing with concepts of negligence in a vehicle accident is a matter of common sense; you probably have a fairly good ideal of the rules of the road. If you are in doubt, however, consider whether either you or the other party violated any state law provision relating to highway safety which contributed to the accident (see Section B below).

A. Who Can Sue Whom?

The owner of a vehicle is the correct person to file a claim for damage to the vehicle, even if he wasn't driving when the damage occurred. Suit for damage to the vehicle should be brought against the negligent driver. If the driver is not the registered owner, suit should also be brought against that person. In other words, both the driver and the registered owner are liable. To find out who owns a car, contact the Department of Motor Vehicles. As long as you can tell them the license number, they can tell you the registered owner.

---

injury; a few states don't allow suits arising out of any vehicle accidents to be brought in Small Claims Court. Check your local rules.

B. Was There a Witness to the Accident?

Because the judge has no way of knowing what happened unless one or more people tell her, a good witness can make or break your case. It is better to have a disinterested witness than a close friend or family member, but any witness is better than no witness. If the other guy is likely to have a witness who supports his point of view (even though it's wrong) and you have none, you will have to work extra hard to develop other evidence to overcome this disadvantage. Re-read Chapter 14 for more information on witnesses. If you do have an eye witness but can't get that person to show up in court voluntarily, bring a written statement.

C. Police Accident Reports

When you have an accident and believe the other person was more at fault than you were, it is almost always wise to call the police so that a police report can be prepared. A police report is admissible as evidence in Small Claims Court in most states. The theory is that an officer investigating the circumstances of the accident at the scene is in a better position to establish the truth of what happened than is any other third party. So, if there was an accident report, buy a copy for a few dollars from the police station. If it supports you, bring it to court. If it doesn't, be prepared to refute what it says. This can best be done with the testimony of an eye witness. If both an eye witness and a police report are against you, try prayer.

Note: Many of you will be reading this book some considerable period of time after your accident. Obviously, my advice to call the police and have an accident report prepared will be of no use. Unfortunately, if the police are not called at the time of the accident, it's too late.

D. Determining Fault

In Chapter 2, I discussed the general concept of negligence. While that discussion is fully applicable to motor vehicle cases (go back and read it if you haven't already), negligence can also be determined in these types of cases by a showing that the other driver caused the accident (in whole or in part) as a result of a Vehicle Code violation or other similar statutory violation. For instance, if Tommy runs a red light (prohibited by state law) and hits a car crossing the intersection, Tommy is negligent (unless he can offer a sufficient excuse for his action). On the other hand, if Tommy is driving without his seatbelt on (also prohibited by most states) and has an accident, the violation cannot be said to have caused the accident and therefore can't be used to determine negligence.

If there is a police report, the reporting officer may have noted any vehicle code violations which occurred relative to the accident. The report may even conclude that a code violation caused the accident. If there is no police report, or the report does not specify any violations, you may wish to do a little research on your own. Your state's vehicle code is available in most large public libraries, all law libraries, and sometimes at the Department of Motor Vehicles. You can use its index to very quickly review dozens of driving rules which may have been violated by the other driver. If you discover any violations that can fairly be said to have contributed to the accident, call them to the attention of the judge. Congratulations, you have gone far towards establishing your negligence claim.

E. Diagrams

With the exception of witnesses and police accident reports, the most effective evidence is a good diagram. I have seen a good case lost because the judge never properly visualized what happened. All courtrooms have blackboards, and it is an excellent idea to draw a diagram of what happened as part of your presentation. If you are nervous about your ability to do this, you may want to prepare your diagram in advance and bring it to court. Use crayons or magic markers and draw on a large piece of paper about three feet square. Do a good job, with attention to detail. Here is a sample drawing that you might prepare to aid your testimony if you were going eastbound on Rose St. and making a right hand turn on Sacramento St. when you were hit by a car that ran a stop sign on Sacramento. Of course, the diagram doesn't tell the whole story—you have to do that.

F. Photos

Photographs can sometimes be of aid in fender bender cases. They can serve to back up your story about how an accident occurred. For example, if you claimed that you were sideswiped while you were parked, a photo showing a long series of scratches down the side of your car would be helpful. It is also a good idea to have pictures of the defendant's car if you can manage to get them, as well as photos of the scene of the accident.

G. Estimates

It is important that you obtain several estimates for the cost of repairing your vehicle. Three is usually a good number. If you have already gotten the work done, bring your cancelled check or receipt from the repair shop, along with the estimates you didn't accept.[2] Be sure to get your estimates from reputable shops. If, for some reason, you get an estimate from someone you later think isn't competent, simply ignore it, and get another. You have no responsibility to get your car fixed by anyone suggested to you by the person who caused the damage. Common sense normally dictates that you don't. Unfortunately, you can't recover money from the other party to cover the time you put in to get estimates, take your car to the repair shop, or to appear in court.

In addition to damage to your car, you can also recover for the fair market value of anything in your car that was destroyed. You must be prepared not only to establish the fact of the damage, but the dollar amount of the loss. You can also recover for alternate transportation while your car is disabled. However, you can only recover for the minimum reasonable time it should take to get your car fixed. Thus, if you could arrange to get a

---

[2]In a few courts, such as in New York City, you must normally have the repairs completed and paid for before you can collect. See your local rules.

fender fixed in two days, you are only entitled to rent a car for two days, even if an overworked mechanic takes four.[3]

Defendant's Note: Sometimes plaintiffs dishonestly try to get already existing damage to their car fixed as part of getting the legitimate accident work done. If you think the repair bill is high, try developing your own evidence that this is so. If you have a picture of the plaintiff's car showing the damage, this can be a big help. Also, remember that the plaintiff is only entitled to get repairs made up to the total value of the car before the accident. If the car was worth only $500 and the repairs would cost $750, the plaintiff is only entitled to $500 (see Chapter 5).

H. Your Demand Letter

Here again, as in almost every other type of Small Claims Court case, you should write a letter to your opponent with an eye to the judge reading it. See the examples in Chapter 6. Here is another:

---

[3]See Chapter 5 for a more thorough discussion of damages.

18 Channing Way
Eugene, OR
August 27, 19__

R. Rigsby Rugg
27 Miramar Crescent
Eugene, OR

Dear Mr. Rugg:

On August 15, 19__ I was eastbound on Rose Street in Eugene, Oregon at about 3:30 on a sunny afternoon. I stopped at the stop sign at the corner of Rose and Sacramento and then proceeded to turn right (south) on Sacramento. As I was making my turn, I saw your car going southbound on Sacramento. You were about 20 feet north of the corner of Rose. Instead of stopping at the stop sign, you proceeded across the intersection and struck my car on the front right fender. By the time I realized that you were coming through the stop sign, there was nothing I could do to get out of your way.

As you remember, after the accident the Eugene police were called and cited you for failure to stop at a stop sign. I have gotten a copy of the police report from the police and it confirms the facts as I have stated them here.

I have obtained three estimates for the work needed on my car. The lowest is $612. I am proceeding to get this work done as I need my car fixed as soon as possible.

I will appreciate receiving a check from you as soon as possible. If you wish to talk about any aspect of this situation, please don't hesitate to call me, evenings at 486-1482.

Sincerely,

Sandy McClatchy

In court, Sandy would present her case like this:

Clerk: "Next case, McClatchy v. Rugg. Please come forward."

Judge: "Please tell me what happened, Ms. McClatchy."

Sandy McClatchy: "Good morning. This dispute involves an auto accident that occurred at Rose and Sacramento Streets on the afternoon of August 15, 19_. I was coming uphill on Rose (that's east) and stopped at the corner. There is a four-way stop sign at the corner. I turned right, or south, on Sacramento Street, and as I was doing so, Mr. Rugg ran the stop sign on Sacramento and crashed into my front fender. Your Honor, may I use the blackboard to make a quick diagram?"

Judge: "Please do. I was about to ask you if you would."

Sandy McClatchy: (makes drawing like the one on page 19:5, points out the movement of the cars in detail and answers several questions from the judge) "Your Honor, before I sit down, I would like to give you several items of evidence. First, I have a copy of the police accident report from the Eugene police which states that Mr. Rugg got a citation for failing to stop at the stop sign. Second, I have some photos which show the damage to the front fender of my car. Third, I have my letter to Mr. Rugg, trying to settle this case and finally I have several estimates as to the cost of repairing the damage to my car. As you can see from my cancelled check, I took the lowest one."

Judge: "Thank you, Ms. McClatchy. Now, Mr. Rugg, it's your turn."

R. Rigsby Rugg: "Your Honor, my case rests on one basic fact. Ms. McClatchy was negligent because she made a wide turn into Sacramento Street. Instead of going from the right hand lane of Rose to the right hand, or inside lane, on Sacramento Street, she turned into the center lane on Sacramento Street. (Mr. Rugg moves to the blackboard and points out what he says happened.) Now it might be true that I made a rolling stop at the corner. You know, I really stopped, but maybe not quite all the way—but I never would have hit anybody if she had kept to her own side of the road. Also, your Honor, I would like to say this—she darted out; she has one of those little foreign cars, and instead of easing out slow, like I do with my Lincoln, she jumped out like a rabbit being chased by a red fox."

Judge: "Do you have anything else to say, Ms. McClatchy?"

Sandy McClatchy: "I am not going to even try to argue about whether Mr. Rugg can be rolling and stopped at the same time. I think the policeman who cited him answered that question. I want to answer his point about my turning into the center lane on Sacramento St., instead of the inside lane. It is true that, after stopping, I had to make a slightly wider turn than usual. If you will look again at the diagram I drew, you will see that a car was parked almost to the corner of Sacramento and Rose on Sacramento. To get around this car, I had to drive a little farther into Sacramento before starting my turn than would have been necessary otherwise. I didn't turn into the center lane, but as I made the turn, my outside fender crossed into the center lane slightly. This is when Mr. Rugg hit me. I feel that since I had the right of way and I had to do what I did to make the turn, I wasn't negligent."

Judge: "Thank you both—you will get my decision in the mail."

(The judge decided in favor of Sandy McClatchy and awarded her $612 plus service of process and filing costs.)

Note: You can win, or partially win, a case involving negligence in most states, even if you were not completely in the right. If the other person was more at fault than you were, you have a case. This concept of "comparative" negligence is a new one in many states. It used to be that if you were even a little at fault, you couldn't recover because of a legal doctrine known as "contributory negligence."

Professional Driver Note: Be particularly wary when you are opposing a bus or truck driver. Many of these people suffer problems on their jobs if they are found to be at fault in too many accidents. As a result, they deny fault almost automatically. Judges usually know this and are often unsympathetic when a bus driver says that there has never been a time when he "didn't look both ways twice, count to ten and say the Lord's Prayer" before pulling out from a bus stop. Still, it never hurts to question the driver in court as to whether his employer has any demerit system or other penalty for being at fault in an accident.

CHAPTER 20

Landlord-Tenant Cases

In most states, Small Claims Court can be used by a tenant to sue for money damages for such things as the failure of a landlord to return a cleaning or damage deposit, invasion of the tenant's privacy by the landlord, the landlord's violation of his duty to provide habitable premises, and rent control violations, to name but a few. Similarly, a landlord can use Small Claims Court to sue a tenant or former tenant for damage done to the rental property and for failure to pay rent. In some states it is also possible for a landlord to use Small Claims Court to evict a tenant. (See Appendix for state-by-state information.) This is an exception to the general rule that only money damage cases can be handed down by Small Claims Court.

Practically, it makes great sense to use Small Claims Court for money damage cases, and sometimes less sense to use it for evictions in many states. Why? Because, Small Claims Court rules, even in those states where evictions are allowed, tend to limit a landlord's rights when it comes to getting the tenant out in the minimum time and getting a judgment for the maximum amount of rent and other damages. In a few states a small claims defendant even has an automatic right to appeal the eviction judgment and to remain living in the rental unit while the appeal is pending, even though no rent is paid.

So before you bring an eviction action in Small Claims Court, check out the following questions in your state rules:

• If you win an eviction order, can you get the sheriff or marshal to enforce it immediately?

• If the defendant appeals, can he or she stay in the dwelling while the appeal is pending?

• Can you sue for enough damages to fully or at least mostly cover your legitimate claim for back rent and damages to the premises?

• If the defendant can stay in the dwelling during an appeal, is there a requirement that he or she must post some money in the form of a bond that will go to you to cover lost rent if the appeal fails?

A. Deposit Cases

The most common landlord-tenant disputes concern the failure of a landlord to return a tenant's cleaning and damage deposits after the tenant moves out. These days, deposits can add up to many hundreds of dollars, and tenants understandably want them returned.

Going to court if a landlord refuses to return a deposit can be easy or difficult, depending upon both the facts of the situation and on how much homework a tenant has done in advance of filing suit. Many landlords are experienced with Small Claims proceedings and come to court prepared with a long list of damaged and dirty conditions that they claim the tenant left behind. All too often, the landlord's presentation leaves the tenant sputtering with righteous indignation. Unfortunately evidence, not indignation, wins cases. Think about it—if the tenant testifies the apartment was clean, and the landlord that it was dirty, the judge (unless he is psychic) is stuck making a decision that is little more than a guess. Faced with this sort of situation, most judges will split the difference.

How should a tenant prepare a case involving failure to return deposits? Ideally, preparation should start when he moves in. Any damage or dirty conditions should be noted as part of the lease or rental agreement. The tenant should also take photographs of substandard conditions and have neighbors or friends look the place over. When the tenant moves out and cleans up, he should do much the same thing—take photos, have friends check the place over, keep receipts for cleaning materials, try to get the landlord to agree that it's in satisfactory condition.

In most states, the burden of proof that conditions exist that justify the landlord keeping all or part of a deposit falls on the landlord. Usually state law also provides that if a deposit is not returned within a short time after the tenant moves out (usually somewhere between 14-30 days, depending on the state), and if the landlord acted in bad faith in retaining the deposits, the tenant may be entitled to "punitive" damages over and above the actual amount of the deposits.[1] Whether or not the tenant actually gets punitive damages is a matter of judicial discretion,

---

[1]California allows $200 as punitive damages, plus interest on the withheld deposit at 2% a month. A large number of states provide for recovery of double (Illinois, New Jersey, Michigan, Ohio, Pennsylvania, and others) or even triple (Georgia & Maryland) the amount wrongfully withheld. Some of these states also provide that the tenant may be awarded attorney's fees if applicable. Texas seems toughest on landlords; there the landlord can be assessed a maximum of $100 plus three times the amount wrongfully withheld plus attorney's fees. To check the law in your state, look under the hearing "Landlord-Tenant" and the subheading "deposits" in your state's legal code.

but it never hurts to bring your suit for an amount that includes them. Remember the general rule that you have to request damages when you file your suit if you wish to receive them.

Now let's assume that you are a tenant and have not gotten $600 in cleaning and damage deposits returned even though you moved out of an apartment three weeks ago, having paid all your rent and having given proper notice. Start by writing the landlord a letter like this:

---

750 Lampost Lane
Costa Mesa, CA
October 15, 19__

Anderson Realty Co.
10 Rose St.
Costa Mesa, California

Dear People:

As you know, until September 30, 19_, I resided in apartment #4 at 300 Oak Street in Costa Mesa and regularly paid my rent to your office. When I moved out, I left the unit cleaner than when I moved in.

As of today, I have received neither my $300 cleaning deposit nor my $300 damage deposit. Indeed, I have never received any accounting from you for any of my money. Please be aware that I know my rights under California Civil Code 1950.5 and that, if I do not receive my money within the next week, I will regard the retention of these deposits as showing "bad faith" on your part and shall sue you, not only for the $600 deposit, but also for the $200 punitive damages allowed by Section 1950.5 of the California Civil Code.

May I hear from you soon.

Sincerely,

Farah Shields

If you get no satisfactory response, file your case. Sometimes it is hard to know who to sue, since rent is often paid to a manager or other agent instead of the owner. In most states, multiple occupancy buildings with two or more units must have ownership information posted on the premises, or list the name of the owner (or his agent for purposes of suit) on the rental agreement. If you are in doubt as to who owns your unit, you are probably safe if you sue both the person to whom you pay your rent, and the person who signed the rental agreement, unless you have received notice that the building has been transferred to a new owner, in which case you would sue that person.

On court day, a well-prepared tenant would show up in court with as many of the following pieces of evidence as possible:

• Photos of the apartment on moving in which show any dirt or damage that already existed.

• Photos of the apartment on moving out which show clean conditions.

• Receipts for cleaning supplies used in the final clean-up.

• A copy of your written lease or rental agreement, if any.

• A copy of a demand letter to the landlord such as the one set out above.

• One, or preferably two, witnesses who were familiar with the property and saw it after you cleaned up, and who will testify that it was immaculate. People who helped in the clean-up are always particularly effective witnesses. If you also have a witness who saw the place when you moved in and who will say that it wasn't so clean (or damage already existed), so much the better.

• A copy of an inventory of conditions when moving in and moving out, signed by the landlord and tenant, if one was prepared.

Proceedings in court should go something like this:

Clerk: "Shields v. Anderson Realty. Please step forward."

Judge: "Good morning. Please tell me your version of the facts, Ms. Shields."

Farah Shields: "I moved into the apartment at 300 Oak St. in Costa Mesa in the spring of 19__. I paid Mr. Anderson here my first and last months' rent which totaled $400. I also paid him a $300 damage security deposit, and a $300 cleaning deposit.

When I moved into #4 at 300 Oak, it was a mess. It's a nice little apartment, but the people who lived there before me were sloppy. The stove was filthy, as was the bathroom, the refrigerator, the floors and just about everything else. In addition, the walls hadn't been painted in years. But I needed a place and this was the best available, so I moved in despite the mess. I painted the whole place—everything. Mr. Anderson's office gave me the paint, but I did all of the work. And I cleaned the place thoroughly too. It took me three days. I like to live in a clean place.

Here are some pictures of what the place looked like when I moved in (*hands photos to clerk who gives them to the judge*). Here is a second set of photos which were taken after I moved out and cleaned up (*again hands pictures to clerk*). Your Honor, I think these pictures tell the story—the place was clean when I moved out. I also have receipts (*hands to clerk*) for cleaning supplies and a rug shampooer that I used during the clean-up. They total $18.25. I have also brought two people who saw the place the day I left and can tell you what it looked like."

Judge: (*looking at one of the witnesses*) "Do you have some personal knowledge of what this apartment looked like?"

John DeBono: "Yes, I helped Farah move in and move out. I simply don't understand what the landlord is fussing about. The place was a smelly mess when she moved in, and it was spotless when Farah moved out."

Judge: (*addressing the second witness*) "Do you have something to add?"

Puna Polaski: "I never saw 300 Oak when Farah moved in because I didn't know her then. But I did help her pack and clean up when she moved out. I can tell you that the windows were washed, the floor waxed and the oven cleaned because I did it.

And I can tell you that the rest of the appartment was clean too, because I saw it."

Judge: "Mr. Anderson, do you want to present your case."

Adam Anderson: "Your Honor, I am not here to argue about whether the place was clean or not. Maybe it was cleaner when Miss Shields moved out than when she moved in. The reason I withheld the deposits is that the walls were all painted odd, bright colors and I have had to paint them all over. Here are some color pictures of the walls taken just after Miss Shields moved out. They show pink and purple walls, two of which are adorned with rainbows. And in one of the bedrooms, there were even animals painted on the walls. I ask you, your Honor, how was I going to rent that place with a purple bulldog painted on the wall? It cost me more than $300 to have the place painted over white."

Judge: (*looks at the pictures and gives up trying to keep a straight face, which is okay, as everyone in the courtroom is laughing except Mr. Anderson*) "Let me ask a few questions. Was it true that the place needed a new coat of paint when you moved in, Ms. Shields?"

Farah Shields: "Yes."

Judge: "Do you agree, Mr. Anderson?"

Adam Anderson: "Yes, that's why my office paid her paint bills although we never would have if we had known about that bulldog, not to mention the rainbows."

Judge: "How much did the paint cost?"

Adam Anderson: "$125."

Judge: "I normally send decisions by mail, but today I am going to explain what I have decided. First, the apartment needed repainting anyway, Mr. Anderson, so I am not going to give you any credit for paying to have the work redone. However, Ms. Shields, even though the place looked quite— shall I say, cheerful—when you moved out, Mr. Anderson does have a point in that you went beyond what is reasonable. Therefore, I feel that it's unfair to make Anderson Realty pay for paint twice. My judgment is this: The $125 for the paint that was given to Ms. Shields is subtracted from the $600 deposits. This means that Anderson Realty owes Farah Shields $475 plus $9.00 for costs."

Note: We have focused here on deposits cases from the tenant's point of view. This is because tenants are the ones who initiate this sort of case. Landlords, who commonly must defend deposit cases, should carefully read the list of evidence that is helpful in court. Often the best witness for a landlord is the new tenant who has just moved in. This person is likely to feel that the place isn't as clean as did the person who moved out.

B. Money Damage Cases —Unpaid Rent

In most states, landlords can initiate Small Claims actions to sue for unpaid rent. Often the tenant has already moved out and doesn't bother to show up in court. If this happens, the landlord wins by default. Sometimes the tenant does show up, but presents no real defense and is only there to request the judge to allow him to make payments over time.

The landlord (or bookkeeper-manager, if you're in a state which allows bookkeepers to appear on behalf of business owners—see Chapter 7) should bring the lease or rental agreement to court and simply state the time periods for which rent is due, but unpaid. Nothing else is required unless the tenant presents a defense as discussed below. Sometimes a landlord will sue for three times the amount of rent owed (triple damages) under a lease or rental agreement that states that he is entitled to them if the tenant fails to pay rent, but stays in the rental unit. Doing this will almost guarantee that the tenant will put up a fight. In my experience, landlords are rarely awarded more than their actual out-of-pocket loss, and it makes little sense to request more.

There are several valid defenses to a suit based on a tenant's failure to pay rent. The principal one is where the tenant claims that rent was withheld because the condition of the premises was "uninhabitable."[2] This amounts to the tenant saying to the landlord: "I won't pay my rent until you make necessary repairs."[3] It is legal to do this in many states by statute or court decision.[4] The important thing for a tenant to understand in all states, however, is that rent withholding is not legal where the landlord refuses to fix some minor defect. For rent to be legally withheld, the condition needing repair must be sufficiently serious as to make the home "uninhabitable," unhealthy or unsafe. In addition, the landlord must have been given reasonable notice to correct the problem. Thus, a broken furnace that a landlord refuses to fix would qualify as a condition making a home uninhabitable in the winter, but lack of heat in the summer would not.

---

[2] In many states, it is legal for a tenant to have repairs done under some circumstances, and to deduct the cost from the rent. Check the index of your state code under "Landlord-Tenant" subtopic "Repairs."

[3] Often a tenant who fails to pay rent is brought to court by the landlord as part of an eviction action. If the tenant can prove that rent was withheld for a valid reason, he or she can't be evicted for exercising this right in the majority of states.

[4] Check with a tenants' rights project or consumer group before withholding rent. Some states, particularly in the South and Midwest, require that tenants living in uninhabitable housing continued to pay rent while bringing legal action to get repairs made. If you live in California, see Moskovitz and Warner, *Tenants' Rights*, Nolo Press, which discusses rent withholding and retaliation eviction in detail.

If you are involved in a rent withholding case as a tenant, your job is to prove (using pictures, witnesses, etc.) that the condition that caused you to withhold rent is indeed serious. Thus, you might call the building inspector or an electrician to testify that the wiring was in a dangerous state of decay. The landlord, of course, will probably testify that the rental unit is in fundamentally sound shape, even though there may be some minor problems. A landlord has the right to inspect the property, as long as she gives the tenant reasonable notice. In many states, 24-hours' notice is presumed by the law to be reasonable in the absence of an emergency.

C. Obnoxious Behavior

Occasionally a particular landlord or tenant can get pretty obnoxious. This is also true of plumbers, physics teachers, and hair stylists, but since this chapter is about landlord-tenant disputes, we will concentrate on these folks.

From the start, there is a major difference between how landlords and tenants handle problems. This is because landlords have two advantages tenants don't have. First, they can charge deposits, and if a tenant fails to pay rent or damages the place, a landlord can often recover her loss by subtracting the amount in question from the deposit. In addition, the landlord usually has the right to ask a tenant to move out. (If the tenant has a lease or the unit is located in a city requiring just cause for eviction, this right is restricted.) Tenants, on the other hand, have neither of these rights and, as a result, are much more likely to sue for money damages in Small Claims Court when they are seriously aggrieved.

Typically, tenants have problems with landlords who cannot stop fidgeting and fussing over their property. Smaller landlords tend to develop this problem to a greater extent than do the larger, more commercial, ones. Nosy landlords are always hanging around or coming by, trying to invite themselves in to look around and generally being pests. In addition, a tenant may also run into a manager who is on a power trip.

If a landlord or manager is difficult or unpleasant to deal with, she can make a tenant's life miserable. There is no law which protects a tenant from a landlord's disagreeable personality, and, if the tenant has no lease, she is especially unprotected from all but the most outrageous invasions of privacy or trespass. However, if the landlord's conduct is truly obnoxious, courts in some states recognize that tenants have a right to sue for the intentional infliction of emotional distress. In the case of *Newby v. Alto Riviera Apts.*, 60 Cal.App.3d 288 (1976),[5] a California court found that it was necessary to prove four things in this sort of lawsuit:

---

[5]Also see *Stoiber v. Honeychuck*, 101 Cal.App.3d 903 (1980), where a court awarded a tenant damages for the mental distress suffered from having to live in slum conditions.

1. Outrageous conduct on the part of the landlord;

2. Intention to cause, or reckless disregard of the probability of causing, emotional distress;

3. Severe emotional suffering;

4. Actual suffering or emotional distress.

D. The Landlord's Right of Entry and the Tenant's Right of Privacy

One area where tenants are easily and understandably upset is when they feel their privacy is invaded. Landlords, on the other hand, have a legal right to enter their rental units in certain situations. Sometimes a tenant's needs to be left alone and a landlord's need to enter conflict. If they do, it is extremely important that both parties understand their rights.

In California, Section 1954 of the Civil Code establishes the circumstances under which a landlord can enter his tenant's home, and Section 1953 (a)(1) provides that these circumstances cannot be expanded, or the tenant's privacy rights waived or modified, by any lease or rental agreement provision. The first thing to realize is that there are only four broad situations in which a landlord may legally enter while a tenant is still in residence. They are:

1. To deal with an emergency;

2. To make needed repairs (or assess the need for them):

3. To show the property to prospective new tenants or purchasers; and

4. When you invite the landlord in.

In most instances (emergencies and tenant invitations excepted), a landlord can enter only during "normal business hours" (9:00 a.m. to 5:00 p.m.) and then only after "reasonable notice," presumed to be 24 hours.

If a landlord does not follow these rules, a tenant's first step is to politely ask him to do so. If violations persist, a letter is in order. If this doesn't help, it is possible to sue in Small Claims Court for invasion of privacy if the landlord's conduct is persistently outrageous.

E.   Evictions

In some states, it is legal to do some types of evictions (known technically as "unlawful detainer," "summary dispossess," and "forcible entry and detainer," depending on the state) in Small Claims Court. A few, including Illinois, New York, and Massachusetts, even have in their larger cities separate "landlord-tenant" courts that amount to Small Claims Courts for this one specific purpose. Without question, landlords should have a simple and cheap way to free themselves of tenants who don't pay their rent. As noted at the beginning of this chapter, in many states, if a landlord wants to be sure to get a tenant out without ridiculous delays, an "unlawful detainer" action must be filed in formal court. Traditionally this has required the expense of a lawyer, but more and more landlords are learning to handle their own eviction actions.

In states where eviction actions are allowed in Small Claims Court, a landlord should check the rules carefully before using the court, especially those governing the tenant's right to appeal. This can be a trap for the unwary. In some states, the defendant has an automatic right to appeal, and there is no requirement that an adequate bond be posted. In this situation, a tenant's appeal can mean a long and costly delay for the landlord who is trying to get the tenant out.

When a landlord gets to Small Claims Court, he must prove that the rent was not paid and that a correct notice was properly served. Bring a copy of the notice to court and "Proof of Service" form filled out by the person doing the service. The fact that a tenant is suffering from some hardship such as illness, poverty, birth of a child, etc., is not a defense to failure to pay rent. Possible tenant defenses are discussed briefly under "Money Damages Cases—Unpaid Rent" in this chapter. In many states, including those that have passed the Uniform Residential Landlord and Tenant Act (URLTA), these include rent withholding because of a condition in the rental property that makes it uninhabitable. A tenant cannot legally raise the existence of a defect for the first time on the day of the court hearing. The landlord must be given reasonable notice that a defect exists before rent is withheld or repairs are made.[6]

---

[6]The length of such "reasonable" notice varies with the situation. For minor problems (dripping faucets, cracked windows, etc.) that doesn't present an immediate threat to health or safety, one month is usually presumed to be reasonable. For no heat in the winter, totally clogged drains or toilets, no hot water, etc., a day or two may be reasonable.

CHAPTER 21

Miscellaneous Cases

By now you should have a clear idea of how a Small Claims case can be presented sensibly. The facts of each situation will vary, but the general approach will not. Here I will discuss a few of the common types of cases not covered in the previous few chapters. If I don't cover your situation in detail, simply make your own outline of steps to be taken, adapting the general approaches I have suggested to your own case.

A. Clothing (Alteration and Cleaning)

Several years ago, before I started attending Small Claims Court regularly, I stopped by one morning when I had a few free moments to kill before a criminal hearing. The case being argued involved an elderly German-American gentleman with a strong accent, suing an equally aged Armenian-born tailor, who was also seriously uncomfortable with the English language. The dispute centered around whether a suitcoat that the tailor had made for the plaintiff should have had two or three buttons. After ten minutes of almost incomprehensible testimony, I understood little more than that the plaintiff had never owned a suit with two buttons and the tailor had never made one with three. The two men ended by standing and facing one another— each pulling a sleeve of the suitcoat and each yelling as loud as he could in his own language, apparently about how many buttons a suit ought to have. Much to their credit, the judge and bailiff just sat and smiled. What happened? I don't know. I was still actively practicing law then and had to bustle off to argue before another judge that my client thought that the two pounds of marijuana he was carrying in a money belt was really oregano. You can probably guess how that argument ended.

While I have never seen another clothing case quite as colorful as that of the two-button suit, I have been consistently surprised at how often I have encountered people in Small Claims Court clutching an injured garment. We must indeed come to view our clothing as an extension of ourselves, because so many of us react with an indignation out of proportion to our monetary loss when some favorite item is damaged. I will never forget the morning I saw a particularly sour-looking fellow with neither word nor smile for anyone, including his obviously long-suffering wife, draw himself up to full height and wax poetic for five minutes about a four-year-old leather vest that a cleaner had mutilated.

Winning a significant victory in a case involving clothing is often difficult. Why? Because, while the liability is often easy to prove (i.e., the seamstress cut off the collar instead of the cuff), a reasonable amount of compensation for damages is difficult or impossible to establish, for the obvious reason that used clothing has little actual market value, even though it may have cost a lot to start with or may have enormous sentimental value to its owner. In theory, a court can award a plaintiff only the fair market value of the damaged clothing, not its replacement cost. But because this rule of law commonly works a severe injustice in clothing cases (a $400 suit bought last week may be worth only $100 this week), many judges tend to bend it a little in favor of the person who has suffered the loss.

They do this by allowing an amount pretty close to the original purchase price when the clothing involved was almost new, even though its fair market value for resale would be much less. Thus, the owner of a $300 dress that had been ruined by a seamstress after only one wearing might recover $250. Judges are not required to take this approach, but many do. With older clothing, I have also seen some judges take a flexible approach. They do this by making a rough estimate of the percentage of total use that remains in a garment and then awarding the plaintiff this percentage of the original purchase price. Thus, if a cleaner ruined a $300 suit that had been worn about 50 percent of its useful life, the plaintiff might recover $150.

Here are some hints:

• Bring the damaged clothing to court. It's hard for a tailor to say much when confronted with a coat that is two sizes too big or has three sleeves.

• Be ready to prove the original purchase price with a cancelled check, newspaper, ad, credit card statement, etc.

• Be sure that the person you are suing (tailor, cleaner, seamstress, etc.) caused the problem. As noted in the example of the suede coat in Chapter 2, some problems that develop during cleaning or alterations may be the responsibility of the manufacturer.

Note: Cleaners are particularly apt to offer "proof" from "independent testing laboratories" that damage caused during cleaning wasn't their fault. You will want to ask: "How much did the cleaner pay the testing lab for the report?" "How many times had the same cleaner used the same testing lab before?" "How did the cleaner know about the testing lab (does it solicit business from cleaners)?" etc.[1]

---

[1] In a creative deviation from the normal, unimaginative way of running Small Claims Court, Minneapolis, Minnesota periodically sets a special day aside in its Small Claims Court for "cleaning" cases. The court has its own independent expert come in and advise it as to who should recover what. Commonly, but not always, the expert finds that the cleaners have been negligent.

B. Dog-Bite Cases

Many states have dog-bite statutes that make dog owners completely liable for injuries their dogs cause, no ifs, ands or buts. Some statutes cover only injuries occurring off the owner's property. Also, some statutes cover only bites, while others apply to any injury (e.g., the dog jumps on you, scratches you and knocks you over) or property damage (e.g., the dog digs up your rose garden) the dog causes. See Chapter 1, Section D, *Legal Research* to find out if your state has a dog-bite statute. If it does, your task in court could be a lot easier.

If your state doesn't, the old "common law" rule probably applies. This means you'll have to prove that the owner was aware of, or should have been aware of, the fact that the dog was vicious. So, if you're bitten by a dog and can show that the dog had snarled, snapped and lunged at people before and that the owner knew about it but let her dog run free anyway, she's probably liable (unless you provoked the dog or offered the dog your hand).

Be ready to prove the extent of the injury, the location where it occurred, time off from work without compensation, doctor's bills etc. If the dog is mean-looking, a picture will be a great help.[2]

---

[2]What you can do when you are injured or annoyed by a dog is discussed in detail in *Dog Law* by Mary Randolph (Nolo Press).

C. Damage to Real Property (Land, Buildings, etc.)

There is no typical case of this nature, as facts vary greatly. So instead of trying to set down general rules, let's look at a situation that happened recently to a friend of mine (let's call her Babette).

Babette owns a cinder-block building that houses two stores. One morning when she came to work, she noticed water pouring in through the back of her building. Because the building was set into a hill, it abutted about eight feet of her uphill neighbor's land (let's call her neighbor Boris). After three days of investigation involving the use of green dye in Boris's plumbing system, it was discovered that the water came from an underground leak in Boris's sewer pipe. At this point, Babette had spent considerable effort and some money to pay helpers to get the water mopped up before it damaged anything in the stores.

Instead of fixing the leak promptly, Boris delayed for four days. All of this time, Babette and her helpers were mopping frantically. Finally, when Boris did get to work, he insisted on digging the pipe out himself, which took another four days. (A plumber with the right equipment could have done it in one.) In the middle of Boris's digging, when his yard looked as though it was being attacked by a herd of giant gophers, it rained. The water filled the holes and trenches instead of running off, as it normally would have. Much of it ran though the ground into Babette's building, bringing a pile of mud with it.

When the flood was finally over, Babette figured out her costs as follows:

First three days (before the source of the water was discovered)	$148 (for help with mopping and cleaning)
Next four days (while Boris refused to cooperate)	$188 (for help with mopping and cleaning)

Final four days (including day it rained)	$262 (for help with mopping and cleaning)
One secondhand water vacuum purchased during rain storm	$200
Her own time, valued at $8.00 per hour.	$600

Assuming that Boris is unwilling to pay Babette's costs, for what amount should she sue and how much is she likely to recover? If you remember the lessons taught in Chapter 2, you will remember that before Babette can recover for her very real loss, she must show that Boris was negligent or caused her loss intentionally. Probably, she can't do this for the first three days no one knew where the water was coming from, and it's probably impossible to show that Boris was negligent because he failed to replace a pipe that up until then had worked fine. However, once the problem was discovered and Boris didn't take immediate steps to fix it, he was clearly negligent, and she can recover at least her out-of-pocket loss ($450 for her labor and $200 for the water vacuum). Can Babette also recover for the value of her own time? The answer to this question is *maybe*. It would depend on the state and the judge. If Babette could show that she had to close her store or take time off from a job to stem the flood, she probably could recover. If I were she, I would sue for about $1,250 ($450 for labor she paid for, $200 for the vacuum, and $600 for the value of her own labor) and count on getting most of it.

D. Police Brutality—False Arrest Cases

Now and then actions against the police end up in Small Claims Court. Usually, the plaintiff is an irate citizen who has tried and failed to get an attorney to represent him in a larger suit and, as a last resort, has filed for the maximum amount.[3] Put simply, most of the people I have seen bringing this sort of case have been run out of court in a hurry. Why? Because the police and jailors have excellent legal advice and aren't afraid to lie to back each other up. The unwritten rule in any law enforcement agency is to protect your own derriere first, and to protect your buddies' derrieres right after that. Police officers are not going to sit still politely and collect black marks on their service records without fighting back. Most law enforcement people have testified many times before and know how to handle themselves in court.

The reason that many plaintiffs must use Small Claims Court to sue law enforcement people pretty much tells the story. Lawyers normally won't invest their time and money in this sort of case because they find them almost impossible to win. Does this mean that I believe that people bringing false arrest, police brutality and similar types of cases are wasting their item? Balancing the trouble involved against the unlikely chance of success, I would have to say *yes*. That said, let me also say that I

---

[3]In most cases of this sort, you will want to sue the city, county, or state government that employs the officer, as well as the individual involved. In most states, before you can sue a government entity, you must file an administrative claim (see Chapter 8).

believe that lots of things that make little sense at a practical level are worthwhile at many other levels. I can't help but admire people who will fight for principle even though they have small chance of winning.

If you do sue a police officer, jailor, or anyone else with a badge, be sure that you have several witnesses who will back you up and won't be intimidated into keeping their mouths shut. Never, never rely on one officer to testify against another. They simply won't do it. It may be cynical, but it is also realistic to assume that all law enforcement personnel will tell whatever lies necessary to protect themselves and each other. This isn't always true, but it happens often enough so that you may as well be prepared for the worst. You would also be wise to spend a few dollars and talk to a lawyer who specializes in criminal cases. For a $75-$100 fee, you can probably pick up some valuable pointers on how to convince the judge that you were treated in an illegal and unreasonable way.

E. Libel, Slander, etc.

In California, libel and slander case may be brought in Small Claims Court. However, many states, among them Colorado, Connecticut, Massachusetts, Michigan, Ohio, and Oklahoma, bar libel and slander cases from Small Claims Court.

Note about false arrest, libel and slander, etc.: Actions for false arrest, libel and slander, malicious prosecution, and other "personal torts" are hard to win, damages are difficult to ascertain, and are therefore commonly barred. Check your state's Small Claims Court laws.

F. Suits Against Airlines or Hotels

Because of overbooking, it is not uncommon for an airline or a hotel to refuse to honor your reservation. In some situations, this can cause considerable financial loss, especially if, in the case of an airline bumping, you miss work or an important meeting. Airlines are not required to provide any amount of compensation, however, public goodwill and trust may move them to. Try contacting the airline's consumer complaint office. If that doesn't work, you can use Small Claims Court to recover. To prepare your case for Small Claims Court, do as much of the following as possible:

• At the airline gate when you are being bumped, tell the airline that you will suffer financial loss if you don't get to your destination promptly and ask that they request other passengers to take a later flight.

• Find out the name of the local airline manager and put him on notice that you will sue if you are bumped.

• Note down all out-of-pocket expenses that the delay causes you.

• Compute any loss of wages, commissions or paid vacation time that the delay causes.

• Write to the airline requesting payment of your loss, and inform them that you will file in Small Claims Court if they don't pay up.

• File your case in Small Claims Court for the amount of your out-of-pocket expenses and lost business. If your claim appears reasonable, the airline may pay voluntarily or allow you to win on a default judgment.

CHAPTER 22

Small Business, Small Claims

More and more, people who own or manage small businesses are turning to Small Claims Court to settle business disputes that they have been unable to compromise. They have learned that Small Claims Court is a relatively fast and cost efficient way to resolve business differences. Recent law changes allowing unincorporated businesses to appear in court in some states without the need for business owners to be present have contributed to this increase in business usage (see Chapter 7).[1]

This chapter didn't appear in the first few editions of this book because I naively assumed that Chapter 18—"Cases In Which Money Is Owed"—provided sufficient information to

---

[1]Of course, in most states, incorporated businesses have long been able to authorize people other than the officers or other principles to appear in court, unfortunately. In a few states, corporations can't sue in Small Claims (see Appendix).

solve the problems of business people. It's here now because I have had so many requests from friends who own their own small businesses asking for additional information. It turned out, of course, that although many disputes between small business people involve a simple failure to pay money, a significant number are more complicated. Commonly, these more complex disputes involve people who have had a continuing business relationship and find themselves in the midst of a major misunderstanding that goes beyond the refusal to pay a bill. Often both parties to the lawsuit are in court because they feel badly used—perhaps even "ripped off" or "cheated" by the other.

I have been asked for advice on preparing Small Claims Court cases by a surprising variety of business people. For example, requests for help have come from a dentist furious at a dental equipment wholesaler, an industrial designer who hadn't been paid for drawing preliminary plans, a typesetter being sued by his former accountant in a dispute involving the value of the latter's services, a landscape architect who was trying to enforce a verbal agreement that he could increase his bid after a client asked for changes in final plans, and an author who claimed that her publisher had taken too long to publish her book. Although these disputes seem quite different from one another at first impression, they all turned out to have one thing in common—in each situation the disputants had enjoyed friendly business relationships at some time in the past. And in each case, at least part of the reason that the plaintiff brought the dispute to court was that he or she was personally upset with (mad at) the other.

A. Organizing Your Case

Business people normally have two advantages over ordinary mortals when it comes to preparing for court. First; as a matter of course, they maintain a record keeping system which includes files, ledgers, and increasingly, computer storage devices. Taken together, these resources normally contain considerable raw material helpful to successfully proving a case. The second advantage is more subtle, but no less real. It involves the average small business person's organizational skill—that is, his or her ability to take a confused mess of facts and organize them into a coherent and convincing narrative. Small business people who don't quickly develop good organizational skills commonly aren't in business long enough to even consider going to court. But the fact that business people begin with a little head start isn't usually much of an advantage when it comes to dealing with another business person. This is because two head starts have a way of cancelling one another out, with the only beneficiary being the judge, who gets to officiate a more coherent dispute.

Here are several hints that may be of real value when thinking about how to present a business case. This material is meant to supplement, not replace, the information contained in the rest of the book, particularly Chapters 2, 6, 13, 14, and 15. If you haven't already done so, I think you will find it helpful to read these chapters before continuing.

1. Contracts

Most business cases involve one person claiming that the other has broken a contract (see Chapter 2). Start by asking yourself the exact nature of the contract which was involved in your case. That is, what were your obligations and expected benefits from the deal, what was the other person supposed to do, and what was he or she going to get out of the deal?

Remember that oral contracts that can be carried out in one year (even if they actually take longer) are legal and enforceable in all states. But remember, too, that oral agreements raise real problems in that they are often difficult to prove.

You should also remember that a written contract need not be a formal document written on parchment and notarized by the Dalai Lama. Any letter or writing can constitute a contract. For example, if Hubert writes to Josephine, "I would like to order 1,000 gopher traps at $14 per trap," and Josephine writes back saying, "Thank you for your order. The traps will be sent next week," there is a contract. Indeed, if Josephine didn't write back at all but simply sent the traps in a reasonable period of time, there would also be a contract implied from the circumstances of the transaction.

You should also be aware that the business usage and practices in a particular field are commonly viewed as being part of a contract and can be introduced as evidence in Small Claims Court to support your case. Thus, if Hubert ordered rodent traps in February and Josephine didn't send them until September, Hubert could present evidence in court that everyone in the rodent control business knows that traps are only saleable in the summer when rodents attack crops and that Josephine's failure to deliver the traps in the correct season constituted a breach of contract.

And keep in mind that contracts can be, and often are, changed many times as negotiations go back and forth and circumstances change. The important agreement is the last one.

2.   Presenting Your Evidence in Court

In addition to the general techniques of presenting evidence efficiently in Court, here are a few more suggestions of special interest to small business people:

• In business disputes, the problem is often having too much evidence, rather than too little. If this occurs, your job is obviously to separate the material that is essential to proving your case from that which is less important. One good way to do this is to organize both your verbal presentation and the backup evidence around the central issue in dispute rather than trying to fill in all the background in an effort to work up to the point. Or, to say the same thing in a different way, you usually want to start with the end of your case rather than the beginning. For example, if Ted did interior decorating work for Alice and she called off the deal, Ted would start his testimony with the fact that a contract existed to do the work and that Alice broke it. The fact that Ted and Alice had had dealings over the last several years which cast light on the present dispute, or that Ted had turned down another job to work for Alice, or that Alice had made a number of unreasonable demands on him, might well constitute good supporting evidence, but should be alluded to only to the extent that they support the main point. All too often I have seen people tell a great but lengthy story in court that put the judge to sleep before the main point was reached.

• Many business people have employees, partners, or business associates who have intimate knowledge of the dispute. By all means, bring them to court as witnesses. A witness who is knowledgeable about the transaction is almost always worth more than a stack of documentary evidence.

• In some situations, having a witness testify as to the normal business practices in a field can be helpful. Thus, if in your business payment is customarily made within thirty days after delivery of goods and the person you are having a dispute with claimed that a 120-day payment schedule was routine, you would want to present an "expert" witness who could testify as to normal business practices.

B. The Drama of the Distraught Designer

Now let's review a case that I was recently asked about. Don is a successful industrial designer who heads his own small company. He has offices in a converted factory building near the University of California and prides himself on doing highly innovative and creative work. Normally he is confident and cheerful, but one day when he stopped by the Nolo office to say hello, he looked more than a little out of sorts.

"What's up?" I asked

"Oh, a couple of late nights of high pressure work," Don replied.

"What's new about that?" I asked him.

"Well, that's not really what's bugging me. Actually, I wonder if you can give me a little advice."

"Sure, what's the problem?"

"Well, I did some design work for an outfit that wants to build a small candle factory and I'm out $2,100. They claim that we never had a contract, but that's simply not true. What really happened is that they gambled and authorized me to do some preliminary work before they got their financing assured. When interest rates went through the roof, the whole deal collapsed. I had already completed my work, but they got uptight and refused to pay."

"So what are you going to do?" I asked him.

"Well, I got Stephanie Carlin, a lawyer who has done some work for me, to write them a letter, but that didn't do any good, so I took Stephanie's advice and filed a Small Claims Court suit against them myself."

"For how much?"

"For the Small Claims maximum. I had to scale down the claim to fit it in, but it was better than paying Stephanie's $125 an hour."

"How can I help?" I asked.

"Believe it or not, I've never been to court and I'm afraid I will overlook something or do something stupid, like calling the judge 'your holiness' instead of 'your honor.' I'm not much on bowing and scraping and the whole court rigmarole has always annoyed me."

"Okay, let me show you how simple your job is. First, how did the candle people (let's call them Wickless) contact you to set up the deal?"

"They are friends of friends. They called and we talked on the phone a couple of times. There was a lot of back and forth about how much I would charge for the whole job and how much for parts of it. After a little garden-variety confusion, we decided that I would start with the preliminary drawings and be paid $2,100. If the whole job came through and we felt good about one another, I would do the whole thing."

"Did you write a contract?"

"No, that's just it. On big jobs I always do, but this one was tiny. They just stopped by the next day and we hashed out the whole thing in person."

"Did you make notes?"

"Sure. In fact, I made a few sketches and then they gave me specifications and sketches they had made."

"Do you still have those?"

"Yes, and also a couple of letters they sent later thanking me for my good ideas and making a few suggestions for changes. And of course, I have copies of the detailed drawings I made and sent them."

"Well, that's it then," I said.

"What do you mean, that's it? You mean that I don't have a case?"

"To the contrary. I mean you have just told me that you can prove that a contract exists. The combination of the sketches they provided and the letters they wrote you pretty well prove that they asked you to do the work. There is a strong presumption in law (called "quantum meruit") that when a person is asked to do work in a situation where compensation is normally expected, she is to be paid when the work is completed.[2] Now, in this sort of situation, I suspect that Wickless will raise one of two defenses if they bother to contest your claim at all. The first is that you were doing your work on speculation—that is, that the deal was that you were to be paid for your preliminary work only if the financing went through, and/or second, that your work was substandard in some way, such as not being what was agreed on."

"But they wrote me that my design was of excellent quality."

"Great, then that takes care of that issue. How about the other one? Do you ever do preliminary work without expecting to be paid unless the deal goes through? And is that a common way to operate in your business?"

"Me? Never! I don't have to. I suppose some designers do, or at least prepare detailed proposals without pay, but I have more work than I can decently do and I make it clear to all potential clients that I charge for preliminary drawings. In this situation, as I said, we agreed on the price in advance."

"What about witnesses to that conversation?"

---

[2]This *"quantum meruit"* concept is discussed briefly in Chapter 2.

"Well, Jim, my partner, sat in on one of the early discussions. We hadn't agreed on the final price yet, but we weren't too far apart."

"Was it clear to Jim that you intended to charge and that Wickless knew you did?"

"Yes, absolutely."

"Great, bring Jim to court with you. Here is how I would proceed. Organize your statement as to what happened so that it takes you no longer than five minutes to present it to the judge. Bring your sketches, and most important, the sketch the Wickless people made, along with the letters they sent you, and show them to the judge. Then have your partner testify to being present when money was discussed. You should have no trouble. If you're nervous about being in court, go down and check it out a few days before. It's just down at Center Street and I'm sure that if you watch for half an hour, you will be raring to go!"

Note: This little scenario is a simplified version of a real case. Don was given a judgment for the entire amount he requested and Wickless paid it.

C. Old Friends Fall Out

Let's look at a typical story. Tom, a true artist when it comes to graphics, is a bit ingenuous when it comes to dollars and cents. Recognizing this, he never prepares his own tax returns. For the past several years, he turned all of his tax affairs over to Phillip, a local C.P.A. Price was discussed the first year, but after that Tom just paid Phillip's bill when the job was done.

One spring, things went wrong. As usual, Tom's records weren't in great shape, and he was late in getting them to Phillip. Phillip was busy and put Tom's tax return together without discussing it with him in detail. When Tom saw the return, he was shocked. He felt that he was being asked to pay way too much to Uncle Sam. He called Phillip and reminded him of a number of deductions that he felt had been overlooked. There was some discussion of whether Phillip should have known about these items or not. At this time, Phillip complained about Tom's sloppy records and his delay in making them available, and Tom told Phillip that he thought that Phillip had done a hurried and substandard job. After some more grumpy talk back and forth, Phillip agreed to make the necessary corrections. In a week this was done and the return was again sent to Tom.

While his tax liability was now less, Tom was still annoyed, feeling that not all of the oversights had been corrected. Tom called Phillip again and this time they quickly got into a shouting match which ended with Phillip very reluctantly agreeing to look at the return a third time and Tom saying that he was taking his business to an accountant who could add. Tom found another accountant and, after several modifications were made which resulted in a slightly lower tax liability, the return was filed. The second accountant stated that as he needed to check all of Phillip's work to satisfy himself that it was correct, he ended up doing almost as much work as if he had started from scratch. He billed Tom for $1,000, saying that this was $250 less than if he had not had the benefit of Phillip's work.

Phillip billed Tom $1,200. Tom was furious and refused to pay. Phillip then sent Tom a demand letter stating that most of the problems were created by Tom's bad records, that he had made a number of changes when requested to do so and had offered to make the final changes at no additional charge. Tom replied with "I'll see you in court." Which is exactly what happened as Phillip went ahead with his suit.

Okay, now it's up to you. Imagine for a moment that you are Phillip. How would you prepare your case? In the spirit of not asking you questions I am afraid to answer myself, here is how I would proceed.

PHILLIP'S CASE

1. Phillip's first job is to write a clear, concise demand letter (see Chapter 6);

2. In court, Phillip will want to prove that he did work that was worth $1,200. Bringing copies of Tom's tax returns as well as his own work sheets is the simplest way to accomplish this. The returns should not be presented to the judge page by page, but as a package. The purpose is to indicate that a lot of work has been done, not go into details;

3. Phillip should then testify as to his hourly rate and how many hours he worked. He should mention that more hours were required than would otherwise have been the case because Tom did not have the raw data well organized. To illustrate his point, Phillip should introduce the raw data Tom gave him into evidence (i.e., a shoe box full of messy receipts);

4. Phillip has now presented his basic case, which is simply that he was hired to do a job, he did it, and he wasn't paid. However, Phillip would be wise to go beyond this and anticipate

at least some of Tom's defenses, which will almost surely involve the poor quality of the work done, as well as a claim that Phillip is simply charging too much. Therefore, were I Phillip, I would close my testimony with a statement along these lines:

"Your honor, when I finished my work my client pointed out that several deductions had been overlooked. I believed then and believe now that this was because the data he provided me with was inadequate, but I did rework the return and corrected several items that were left out. When my client told me that he felt even the revised draft needed work, I again told him that I would work with him to make any necessary changes. It was at this point that he refused to let me see the returns and hired another accountant. In my professional opinion, very little work remained to be done at this stage—certainly nothing that couldn't be accomplished in an hour or two. Now, as to the amount charged, it took me ten hours to reconstruct what went on in the typesetting business from the mess of incomplete and incoherent records I was given. At $60 per hour, this means that $600 of my bill involved work that had to be done prior to actually preparing the return. Taking into consideration the difficult circumstances, I believe I charged fairly for the work I did, and that I did my work well."

TOM'S CASE

Okay, so much for getting into the head of an indignant accountant. Now let's see how Tom, the upset typesetter, might defend his case.

1. Tom should write a letter of his own, rebutting Phillip's demand letter point by point (see Chapter 6). He should bring this letter to court and give it to the judge.

2. Next, Tom should testify that he refused to pay the bill because he felt that Phillip's work was so poorly done that he didn't trust Phillip to finish the job. Tom should testify as to the details of several of the points that Phillip overlooked. Thus, if Tom provided Phillip with information concerning equipment purchases and Phillip forgot to claim depreciation, this would be important evidence. But Tom should be careful to make his points relatively brief and understandable. He won't gain by a long and boring rehash of his entire return.

3. Now, to really make his case, Tom should present more detailed evidence that supports his claim that Phillip did poor work. The tax return as correctly prepared by the new accountant would be of some help, but far more valuable would be having the second accountant come to court to testify. Unfortunately, professionals are commonly reluctant to testify against one another, so this may be difficult to arrange. But Tom should at the very least be able to get a letter from the new accountant outlining the things that he found it necessary to do to change the return as prepared by Phillip.

4. Tom should also present to the court his cancelled checks, establishing the amounts paid Phillip for the last several years' returns, assuming, of course, that Phillip's previous bills were much less. For example, if Tom had been billed $400 and $500 in the two previous years, it would raise some questions as to whether Phillip's bill of $1,200 for the current year was reasonable.

5. Tom should also present the bill from the second accountant to the court as well as his note explaining that his $1,000 charge was $250 less than his normal bill for the whole job.

Note: After (or perhaps during) Phillip's and Tom's testimony, the judge is almost certain to ask a number of questions. In addition, he will probably give each an opportunity to rebut the statements of the other. I don't have space to discuss how this might go in detail, but in rebuttal, it's important to focus on the one or two points that you think the judge has missed or is in danger of getting wrong. This is not a time to attempt to restate your entire case.

WHAT HAPPENED?

Phillip was given a judgment for $700. The judge didn't explain his reasoning, but apparently felt that there was some right on each side and split the difference with a little edge to Tom. This sort of decision where each side is given something is common in Small Claims Court and again illustrates the wisdom of the parties' working out their own compromise. Even if Tom and Phillip had arrived at a solution where one or the other gave up a little more than the judge ordered, there would have been a saving in time and aggravation that probably would have more than made up the difference.

Bad Check Note: Every merchant is stuck with a rubber check now and then. Until recently, it usually didn't pay to take a bad check writer to court, especially for smaller checks. Today, over a dozen states permit a person holding a bad check to obtain a judgment for a specified amount of money in damages in addition to the amount of the check. I discuss how to take advantage of these laws in Chapter 4, "Bad Checks."

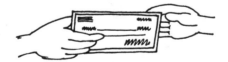

CHAPTER 23

Judgment and Appeal

A. The Judgment

In most states, including California, the decision in your case will be mailed to the address on record with the clerk any time from a few days to a few weeks after your case is heard. The exception to this rule occurs when one side doesn't show up (or doesn't file an answer within the proper time, in states that require it), and the other wins by default. Default judgments are normally announced in the courtroom.[1] The truth is that in the

---

[1]Chapters 10, 12 and 15 discuss default judgments and the fact that people who have had defaults entered against them can often get them set aside if (1) they have a decent excuse for not being present, and (2) they notified the court clerk immediately of their desire to have the judgment set aside. In most states, a motion to vacate a default judgment must be filed immediately if the defaulting party was properly notified of the case to start with. If the defaulting defendant was never properly served, he or she must move to set aside the default as soon as the default is discovered.

vast majority of contested cases the judge has already made up his mind at the time the case is heard and notes down his decision before the parties leave the courtroom. Traditionally, decisions have been sent by mail because the court didn't want to deal with angry, unhappy losers, especially those few who might get violent. More recently, however, some judges have begun explaining their decisions in court, on the theory that both parties are entitled to know why a particular decision was reached. One progressive judge explained his policy in this regard as follows: "The only time I don't announce in court is when I have phoning or research to do or if I feel that the losing party will be unnecessarily embarrassed in front of the audience."

Often when a judgment is entered against a person, she feels that the judge would surely have made a different decision if he hadn't gotten mixed up, or overlooked some crucial fact, or had properly understood an argument. On the basis of my experience on the bench, I can tell you that in the vast majority of Small Claims cases, there is little likelihood that the judge would change his decision even if you had a chance to argue the whole case over. In any event, you don't. You have had your chance and the decision has gone against you. It won't help you to call the judge, or go to see him, or send him documents through the mail (see Section D below for appeal rights).

Note: Now that a judgment has been entered, we need to expand our vocabulary slightly. The person who wins the case (gets the judgment) now becomes "the judgment creditor" and the loser is known as "the judgment debtor."

B. Time Payments

I have mentioned the fact that in a great many states, including California, Connecticut, Michigan, New York, and Minnesota, a judge may order that the loser be allowed to pay the winner over a period of time, rather than all at once.[2] The judge won't normally make this sort of order unless you request it. If you are in a state in which the judge announces her decision in court, this is not a problem, as you are present to ask for time payments if you lose. If you're in a state in which decisions are sent by mail, and if you have no real defense to a claim, or if you have a fairly good case but aren't sure which way the judge will go, be sure that the judge knows that, if the judgment goes against you, you wish to pay in installments. You might put your request this way:

• "In closing my presentation, I would like to say that I believe I have a convincing case and should be awarded the judgment, but in the event that you rule for my opponent, I would like you to allow me time payments of no more than (whatever amount is convenient) per month."

Or, if you have no real defense:

• "Your Honor, I request that you enter the judgment against me for no more than (an amount convenient to you) per month."

If you neglect to ask for time payments in court and wish to make this request after you receive the judgment, first contact the other party to see if she will voluntarily agree to accept her money on a schedule you can afford to pay. If she agrees, it is wise to write your agreement down and each sign it. If your opponent is an all-or-nothing sort of person and refuses payments, promptly contact the court clerk and ask that the case again be brought before the judge—not as to the facts, but only to set up a payment schedule that you can live with. The clerk should arrange things for you, but if there is a problem, write a letter like this one to the judge:

---

[2]Many other states also allow time payments. Be sure to ask about this possibility in your Small Claims Court.

47 West Adams St.
Brooklyn, NY
October 17, 19__

Honorable Felix Hamburg
Judge of the Small Claims Court
111 Center St.
New York, NY

Re: Elliot v. Toller

Index No.__

Dear Judge Hamburg:

I recently appeared before you in the case of Elliot v. Toller (Index No. _____). Mr. Elliot was awarded a judgment in the amount of $526. Paying this amount all at once would be nearly impossible because of (lack of employment, illness, or whatever). I can pay $25 per month.

Please change the order in this case to allow for a $25 per month payment. If it is necessary for me to make this request in court, please inform me of the time I should be present.

Sincerely,

John Toller

Name and Address of Court:

SMALL CLAIMS CASE NO.

PLAINTIFF/DEMANDANTE (name, address, and telephone number of each):

John Toller

Telephone No.:

Telephone No.:

DEFENDANT/DEMANDADO (Name, address, and telephone number of each):

Mildred Edwards

Telephone No.:

Telephone No.:

☐ See attached sheet for additional plaintiffs and defendants.

REQUEST TO PAY JUDGMENT IN INSTALLMENTS

1. I request the court to allow me to make installment payments on the judgment entered against me in this case in the amount and manner stated below.
2. My request is based on this declaration, the court records, my completed financial declaration (Form EJ-165 — *obtain from court clerk*) attached to this declaration, and any other evidence that may be presented.
    NOTE: YOU MUST ATTACH A COMPLETED FINANCIAL DECLARATION WITH THIS REQUEST TO MAKE INSTALLMENT PAYMENTS.
3. Judgment was entered against me in this matter on *(date)*: (fill in) in the amount of *(specify)*: $526.00
4. Payment of the entire amount of the judgment at one time will be a hardship on me because *(specify)*:
    (lack of employment, illness or whatever)
5. I can and will make payments toward the judgment in the amount of *(specify)*: $25.00   per ☐ week ☒ month.
6. I request the court to order that I make payments as specified in item 5 and that execution on the judgment be stayed as long as I make payments according to this schedule.

    I declare under penalty of perjury under the laws of the State of California that the foregoing is true and correct.

Date:

..... Mildred Edwards ....   ▶ *Mildred Edwards*
         (TYPE OR PRINT NAME)   (SIGNATURE OF JUDGMENT DEBTOR)

NOTICE TO JUDGMENT CREDITOR

The judgment debtor has requested the court to allow payment of the judgment in installments. Complete the following and return this form to the court within 10 days. You will be notified of the court's order, or, if a hearing is necessary, the date of the hearing.

1. I am the judgment creditor, and I have read and considered the judgment debtor's request to make installment payments on the judgment.
2. a. ☒ I am willing to accept the payment schedule the judgment debtor has requested.
    b. ☐ I am willing to accept payments in the amount of *(specify)*: $ per ☐ week ☐ month.
    c. ☐ I am opposed to accepting installment payments because *(specify)*:

    I declare under penalty of perjury under the laws of the State of California that the foregoing is true and correct.

Date:

..... John Toller ....   ▶ *John Toller*
         (TYPE OR PRINT NAME)   (SIGNATURE OF JUDGMENT CREDITOR)

SEE REVERSE FOR HEARING DATE, IF ANY.
(Continued on reverse)

Form Approved by the
Judicial Council of California
SC-106 [New January 1, 1992]

REQUEST TO PAY JUDGMENT IN INSTALLMENTS
(Small Claims)

Code of Civil Procedure, § 116.620(b)

ORDER

Judgment to be paid $25.00 on the first day of each month until fully paid. Should the judgment debtor fail to make one or more payments, the judgment creditor may file an affidavit so stating with this court and the above order shall thereby be vacated and the clerk shall proceed as if it had not been made.

DATED:_____   _____
                                    JUDGE

C. The Satisfaction of Judgment[3]

In all states, once a judgment is paid, whether in installments or a lump sum, a "judgment creditor" must file a "satisfaction of judgment" form with the court. If a judgment creditor who receives payment in full on a judgment fails to do this, the judgment debtor should send a written demand that this be done. A first class letter is adequate. It's important to do this because otherwise the judgment will continue to appear on credit records as unpaid and may result in the judgment debtor being denied credit. If, after written demand, the judgment creditor doesn't file his satisfaction within a number of days of the request (usually between 15 and 30—check your local rules), and without just cause, many states provide that the judgment debtor is entitled to recover all actual damages he or she may sustain by reason of such failure (i.e., for denial of a credit application) and, in addition, in some states, a sum of money (California provides a $50 fine).

Here is a sample "Satisfaction of Judgment" form which is used in California. Again, it should be signed by the judgment creditor when the judgment is paid and filed with the court clerk Don't forget to do this; otherwise, you may have to track down the other party later.

Note: If either party ever needs it, the clerk, for a small fee, will provide a certified copy of this form to prove that the judgment has been paid.

Sometimes people forget to get a "Satisfaction of Judgment" form signed when they pay a judgment, only to find later that they can't locate the judgment creditor. If this happens and you need a satisfaction of judgment to clean up your credit record or for some other reason, you can get it if you present the court with proof that the judgment was paid. The following documents will help you:

---

[3]The rules I discuss here, including time limits, fees, etc., are for California. Other states have similar regulations.

ATTORNEY OR PARTY WITHOUT ATTORNEY (Name and Address):	TELEPHONE NO.:	FOR RECORDER'S OR SECRETARY OF STATE'S USE ONLY

ATTORNEY FOR (Name):

NAME OF COURT:
STREET ADDRESS:
MAILING ADDRESS:
CITY AND ZIP CODE:
BRANCH NAME:

PLAINTIFF:

DEFENDANT:

ACKNOWLEDGMENT OF SATISFACTION OF JUDGMENT

☐ FULL   ☐ PARTIAL   ☐ MATURED INSTALLMENT

CASE NUMBER:

FOR COURT USE ONLY

1. Satisfaction of the judgment is acknowledged as follows (see footnote* before completing):

   a. ☐ Full satisfaction
     (1) ☐ Judgment is satisfied in full.
     (2) ☐ The judgment creditor has accepted payment or performance other than that specified in the judgment in full satisfaction of the judgment.

   b. ☐ Partial satisfaction
     The amount received in partial satisfaction of the judgment is
     $

   c. ☐ Matured installment
     All matured installments under the installment judgment have been satisfied as of (date):

2. Full name and address of judgment creditor:

3. Full name and address of assignee of record, if any:

4. Full name and address of judgment debtor being fully or partially released:

5. a. Judgment entered on (date):
     ☐ (1) in judgment book volume no.:   (2) page no.:
   b. ☐ Renewal entered on (date):
     ☐ (1) in judgment book volume no.:   (2) page no.:

6. ☐ An ☐ abstract of judgment ☐ certified copy of the judgment has been recorded as follows (complete all information for each county where recorded):

COUNTY	DATE OF RECORDING	BOOK NUMBER	PAGE NUMBER

7. ☐ A notice of judgment lien has been filed in the office of the Secretary of State as file number (specify):

NOTICE TO JUDGMENT DEBTOR: If this is an acknowledgment of full satisfaction of judgment, it will have to be recorded in each county shown in item 6 above, if any, in order to release the judgment lien, and will have to be filed in the office of the Secretary of State to terminate any judgment lien on personal property.

Date:

▶

(SIGNATURE OF JUDGMENT CREDITOR OR ASSIGNEE OF CREDITOR OR ATTORNEY)

*The names of the judgment creditor and judgment debtor must be stated as shown in any Abstract of Judgment which was recorded and is being released by this satisfaction. A separate notary acknowledgment must be attached for each signature.

Form Approved by the
Judicial Council of California
EJ-100 (Rev. July 1, 1983)(Cor. 7/84)

ACKNOWLEDGMENT OF SATISFACTION OF JUDGMENT

CCP 724.060, 724.120, 724.250

1. A cancelled check or money order written after the date the court awarded judgment by the judgment debtor for the full amount of the judgment, or a cash receipt for the full amount of the judgment signed by the judgment creditor; and

2. A statement signed by the judgment debtor under penalty of perjury stating all of the following:

• The judgment creditor has been paid the full amount of the judgment and costs;

• The judgment creditor has been requested to file a satisfaction of judgment and refuses to do so or can't be located;

• The documents attached (e.g., the check or money order) constitute evidence of the judgment debtor's receipt of the payment.

Check with the clerk of your state for your local rules.

SAMPLE STATEMENT

My name is John Elliot. On January 11, 19__ , a judgment was awarded against me in Small Claims Court in Ithaca, New York (Case # 1234). On March 20, 19__ I paid Beatrice Small, the prevailing party $1,200, the full amount of this judgment [or, if payments were made in installments—"I paid Beatrice Small, the prevailing party in this action, the final installment necessary to pay this judgment in full."]

I attach to this statement a cancelled check for the full amount of the judgment endorsed by Beatrice Small.[4]

Beatrice Small did not voluntarily file a Satisfaction of Judgment. When I tried to contact her, I learned that she had moved and had left no forwarding address.[5]

Sincerely,

John Elliot

---

[4]If payment was made by money order or cash (with a receipt), modify this statement as needed.

[5]If the judgment creditor refuses to sign a Satisfaction of Judgment, or is otherwise not available to do so, modify this statement as necessary.

D. The Appeal

Unlike Small Claims Court itself, where rules and procedures are remarkably the same throughout the United States, the rules that cover appeals from Small Claims Court judgments vary greatly from one state to the next. A few, such as Connecticut and Hawaii, allow no appeal.[6] New York allows an appeal of a judge's decision, but not an attorney-arbitrator's. California,[7] Massachusetts and a few other states allow a losing defendant to appeal, but do not permit the person who brought the suit (the plaintiff) to do so; in these states, if you are a losing plaintiff, you are finished when it comes to judgments rendered on claims you initiated.[8] In the Appendix you will find a very brief summary of the appeal procedures of every state.

Determining whether you are eligible to appeal is important, but it is only part of the information you need. It is just as important to determine what kind of appeal is permitted in your state. While it may be true, as Gertrude Stein suggested, that "rose is a rose is a rose," Small Claims appeals are not nearly so consistent. Some states allow an appeal only on questions of law, while others allow the whole case to be replayed from scratch. Let's pause for a moment and look at some of the differences.

Note: You Can't Appeal If You Didn't Show Up in Small Claims Court: Appeal rights are almost always restricted to those who showed up in Small Claims Court, argued their case and lost. If you defaulted (didn't show up), you normally can't appeal unless and until you get the default set aside. Normally, you must file paperwork to do this almost immediately, or the Small Claims judgment will become final and unappealable. (See Chapter 10, Section F, "If One Party Doesn't Show Up.")

---

[6]Other states which allow no appeal include Michigan, North Dakota and South Dakota.

[7]California allows losing plaintiffs to file a motion with the Small Claims Court itself to correct or vacate a judgment on the basis or claim that a legal or clerical mistake was made. CCP Sec. 116.725.

[8]In these states, losing plaintiffs can appeal from claims initiated by the defendant. That is, if the plaintiff sues and the defendant countersues and wins, the plaintiff can appeal.

1. New Trial on Appeal

In several states, including Pennsylvania and Texas, either party can appeal and have the case heard over from scratch. In other states, including California, Rhode Island and Massachusetts, only the defendant can normally appeal, but if she does, the whole case is also presented again by both sides, as if the first trial hadn't occurred. When a whole new trial is allowed on appeal (it's called a trial "de novo," in legalese), you simply argue the case over, presenting all necessary witnesses, documents and testimony. Starting from scratch is required because no records are normally kept at Small Claims Court hearings. However, in a few Small Claims courts, judges now tape record hearings, and these recordings are available to the judge who considers the appeal, as part of the reargument of the case.

On appeal, both sides should give careful thought to how their presentation can be improved. This is particularly true if you are the person who lost. Ask yourself: Did the judge decide against me because I presented my case poorly or because I didn't support my statements with evidence? Or did the judge simply misapply the law? To answer these questions, you may have to do some additional legal research. (See Chapter 1, Section D, for some tips on how to do this.) Once you have decided how to improve your case, practice presenting it to an objective friend. When you are done, ask your friend which parts of your presentation were convincing and which need more work.

Depending on your state's court rules and judicial attitudes, your appellate presentation may be allowed to be as informal as was your Small Claims Court case. At the other extreme, however, a state's Small Claims Court appeal rules may require that it be conducted with all the pomp and circumstance of a regular trial court. Because procedures can differ even within the same state, I can't tell you exactly what type of hearing you will face. This means rule number one is to take the time to check out exactly what type of hearing you will encounter. For example, you may learn you'll need to be prepared to present your testimony while sitting in the witness box, or question your witnesses and introduce evidence using the formal lawyer style you have seen so often on TV.

What should you do if you see that your appeal will be conducted in a style you find intimidating?

• Read *Represent Yourself in Court,* by Paul Bergman and Sara Berman-Barrett (Nolo Press). This book beautifully explains how to conduct a contested civil trial in a formal courtroom setting, including how to present testimony and cross-examine witnesses. It should quickly increase your comfort level.

• Ask the judge, in advance, to conduct your appeal as informally as possible. You can do this on the day of your hearing, or better yet, by writing a brief, polite letter to the court ahead of time. Explain that, as a nonlawyer, you are thoroughly prepared to present the facts of your case, but that since you are unfamiliar with formal rules of evidence and procedure, you will appreciate it if your Small Claims appeal is conducted so that a citizen who has not spent three years at law school is given a fair opportunity to be heard.

• During your Small Claims appeal, if there is some procedure you don't understand, politely ask the judge for an explanation. If necessary, remind the judge that, as a taxpayer and a citizen, you are entitled to understand the rules and procedures that control the presentation of your case.

Note: Is the Deck Stacked Against You? It is probably true that some judges have a bias toward the person who won the first time. Some may even believe that Small Claims Court appeals are not worth the time they take, and upholding the original judgment is a good way to discourage them. However, it's my experience that most judges will give you a fair hearing on appeal if you are well-prepared and able to present a convincing case. So, if you believe you were victimized by a bad decision in Small Claims Court and your case involves enough money to make a further investment of time and energy worthwhile, by all means appeal.

2. Appeal on Questions of Law Only

In over 20 states, including Wisconsin and Vermont, appeals can be based only on questions of law, not on the facts of the case. (See Appendix for the other states.) This is the sort of appeal that the United States Supreme Court and the other formal appellate courts normally hear.

Example 1: Your Small Claims case involves your contention that a car mechanic botched fixing your car. After listening to both sides, the judge rules for the car mechanic, based on her conclusion that the repairs were made properly and something else was wrong with your car. You disagree, contending that the repairperson really did mess up the job. Too bad—you are not eligible to appeal, because this is a factual dispute.

Example 2: Assume you are a tenant suing for the return of a cleaning deposit withheld by the landlord. The appeals court agrees with you and awards you the amount of the deposit plus $500 in punitive damages. The landlord appeals, claiming that under the law of your state, the judge only has the power to award punitive damages in the amount of $250. Since this appeal claims a mistake was made in applying the law, it is proper and will be considered.

In most states, appeals made on the basis of a mistake of law must be backed up by a written outline of what the claimed mistakes are. This can put nonlawyers at a disadvantage because they are unfamiliar with legal research and legal writing techniques. Start by contacting the court clerk and requesting all forms and rules governing appeals. While you should take these seriously and do your best to comply, the good news is that most appellate judges will consider any well-reasoned written statement you submit claiming that the Small Claims judge made a legal error.

Here is a brief example of appropriate paperwork:

Appeal from Small Claims Judgment #___, Based on Legal Error: Under the laws of the state of _____.

A Small Claims judgment may be set aside if it is based on a legal error or mistake. In my personal injury case, the court incorrectly applied the statute of limitations, because it did not take into consideration the fact that I was a minor when the accident occurred.

My case is based on a personal injury I suffered on January 23, 1992, when I was 17 years and two months old. The Small Claims judge dismissed my case because it was not filed within one year after my injury, as is required by the statute of limitations. This was an incorrect application of the law.

It's true that under the terms of Code of Civil Procedure Sec. 340, a personal injury case must normally be filed within one year of the date of the injury, which in my case occurred on January 23, 1992. However, Sec.

The appeal fee is often higher than the original filing fee; $20–$40 is average. You are now going into formal court and you must pay according to the formal court's fee schedule. If you ultimately win your appeal (that is, get the original decision turned around in your favor), you can add these court costs to the judgment. In many states, the party filing an appeal must post a bond (or written guarantee by financially solvent adults) to cover the amount of the judgment if he loses. This is not required in California and some other states.

It is absolutely essential that you get and study a copy of your state's Small Claims appeal rules. They vary considerably, especially between those states where you can only appeal questions of law and those where you are entitled to a complete new trial.

The following illustrates an appeal notice in use in Massachusetts, where juries are allowed on appeal. The one in use in your state may look different, but the information requested will be similar.

Note: Appeal rights are almost always restricted to those who showed up in Small Claims Court, argued their case, and lost. If you defaulted (didn't show up), you normally can't appeal until you get the default set aside. You must act to do this almost immediately (see Chapter 10, "If One Party Doesn't Show Up").

Because many states start counting your time to appeal from the date the judgment was mailed, this date, which should appear on the judgment, is critical. If for some reason attributable to the magic of the U.S. Postal Service your judgment doesn't show up within the number of days in which you are allowed to appeal, call the Small Claims clerk immediately and request help in getting an extension of time to file your appeal.

Appeals must usually be filed using a form supplied by the Small Claims Court.

2. Appeal Fees

The appeal fee is often higher than the original filing fee; $20-$60 is typical. If you ultimately win your appeal (that is, get the original decision turned around in your favor), you can add these court costs to the judgment. In many states, the party filing an appeal must post a cash bond (or written guarantee by financially solvent adults) to cover the amount of the judgment if he loses. This is not required in California and some other states.

F.   Arguing Your Appeal Without a Lawyer

You are entitled to have an attorney in formal court, where Small Claims Court appeals are heard. But since by definition your Small Claims case is not worth big bucks, you will probably decide that it is not wise to hire one. Indeed, there should be little practical reason for an attorney, as you probably have an excellent grasp of the issues by this time.

But what if your opponent hires a lawyer? Aren't you at a disadvantage if you represent yourself? Not necessarily. As noted in Section D, above, in many states, the appeals court must follow informal rules, similar to those used in Small Claims Court, thus placing you on a relatively equal footing, even if your opponent has a lawyer. If you have prepared carefully, you may even have an advantage; you carry with you the honest conviction that you are right while a lawyer arguing a Small Claims appeal always seems a bit pathetic. If, despite this common sense view of the situation, you still feel a little intimidated, the best cure is to go watch a few Small Claims appeals. Ask the court clerk when they are scheduled. Again, as noted above, since some states follow formal court rules for Small Claims appeals, you really do want to be prepared.

Jury Trial Note: A few states, including North Carolina and Virginia permit jury trials on appeal. Most states don't. Check with your county clerk.

Discovery Note: Most states allow you to subpoena documents for your original hearing (see Chapter 14, Section C, "Subpoenaing Documents"). Other formal discovery techniques, such as taking the deposition of your opponent and witnesses or requesting that she answer a series of written questions, are normally prohibited in Small Claims Court. Unfortunately, in a few states, some of these discovery techniques are allowed for appeals. This is a mistake, since these techniques are expensive and time-consuming at the same time that they favor lawyers who know all the tricks. We look forward to the day when it is clear that they have been eliminated in all states.

Appeals from the Appeal: If a defendant loses the appeal, there is normally no right to file a second appeal. However, it is usually possible to file an "extraordinary writ" (a special request for review based on extraordinary circumstances) to the Court of Appeal claiming that the case involves an important question of law. (In some states, the lower court judge also may recommend that the Court of Appeal hear the case.) Because of the small amounts of money involved, extraordinary writs based on Small Claims judgments are almost never filed. When they are, they are seldom granted. For these reasons, I do not cover this procedure here.

CHAPTER 24

Collecting Your Money

You won. You are entitled to the dollar amount of the judgment from the opposing party or parties. How are you going to get it? Your first job is to be patient for a short while longer. Here's why.

Appeals

If the other party appeared in court and fought the case, you must wait to see if he files an appeal. Depending on your state's rules, an appeal must normally be filed in ten to 30 days.

Exception: In a few states, no appeals are allowed, and in several more, only a losing defendant can appeal. (See Appendix.) If the other party can't appeal, you can begin collection activities immediately.

Default Judgments

If you got your judgment because the defendant defaulted (that is, the defendant didn't show up), the defendant normally can't appeal until she first asks the court to set aside the default and allow her to defend the case. Most defendants who didn't show up in the first place don't bother to do this. Nevertheless, in some states, such as California, you must wait the time period in which the losing party is allowed to ask the court to set aside the default judgment. (See Chapter 10.) And even if waiting isn't required, it's always a good idea if you are in a state that allows a defendant a certain number of days in which to petition the court to set aside the default judgment. The reason is simple. If you move to collect your judgment immediately, you may alert the defendant to try and set it aside.

Assume now that you do face a short waiting period before you can initiate official collections procedures, such as a wage attachment—is it a good idea to use this time to ask the losing party to pay up voluntarily? No. While it is not illegal to ask for your money during these waiting periods, it is unwise. If you make your request for money, you are likely to remind the defendant to take advantage of his right to appeal or set aside a default judgment. In short, if there is ever a time when you should "let sleeping dogs lie," this is it.

Once any waiting period is up, what should you do? Try asking politely for your money. This works in many cases, especially if you have sued a responsible person or business. If you don't have personal contact with the person who owes you money, try a note like the following:

Sample Collection Note

P.O. Box 66
Springfield, IL
February 15, 19___

Mildred Edwards
11 Milvia Street
Springfield, IL

Dear Mrs. Edwards:

As you know, a judgment was entered against you in Small Claims Court on January 15 in the amount of $1,457.86. As the judgment creditor, I will appreciate your paying this amount within 10 days.

Thank you for your consideration.

Very truly yours,

David Osaki

If you receive no payment after sending your polite note, you will have to get serious about collecting your money or forget it. The emphasis in the previous sentence should be on the word "you." Much to many people's surprise, the court does not enforce its judgments and collect money for you—you have to do it yourself.[1]

However, don't get so carried away in your efforts that you harass the debtor or treat her unfairly or dishonestly! If you do, you could find yourself on the other end of a lawsuit.

A few of the ways to collect money from a debtor are relatively easy. I mentioned these briefly in Chapter 3. Hopefully,

---

[1]Some courts, such as California, allow the debtor to pay the court directly. The court then forwards the money to you. If you are interested, ask the court clerk for details.

you gave some thought to collection before you brought your case. Should you only realize now that your opponent doesn't have the money to buy a toothbrush and never will, you are better off not wasting more time and money trying to get him to pay up, at least for the present. Remember, though—a judgment is valid for many years (between 10 and 20 years in most states) and can be renewed for an additional period of years if you can show that you have tried to collect it, but failed. In some situations you may simply want to sit on your judgment, with the hope that your judgment debtor will show a few signs of life in the future.[2]

Important: A few states, such as New York, are putting teeth in their collection rules. In New York, if a judgment debtor that has the ability to do so doesn't pay three or more Small Claims Court judgments, a judgment creditor can get triple the judgment as damages, plus attorney fees. If you are in New York, contact the Small Claims Court clerk for details.

---

[2]Especially, if a substantial amount of money is involved, it's a good idea to establish liens on the debtor's property, even if he's unlikely to buy or sell real property in the near future. (See Section A, below.)

When the Debtor Pays By Check

Always make copies of checks written by the debtor to pay the judgment. Should you receive only partial payment and later want to collect the rest, you'll have information on where the debtor has been banking.[3] If the debtor's check bounces, you may, depending on your state's law, be entitled to:

• sue in small claims court (or in municipal court if there is no small claims court in your area), for the original amount of the bounced check plus damages. First you must usually send a demand letter to the debtor;[4] or

• see if your county's district attorney's office will prosecute the debtor or refer the debtor to a bad check diversion program. These generally allow the person who wrote the bad check to avoid prosecution by making the check good and complying with other rules. Usually, you cannot seek damages if you enlist the district attorney's help—but you'll be spared the hassle of another lawsuit.

A. Create Property Liens

One important collection device used by judgment creditors is the property lien. In a little under half of the states, the entry of a court judgment automatically creates a lien on any real property the debtor owns in the county where the judgment was obtained. In the rest of the states, you must record the judgment with the

---

[3]If the judgment debtor sends you a check for partial payment marked "cashing this check constitutes payment in full" or something similar, it's best not to cash the check, unless you clearly establish that such a statement is not valid in your state. Otherwise, you may be barred from collecting the balance. See *Money Troubles: Legal Strategies to Cope With Your Debts*, by Robin Leonard (Nolo Press).

[4]For information about specific states' bad check laws, see *Money Troubles: Legal Strategies to Cope With Your Debts*, by Robin Leonard (Nolo Press).

county to create a lien on the debtor's real property. In Alabama, Georgia, Massachusetts and Mississippi, the lien is on the debtor's real and personal property.[5]

Once you have a lien on the judgment debtor's property, especially real property, there is a good chance you'll eventually be paid. It usually works like this. When the debtor sells or refinances her property, the buyer will see your lien on the property. In the case of a sale, you will normally be notified and paid out of the proceeds. If property is refinanced, the lender will normally insist on the existing liens being paid off.

Instead of waiting for the debtor to sell her property, you may be able to execute on the lien—that is, have the sheriff seize the property (typically a house) and arrange for a public sale from which you are paid out of the proceeds. This is unusual, however, because arranging a public sale is time-consuming and expensive. Furthermore, you may not get much money by selling property at this kind of sale, called a distress sale. Any mortgage holder, government taxing authority or other creditor who has placed a lien on the debtor's property before you is paid first. In addition, in most states, a portion of the debtor's equity is protected by "homestead laws." Only if the debtor has money over and above what he already owes on the real property and the amount of any homestead exemptions, can you collect your judgment.

In many states, here's how to record your judgment against real property. First get an Abstract of Judgment from the Small Claims clerk's office. The clerk will prepare this paper for you. Then take the Abstract of Judgment to the county recorder's office in the county where the property is located, pay a fee and give the recorder the mailing address of the judgment debtor so that he can be notified. Check with your Small Claims Court for the exact procedures.

---

[5]In some states where you do not get a lien on personal property after the judgment is entered or recorded, you may be able to get a lien on the debtor's personal property by filing the judgment with the Secretary of State. See *Money Troubles: Legal Strategies to Cope With Your Debts*, Leonard (Nolo Press), for a comprehensive listing of different state's lien laws.

Note: In some states, you have to specifically identify the property you're putting the lien on.

B. Levying On Wages, Bank Accounts, Business Assets, Real Property, etc.

If a polite letter doesn't work (ten days is plenty of time to wait), and you know that the judgment debtor has the money, you will have to start acting like a collection agency. It is also possible to turn your debt over to a real collection agency, but this probably doesn't make too much sense as the agency usually takes up to 50% of what it collects. Unless you are a regular customer, the agency probably won't treat your debt with much priority unless it believes that it is easy to collect. If it is easy for the agency to collect, it probably won't be hard for you to do it yourself and save the fee.

If you know where the judgment debtor works, you are in good shape. In most states, you can get up to 25% of a person's net wages to satisfy a debt.[6] As mentioned, knowing where a judgment debtor banks can also be extremely valuable, as you can order a sheriff, marshal or constable to levy on a bank account and get whatever it contains at the time of the levy.[7] Of course, a bank account levy will only work once at a given bank,

---

[6] If a person has a very low income, the amount you can recover can be considerably less than 25%. Wage garnishments are not allowed in Texas. Some other states make it difficult to garnish the wages of a head of family in a situation where the family has a low income and needs all of its income to survive. A few states, such as New York, limit garnishments to 10% of a person's wages. The sheriff or marshal's office in your area can supply you with rules in your state.

[7] Bank account levies are subject to exempt property laws. In most states, approximately 75% of wages placed in a bank account are exempt (100% if there has been a previous wage attachment involving the same money) for 30 days after payment. Social Security money and deposits from other public benefits, such as AFDC, unemployment insurance and veteran's benefits are totally exempt.

as the debtor is pretty sure to move his account when he realizes that you have access to it.

Stocks, bonds, mutual funds and other securities are normally not difficult to levy on if you know where they are held.

Other types of property are normally much more difficult to grab. Why? Because all states have a number of "exemption" laws which say that, even though a person owes money, certain types of her property can't be taken to satisfy the debt. Items protected typically include a portion or all equity in a family house, furniture, clothes, and much more.[8] Practically speaking, the only assets other than wages and bank accounts and securities that are normally worth thinking about to satisfy a Small Claims judgment are the receipts of an operating business (Section 4, below) and a motor vehicle (Section 5, below) in which the judgment debtor has an equity considerably in excess of the exemption amount in effect in your state. Theoretically, there are many other assets that you could reach, but in most cases they are not worth the time and expense involved, considering that your judgment is for the Small Claims maximum, or less.

Real Property Note: As discussed in Section A, above, while it doesn't usually make sense to try and force a sale of a judgment debtor's house or other real property to collect a small claims judgment, placing a lien against real property is sensible—sooner or later the judgment debtor will sell or refinance, and chances are good your judgment will be paid, plus interest.

1. The Writ of Execution

Before you can levy on a person's wages or other property, you must get court permission, usually in a document called a

---

[8] All states exempt some property from attachment, but the details vary considerably. For more information, see *Money Troubles: Legal Strategies to Cope With Your Debts,* by Robin Leonard (Nolo Press).

Writ of Execution, Writ of Garnishment or similar title. Some courts also require that you complete a short application for the Writ. If you have a Small Claims judgment, you are entitled to this Writ. You get your Writ in most states from the Small Claims Court clerk who will help you fill it out. There is often a small fee, which is a recoverable cost (see Section D, "Recovering Collection Costs and Interest," later in this chapter).

2. The Sheriff (or Marshal or Constable)

Once you obtain a Writ, the procedure to collect your money will be as follows in most states: Take or send the writ to the sheriff, marshal or constable in the county in which the assets are located.[9] The Small Claims Court clerk will direct you. Do it right away because the Writ of Execution expires within a certain period (often 60-180 days) if it is not served by the sheriff or marshal. If this time runs out, you will have to go back to the Small Claims Court clerk and get another Writ issued. Give the sheriff, marshal or Small Claims clerk the following:

• The Writ (original) and one to three or more copies, depending on the asset to be collected. Remember to keep a copy of the Writ for your files.

• The required fees for collecting (this will vary as to the type of asset); call ahead to inquire.

Instructions on what type of asset to collect and where it is located. The sheriff, marshal, constable or Small Claims clerk may have a form they wish you to use when providing these instructions. Or the instructions might be a part of the Writ form itself. Normally, however, they will accept a letter if it contains all the necessary information.

---

[9] In some states, collection papers may be given to the Small Claims Court clerk, who will transmit them to the sheriff, marshal, or constable for you.

3. How to Levy on Wages and Bank Accounts

To seize a person's wages or bank account, you need the original, copies of the Writ for the sheriff, marshal or constable, and a letter of instruction like that shown below. If your state has a special wage garnishment form, use that—your Small Claims advisor should know.

P.O. Box 66-D
Jackson, Wyoming 83001
March 1, 19__

Sheriff (Civil Division)
Cheyenne, Wyoming

Re: Carol Lamp vs. Frank Post

Small Claims Court No. 81-52

To Whom It May Concern:

Enclosed you will find the original and one copy of a Writ of Garnishment issued by the Small Claims Court in the amount of $__(fill in total due)__. I also enclose a check for your fee in the amount of $_____.

I hereby instruct you to levy on the wages of Frank Post, who works at the Graphite Oil Co., 1341 Chester St., Cheyenne, Wyoming. Please serve the Writ on or before March 15, 19__.[10]

Very truly yours,

Carol Lamp

---

[10]For a bank account, you would simply substitute "all monies in all accounts of Frank Post, located at the Bank of Trade, 11 City St., Cheyenne, Wyoming." You generally do not need to know the account number. If a bank account is in the name of defendant and someone else, you may have to post a bond, depending on your state's laws. Ask the levying officer for details.

4. Business Assets

In many states, it is possible to have someone from the sheriff, marshal or constable's office sent to the business of a person who owes you money to collect it from the cash on hand. You will want to ask your court clerk about your local rules. In many states, this can be done with a "till tap" or "keeper."

A till tap consists of a one-time removal of all cash receipts from the business. For a keeper, a deputy from the sheriff, marshal or constable's office goes to the place of business, takes all the money in the cash register, and then stays there for a set period of time (an "8-hour keeper," a "24-hour keeper," or a "48-hour keeper") to take more money as it comes in. Keepers' fees are high; a 48-hour keeper can cost as much as $400. It is also possible for the business' property to be seized and sold. But costs of doing so are often prohibitive.

Talk to the sheriff, marshal or constable in your area to get more details. He will want an original and copies of your Writ as well as instructions telling him where and when to go. Fees are recoverable from the judgment debtor if enough money comes in to cover them, plus the judgment.

5. Levying on Motor Vehicles (Including Planes, Boats and RV's)

Selling a person's motor vehicle tends to be difficult for several reasons, including the following:

• A portion of the equity in a car is exempt from your levy in many states. For instance, Oregon exempts $1,200.[11]

Example: A judgment debtor in Oregon has a car worth $4,000 on which he owes $3,000 to a bank. This means that his equity is

---

[11]Some states have no exemption for motor vehicles and some exempt a higher amount of equity. Check your state legal codes, call your local sheriff or marshal's office, or consult. *Money Troubles: Legal Strategies to Cope With Your Debts*, by Robin Leonard (Nolo Press).

$1,000—the bank owns the rest. As an equity of $1,200 is exempt under Oregon law, you would end up with nothing.

• You may not be able to instruct the sheriff to pick up the car from a garage or other private place unless you first go to court and obtain a judge's permission.

• The judgment debtor may not own the car she drives. It may be in someone else's name, belong to her employer, or she may owe a bank or finance company as much or more than the car is worth.

To find out if a judgment debtor owns the car he drives, go to the Department of Motor Vehicles. In most states, for a small fee, they will tell you who owns the car, including whether or not a bank or finance company is involved. Once you have this information, you can determine whether selling the car is likely to yield enough to pay off any loan you discover, provide the debtor with her exemption amount, cover the costs of sale, and still leave enough to pay off all, or at least a substantial part of, your judgment. If you are convinced that the vehicle is worth enough to cover these costs, as would be the case if it is relatively new and owned by the debtor free and clear, have the sheriff pick up the car and sell it. But remember, the sheriff fees to do this are relatively high (usually $400 or more) and must be paid in advance. Also, the sale price at a public auction will fetch far less than at a private sale. Your costs are recoverable when the vehicle is sold.

Call the sheriff, marshal, or constable of the county in which the car is located to find out how much money he requires as a deposit with your Writ and how many copies of the Writ you need. Then write a letter such as this:

P.O. Box 66-D
Jackson, WY 83001
March 1, 19__

Sheriff (Civil Division)
Cheyenne, Wyoming

Re: Carol Lamp v. Frank Post
Small Claims Court
No. SC 81-52

To Whom It May Concern:

You are hereby instructed, under the authority of the enclosed Writ, to levy upon and sell all of the right, title and interest of Frank Post, judgment debtor, in the following motor vehicle:

[Type the description of the car as it appears on your D.M.V. report, including the license number.]

The vehicle is registered in the name(s) of Frank Post, and is regularly found at the following address(es):

[List home and work address of owner. Remember that the car might have to be parked in a public place.]

Enclosed is my check for $_____ to cover your costs of levy and sale.

Very truly yours,

Carol Lamp

352 of the Code of Civil Procedure also states: 'If a person entitled to bring an action, mentioned in Chapter 3 of this title, be, at the time the cause of action occurred, ...under the age of majority...the time of such disability is not a part of the time limited for the commencement of the action.'

Since I was still a minor until November 23, 1993 (at which point I became 18), under the terms of CCP Sec. 352, it was from this date (not from January 23, 1992) that the court should have begun counting the one-year statute of limitations for personal injury actions. Therefore, I was entitled to file my case until November 22, 1994. In fact, since I filed on June 27, 1994, I filed well within the allowed time."

In conclusion, I request that the judgment in this case be vacated and that I be granted a new Small Claims Court hearing.

E. Filing Your Appeal

If you haven't already done so, it is absolutely essential that you get and study a copy of your state's Small Claims appeal rules. They vary considerably, especially between those states where you can only appeal questions of law and those where you are entitled to a complete new trial.

1. File Your Appeal Promptly

In all states, appeals must be filed promptly, so wherever you are, don't delay. In California, New York and many other states, the defendant must file a notice of appeal within 30 days of the day the court clerk mails the judgment to the parties (or hands it over, if a decision is made in the courtroom). This means that if the decision was mailed, there will be less than 30 days to file an appeal from the day that the defendant receives the judgment. In a number of other states, including Massachusetts and Montana, appeals must be filed within ten days, while Washington, D.C. requires that appeals be on file within three days.

tions. You'll need to check your state laws to find out if retirement accounts are fair game.[12] If you're entitled to go after this money, you can do so just as you do any other money kept in a bank. Of course, you need to know where the money is.

Private company retirement plans and state or local government retirement plans generally can't be touched until the money is paid over to the employee. Even then, the judgment debtor might claim those amounts as exempt.

Federal government pension and retirement benefits may not be garnished to satisfy any debts, except those for alimony and child support.

C. Finding Phantom Assets

As you now understand from reading the above sections, collecting on your Small Claims judgment isn't normally difficult if the judgment debtor has some money or property and you know where it is. But what do you do when you suspect that money or property exists, but have no idea how to find it? For example, you may know that a person works, but not where, or that he has money in the bank, but not which one. Wouldn't it be nice to simply ask the judgment debtor a few questions which he must answer?

Well, you often can. In a number of states, when a Small Claims Court judgment is entered against a person (or business) the loser (judgment debtor) must fill out a statement of assets form. This form must be sent by the judgment debtor to the person who won the case (the judgment creditor) within a required number of days after Notice of Entry of Judgment is mailed out by the clerk *unless* the judgment debtor pays off the judgment, appeals or makes a motion to set aside or vacate the judgment.

---

[12]See *Money Troubles: Legal Strategies to Cope With Your Debts*, by Robin Leonard (Nolo Press) or check with your court's Small Claims advisor, if there is one, or the Sheriff's office.

If a judgment debtor does not fill out this statement of assets form when required to do so (or if no such form exists), the judgment creditor can ask the court clerk to issue an order requiring the judgment debtor to appear in court in person to be questioned. In some states, this is called an Order of Examination or Judgment Debtors Examination. This order, which must be properly served on the judgment debtor, requires the debtor to show up in court and provide the information personally. If the debtor fails to show up, the judge can issue a bench warrant for his arrest. Oh, and one hint. In many states, at the Order of Examination hearing, the judgment creditor can ask if the debtor has any cash in her possession. If so, this can be taken to satisfy at least a portion of the debt right on the spot.

D.   Recovering Collection Costs and Interest

Costs (including the filing fee, costs of service, etc.) incurred prior to recovering a judgment should be included in the judgment total when it is entered by the judge. I discuss this in Chapter 15, "Don't Forget to Ask for Your Costs."

Here I am concerned with costs incurred after judgment. These are the costs that result when the judgment debtor doesn't pay voluntarily and you have to levy on his or her assets. This can be expensive and you will want to make the judgment debtor pay, if possible. Many costs of collecting a judgment are recoverable; a few are not. Generally speaking, you can recover your direct costs of collecting which include such things as sheriff, marshal or constable fees,[13] costs to get copies of required papers issued by the court (such as a Writ of Execution or Abstract of Judgment) and recording fees. Indirect costs such as babysitting costs, time off work, postage, photocopying gasoline, etc., can't be recovered. Check with your clerk for rules.

---

[13]In most states, law enforcement agencies will demand a deposit up front to cover their collection fees, but will reimburse you over and above the amount of the judgment if they are successful in collecting.

You can also recover interest on the judgment. The interest rate depends on your state's laws; 8% to 12% per year is usual.

E. Renew Your Judgment

Judgments expire after a certain number of years—usually five to 10, depending on the state.[14] Fortunately, you are entitled to renew your judgment—and any liens based on them—if you do so before the expiration date. For information on how to renew a judgment, contact your Small Claims Court clerk's office.

---

[14]The time limit can be as soon as three years (District of Columbia) or as late as 20 years.

C H A P T E R   2 5

Where Do We Go
From Here?

It's easy to criticize the existing legal system—almost everyone knows that it's on the rocks. The $1,000 a day experts with
their degrees, titles, and well-funded consulting companies have
studied the problem to death with no positive results. And this is
hardly surprising, since most of the experts involved in the
studies, and in the resulting decisions, are lawyers who, at bot-
tom, are unable to understand a problem of which they are so
thoroughly a part.[1]

---

[1]Not everyone believes that a rotten court system is a bad thing. David
Hapgood, in his interesting book, *The Average Man Fights Back*,
Doubleday, reports the following statement by the Chinese Emperor
K'ang-hsi " ...lawsuits would tend to increase to a frightening extent if
people were not afraid of the tribunals and if they felt confident of
always finding in them ready and perfect justice . . . I desire therefore
that those who have recourse to the tribunals should be treated without

But instead of my lecturing you about all the things that are wrong at the local courthouse, let's sit down at the kitchen table with a pot of tea and a bowl of raspberries and see if we can't design a better system. After all, this republic was founded by ordinary people taking things into their own hands —they had to, because most of the governor, judge and lawyer-types were quite comfortable in England, thank you. And don't forget that we have already agreed that the present legal structure doesn't work, so we obviously have nothing to lose by making our own suggestions. Hey, leave a few raspberries for me, and why don't you jot down a few of your own ideas as we go along, so that this becomes a two-way communication.

Before we get to specific suggestions for change, let's take a brief look around to see from where we are starting. As a society, we obviously have a fixation with trying to solve problems by suing one another. Nowhere in the world do people even come close to being as litigious as we are. The result of this love of lawsuits, or perhaps its cause—it's one of those chicken and egg problems—is the fact that whenever we get into any sort of spat with anyone, or even think that we might get into one in the future, we run to a lawyer.[2] It's gotten so bad that people who suffer an injury have been known to call their lawyer before their doctor. But there is an odd paradox here. At the same time that we tolerate vast numbers of lawyers eating at the top end of our societal trough, and are more and more likely to use them, public opinion polls tell us that our respect for lawyers has fallen, so that we rate their trustworthiness below that of used-car sales-people, undertakers, and loan sharks. It's as if the less we respect lawyers, the more we use them. Perhaps we're afraid that if we don't sue first, someone will get the jump on us. If you eat one more of those raspberries, I'll see you in court.

Have you ever thought about how people solved their disputes in simpler societies? Let's pretend, for a moment, that

---

pity and in such a manner that they shall be disgusted with law and tremble to appear before a magistrate."

[2]There are close to 1,000,000 lawyers in the United States, and another 140,000 in law school. California alone has more than 135,000. There are more judges in Los Angeles County than there are in all of France.

we are members of a tribe of deer hunters in a pre-industrial age.[3] One fine fall morning, we both set out, bow in hand, you to the east and I to the west. Before long, you hit a high cliff and turn north. My way is blocked by a swift river, and I too turn north. Without our realizing it, our paths converge. Suddenly, a great stag jumps from the underbrush and we both pull back our bows and let fly. Our arrows pierce the deer's heart from opposite sides, seemingly at the same instant.

For a moment, we stand frozen, each surprised by the presence of the other. Then we realize what has happened and that we have a problem. To whom does the deer belong? We carry the deer back to the village, each unwilling to surrender it to the other. After the deer is gutted and hung, we speak to the chief of our group about our problem. He convenes a council of elders to meet late in the afternoon to consider it. Each of us has his say as to what happened. The deer carcass is examined. Anyone else who has knowledge of our dispute is invited to speak. Tribal customs (laws) are consulted, our credibility is weighed, and a decision is made—in time for dinner.

---

[3]Anthropologists will, I hope, accept this little fable as just that.

Now, let's ask ourselves what would happen today if you and I simultaneously shot a deer (instead of each other) on the first day of hunting season and were unable to agree on to whom it belonged. Assuming we didn't fight it out on the spot but wanted the dispute resolved by "proper" legal procedures, lawyers would have to be consulted, court papers filed and responded to, a court appearance scheduled, words spoken in legalese, and a formal court decision written and issued. All of this for a deer that would have long since rotted away unless it had been put in cold storage. If the deer had been frozen, the storage costs would have to be added to court costs and attorney fees, which, all together, would surely add up to a lot more than the value of the deer.

Seriously, what where the differences between the ways that the two societies resolved the problem of who owned the deer? The so-called primitive one did a better job, but why? Obviously because their solution was in proportion to the problem, while today we make the solution process so cumbersome and expensive that it dwarfs the dispute. The hunting society handled the disagreement quickly, cheaply, and, most importantly, with a process that allowed the disputing parties to participate in and understand what was going on. Simple, you say. Why then can't our dispute resolution procedure achieve even one of these goals? In large measure, because lawyers have vested financial and psychic interests in the present cumbersome way of doing things and have neither the motivation nor the perspective to make changes.

But isn't my view a bit radical? Isn't there something uniquely valuable about the great sweep of the common law as it has evolved through the ages? Doesn't the majestic black-robed judge sitting on his throne mumbling age-old mantras somehow guarantee that God is in heaven, the republic safe, and "justice will be done?" Not necessarily. History is arbitrary—our dispute resolution mechanisms could have developed in a number of alternative ways. If our present system worked well, imposing it on the future would make sense. As, in fact, it hardly works at all, continuing it is silly. Those who get quite misty-eyed recounting the history, traditions and time-tested forms behind our present ways of resolving disputes are almost always people that benefit by its continuance. Consider, too, that in the United States, we have no pure legal tradition, having borrowed large hunks of our jurisprudence on a catch-as-catch-can basis from England, Spain, France, Holland, and Germany, as well as various Native American cultures.

Okay, granted that there have been legal systems that worked better than ours, and granted that at least some change is overdue, what should we do? One significant reform would be to expand Small Claims Court. Like the system followed by the deer hunters, but unlike most of the rest of our legal system, Small Claims Court is simple, fast, cheap, and allows for the direct participation of the disputing parties. Never mind that up to now Small Claims Court has been tolerated as a way to keep lawyers' offices clear of penny-ante people with penny-ante disputes. It's there, it works, and we can expand it to play a meaningful role in our lives.

As you know by now, Small Claims Court as it is presently set up has several disadvantages. First, the amount for which suit can be brought is ridiculously low. Second, in most instances, the court only has the power to make judgments that can be satisfied by the payment of money damages. Third, many kinds of cases, such as divorces, adoptions, etc. aren't permitted in Small Claims at all. Fourth, many states still allow lawyers to represent people in Small Claims Court, even though a recent study by the National Center for State Courts indicates that people win just as often without lawyers. Why not start our effort to improve things by doing away with these disadvantages? Let's raise the maximum   amount for which suit can be brought to $10,000.[4]. I would like to suggest $20,000, but perhaps we should take one step at a time, to limit attorney opposition. An increase to $10,000 would be a significant reform, allowing tens of thousands of disputes to be removed from our formal legal system.

---

[4]While most states limit Small Claims jurisdiction to the $1,500-$5,000 range, there are exceptions. For example, the United States Tax Court has a very successful Small Claims procedure which allows claims up to $10,000.

One logical reason to pick $10,000 is that people can't afford lawyers to handle disputes for amounts below this.[5]

To illustrate, let's take a situation in which Randy the carpenter agrees to do $20,000 worth of rehabilitation to Al's home. When the work is completed, an argument develops about whether the work was done properly according to the agreement. Al pays Randy $15,000, leaving $5,000 in dispute. Randy goes to his lawyer and Al to his. Each has several preliminary conferences, after which the lawyers exchange several letters and telephone calls. Eventually, a lawsuit is filed and answered, a court date is obtained many months in the future and then changed several times, and finally a two-hour trial is held. Randy's lawyer bills him $1,250 (12.5 hours x $100 per hour) and Al's charges $960 (12 hours x $80 per hour), for a total fee of $2,210. The dispute takes eleven months to be decided. In the end, Randy is awarded $3,500.[6]

---

[5]I believe that there are persuasive reasons for limiting the role of lawyers, in addition to the fact that they cost too much. Such a limitation would require fundamental changes in our adversary system and is the subject for a broader book. For a good history of how our adversary system evolved from barbaric practices such as trial by battle, how it all too often serves to obscure rather than expose the truth, and how it protects the interests of the already strong and powerful (those who can afford a good mouthpiece) at the expense of everyone else, see *Injustice for All*, Strick, Putnam, $8.95.

[6]A lawyer might argue that many cases of this type are settled with a few letters and phone calls. This is true, but by the time you allow for client conferences and the fact that many lawyers charge considerably more than the fees I list here, the cost to settle would probably be comparable.

This is a typical case with a typical solution. Between them, the lawyers collected almost half of the amount in dispute and took most of a year to arrive at a solution that very likely left both Randy and Al frustrated. Don't you think that Randy and Al would have preferred presenting their case in Small Claims Court, in which it would have been heard and decided in a month? Of course, either of them could have done worse arguing the case himself, but remember, when the legal fees are taken into consideration, the loser would have had to do a *lot* worse in Small Claims before he would have ended up in worse financial shape. Randy recovered $3,500 with a lawyer, but after subtracting the $1,250 lawyer fee, his net gain was only $2,250. Al ended up paying $4,460 ($3,500 for the judgment and $960 for his attorney). Thus, if a Small Claims Court judge had awarded Randy any amount from $2,246 to $4,459, both men would have done better than they did with lawyers. Of course, if this sort of case were permitted in Small Claims Court, there would be two big losers—the lawyers.

The second great barrier to bringing cases in Small Claims Court is the fact that, with minor exceptions, the court is limited to making money judgments. Think back for a moment to our problems with the twice-shot deer. How does the award of money make sense in this situation? In Small Claims Courts, the tribesman who didn't end up with the carcass would have had to sue the other for the fair market value of the deer. What nonsense—if we are going to have a dispute resolution procedure, why not permit a broad range of solutions, such as the deer being cut in half, or the deer going to one hunter and six ducks going to the other in compensation, or maybe even the deer going to the person who needed it most. Using an example more common at the end of the 20th century, why not allow a Small Claims Court judge to order that an apartment be cleaned, a garage repainted, or a car properly fixed, instead of simply telling one person to pay X dollars to the other. One advantage of this sort of flexibility is that more judgments would be meaningful. Under our present system, tens of thousands of judgments can't be collected because the loser has no obvious source of income. We need to get away from the notion that people who are broke have neither rights nor responsibilities. To have a decent life, people need both.

Lawyers and judges often contend that it would be impossible to enforce non-money judgments. Perhaps some would be hard to keep track of. Certainly it might require some experimentation to find out what types of judgments are practical and which are not; however, since it is often impossible to collect a judgment under the present system, it can't hurt to try some alternatives.

The third big change that I propose, and the one that would truly make over our court system, involves expanding the types of cases that can be heard in Small Claims Court. Why not be brave and take the 20 most common legal problems and adopt simplified procedures enabling all of them to be handled by the people themselves, without lawyers? Why not open up our courthouses to the average person who, after all, pays the bills?

To accomplish this democratization of our dispute resolution procedures, it may be practical to divide Small Claims Court into several separate divisions, each one responsible for a broad area of common concern. For example, there could be a landlord-tenant and a domestic relations division.[7] Each division would have the authority to consider a broad range of problems and solutions falling within its area of concern. Today, if you have a claim against your landlord (or he against you) for money damages, you can use Small Claims Court only if the claim is under the dollar limit. If you want to have a roof fixed, to have a tenant evicted, or to protect your privacy, etc., most Small Claims Courts can't help you, except possibly to award a money judgment for the intentional infliction of emotional distress.[8] The Canadian province of British Columbia and a few East Coast cities have already put all landlord-tenant disputes into what amounts to a Small Claims Court format, easily and cheaply

---

[7]There is nothing new about the idea of dividing a court by subject matter. This is already done in our formal trial courts and works well.

[8]As I pointed out in Chapter 20, some evictions can be brought in Small Claims if a number of conditions are met, but it is commonly unwise to do so.

available to both landlord and tenant. Why can't this be done everywhere?

A domestic relations Small Claims Court could include simplified procedures to help people handle their own uncontested divorces, adoptions, name changes, guardianships, etc., safely and cheaply. And why not? Even with considerable hostility from lawyers and court personnel, over 30 percent of the divorces in California are already handled without a lawyer by people who deal with the absurd procedures inherent in going to formal court. I'm not advocating that sensible safeguards be dropped. For example, if a divorce involves children, you would want to have someone trained in the field carefully examine the parents' plans for custody, visitation, and support to see if they are reasonable.

Without going into detail, I suggest that if we took lawyers out of our domestic relations courts we would not only save millions of dollars and hours, but more importantly, we would lighten the heavy burden of hostility and anxiety that divorcing spouses must now bear. Our present system, in which parents and children become clients to a "hired gun" (the lawyer), is a bad one. By definition, the client role is weak and the gun fighter role strong.[9] This imbalance commonly results in lawyers making critical decisions affecting their clients' lives, sometimes obviously, sometimes subtly. All too often, these decisions benefit the lawyer and his bank balance to the detriment of both the clients' psyche and pocketbook. The lawyer, after all, is paid more to fight, or at least to pretend to fight, than to compromise. I have seen dozens of situations in which lawyers have played on people's worst instincts (paranoia, greed, ego, one-upsmanship) to fan nasty little disagreements into flaming battles. Perhaps mercifully, the battles normally last only as long as the lawyers' bills are paid.

---

[9]In an interesting article entitled "Valuable Deficiencies, A Service Economy Needs People in Need," in the Fall 1977 *Co-Evolution Quarterly*, John McNight points out that "The Latin root of the word 'client' translates to 'to hear,' 'to obey.'"

I could list a number of other areas of law that could be converted to a Small Claims approach (auto accidents, simple probates, perhaps even some criminal cases), but I am sure you get the point. We must take control of the decision-making processes that affect our lives. We must make ourselves welcome in our own courts and legislatures. We must stop looking at ourselves as clients who hear and obey and start taking responsibility for our own legal decisions.

Let's assume now that the obstacles can be overcome and the role of Small Claims Court will be greatly expanded. In the process of doing so, we will need to make a number of changes in the way the court now operates. It will be a good opportunity to throw out a number of existing procedures that owe more to history than to common sense. Here are a few specific ideas for changes:

1. Let's make Small Claims Court easily accessible. This means holding weekend and evening sessions. This is being done now experimentally in a few areas, but such sessions should be as routinely available everywhere else as they are in New York City. When court is held at 9 a.m. on weekdays, it often costs more in lost time from work for all the principals and witnesses to show up than the case is worth.

2. Let's get the judge out of the black robe and off of the throne. There is a part of all of us that loves the drama involved in seeing our magistrate sitting on high like the king of England, but I am convinced by my own brief experience as a "pro tem" judge that this pomp and circumstance is counterproductive. We would have a lot less confrontation and a lot more willingness to compromise if we got rid of some of the drama.

3. Let's ban lawyers and collection agencies in states where they are currently allowed.[10]

---

[10]Because of the so-called constitutional right to be represented by a lawyer if you want one, there will be problems barring lawyers from Small Claims Court itself and eliminating the defendant's right to appeal (or transfer) to a court where they can have a lawyer. One way to solve this dilemma is to create a simplified (voluntary) Small Claims procedure with no lawyers allowed that is so desirable that very few

4. While we're making changes, let's make a big one—let's put strict limits on the adversary system.[11] It contributes a great deal to the posturing of the litigants and obfuscation of the dispute and very little to settling disputes efficiently. We must move toward systems of mediation and arbitration in which, instead of a traditional judge, we have someone whose role is to facilitate the parties arriving at their own solution—imposing a decision only if they arrive at a hopeless impasse. Big business, big labor, and increasingly even lawyers are coming to realize that arbitration and mediation are good ways to solve problems. What I have in mind is something like this: All parties to the dispute would sit down at a table with a Small Claims Court referee (let's drop the word "judge."). This person, who would be trained for the job, would not necessarily be a lawyer. The referee would help the parties search for areas of agreement and possible compromise, and, if this wasn't possible, at least help them define the area in dispute. Only if the dispute couldn't be resolved by the parties would the referee decide it.[12]

5. Appeal rules should also be changed. In many states, existing rules allow only the defendant to appeal, allow litigants to have lawyers on appeal, and even allow the parties to start the whole case over. This is nuts. All too often, corporate defendants who have lawyers on retainer use the present system to frustrate consumers who have won in Small Claims Court. It is my belief that no appeal should be allowed in Small Claims Court—the amounts in question just aren't worth it. If appeals are allowed,

---

defendants will want their cases transferred to a formal court where lawyers are allowed.

[11]Roscoe Pound, distinguished legal scholar, made this point better than I can, "The doctrine of contentious procedure...is peculiar to Anglo-American law...(it) disfigures our judicial administration at every point...(it) gives to the whole community a false notion of the purpose and end of law...Thus, the courts...are made agents or abettors of lawlessness."

[12]An alternate approach also worth a try would be for the Small Claims Court clerk to divert willing parties to a separate mediation procedure. If mediation was not successful, they could return to Small Claims, where a decision would be rendered.

they should be limited to obvious mistakes of law, and lawyers should be prohibited.[13]

I don't mean to suggest that the changes I propose in this short chapter are the only ones necessary. If we are going to put the majority of our routine legal work in Small Claims, it will require turning our dispute resolution process on its head. Legal information must be stored and decoded so that it is available to the average person. Clerk's offices and the other support systems surrounding our courts must be expanded and geared to serve the nonlawyer. Legal forms must be translated from "legalese" into English. Computer systems must be developed to bring legal information into our offices and living rooms.

Let's illustrate how things might change by looking at a case I recently saw argued in a Northern California Small Claims Court. One party to the dispute (let's call her Sally) arranged fishing charters for business and club groups. The other (let's call him Ben) owned several fishing boats. Sally often hired Ben's boats for her charters. Their relationship was of long standing and had been profitable to both. However, as the fishing charter business grew, both Sally and Ben began to enlarge their operations. Sally got a boat or two of her own and Ben began getting into the charter booking business. Eventually, they stepped on one another's toes and their friendly relationship was replaced by tension and arguments. One day a blow-up occurred over some inconsequential detail, phones were slammed down, and Sally and Ben each swore never to do business with the other again.

---

[13]Because of the so-called constitutional right to be represented by a lawyer if you want one, there will be problems barring lawyers from Small Claims Court itself and eliminating the defendant's right to appeal (or transfer) to a court where they can have a lawyer. One way to solve this dilemma is to create a simplified (voluntary) Small Claims procedure with no lawyers allowed that is so desirable that very few defendants will want their cases transferred to a formal court where lawyers are allowed.

Before the day of the final fight, Sally had organized two charters on Ben's boat. These were to have taken place a week after the phones were slammed down. For reasons unconnected with the argument, the charters were cancelled by the clubs that had organized them. Ben had about a weeks' notice of cancellation. He also had $600 in deposit that Sally had paid him. He refused to refund the deposits. Sally sued him in Small Claims Court for $700 ($600 for the charter fee and $100 for general inconvenience.)[14]

Testimony in court made it clear that charters were commonly canceled and were often replaced by others booked at the last minute. Ben and Sally had signed a "Standard Marine Charter Agreement," which dealt with the issue of canceled charters because it was required by the Coast Guard, although they had never in the past paid attention to its terms. They had always worked out sensible adjustments on a situation-by-situation basis, depending on whether substitute charters were available and whether the club or business canceling had paid money up front, etc.

When Ben and Sally first presented their arguments about the $700, it seemed that they were not too far apart as to what would be a fair compromise. Unfortunately, the adversary nature of the court system encouraged each to overstate his (her) case and to dredge up all sorts of irrelevant side issues. "What about the times you overloaded my boat?" Ben demanded. "How about those holidays when you price-gouged me?" Sally replied. As the arguments went back and forth, each person got angrier and angrier and was less and less able to listen to the other.

The result was that after an hour of testimony, the judge was left with a confused mishmash of custom, habit, maritime charter contracts, promises made or not made, past performance, etc. No decision that he arrived at was likely to be accepted as fair by both Ben and Sally. Indeed, unless the judge gave one or the other everything he or she requested, both of them would surely feel cheated. That is not to say that the hearing was all bad. Some

---

[14]As we learned earlier, Sally can't recover for inconvenience, so her maximum recovery would be $600.

good things did occur. The dispute was presented quickly, and cheaply, and each person got to have his or her say and blow off some steam. All of these things would have been impossible in our formal court system. However, if Small Claims Court could be changed along the lines suggested above, a better result might have been reached.

Suppose that instead of a formal courtroom confrontation, Ben and Sally are first encouraged to talk the dispute out themselves. If this fails, then the next step is for the two of them to sit down in a non-courtroom setting with a court employee who is trained as a mediator and whose job is to help Ben and Sally arrive at a fair compromise—a compromise which will hopefully provide a foundation for Ben and Sally to continue to work together in the future. Only if compromise is impossible would there be recourse to a more formal court hearing—I am convinced that if this sort of three-tiered approach was available, that Ben and Sally would have worked out a compromise at the first or second stage.

APPENDIX

Small Claims Court Rules for the 50 States (and the District of Columbia)

Please Read This

The following state-by-state Small Claims rules are for general reference only. They are not a substitute for getting a copy of your local Small Claims Court rules. Please do not make decisions based solely on the summary of state laws you read here. Our information is as sound as we can make it, but we might have inadvertently omitted or inaccurately stated a detail of particular importance to you. This can occur because laws have changed since we went to press or because the laws of many states vary from one county to the next and we haven't been able to include every local difference. So, whether you are a plaintiff or defendant, please call your Small Claims clerk for accurate up-to-date information.

ALABAMA

Small Claims Docket (District Court)

Statutes: Code of Alabama: Title 12, Chapter 12, Secs. 31, 70 and 71 and Alabama Small Claims Rules, Rules A to N; Ala. Rules of Judicial Administration Rule 17.

Dollar Limit: $1,500.

Where to Sue: County or district where any defendant resides, or injury or property damage occurred. A corporation "resides" wherever it is doing business.

Service of Process: Sheriff, adult approved by court or certified mail.

Transfer: No provision.

Attorneys: Allowed; required for assignees (collection agencies).

Appeals: Allowed by either party within 14 days to Circuit Court for new trial.

Evictions: No; must go on regular district court docket.

Notes: (1) The defendant must file a written answer within 14 days of service or will lose by default.

(2) Equitable relief is available.

(3) Director of Courts publishes guide to Alabama Small Claims rules.

ALASKA

Small Claims (District Court Judges and Magistrates)

Statutes: Alaska Statutes Title 22, Ch. 15, Sec. 040 District Court Rules of Civil Procedure, Rules 8 to 22.

Dollar Limit: $5,000.

Where to Sue: Court nearest to the defendant's residence or place of employment, district in which injury or property damage occurred or district where defendant does business.

Service of Process: Peace officer or registered or certified mail. Certified or registered mail service is binding on defendant who refuses to accept and sign for the letter. After such refusal, the clerk remails it regular first class, and service is assumed.

Transfer: Defendant (or plaintiff against whom a counterclaim has been filed) or judge may transfer case to regular District Court.

Attorneys or Legal Interns: Allowed; required for assignees (collection agencies).

Appeals: For claims over $50, allowed by either party, on law—not facts.

Evictions: No.

Note: (1) The defendant must file a written answer within 20 days of service or will lose by default.

(2) The state cannot be sued in Small Claims Court.

ARIZONA

Justice of Peace (Small Claims Division) and Regular Justice Court

Statutes: Arizona Revised Statutes: Secs. 22-201 through 22-283 (Justice Court); Secs. 22-501 through 22-523 (Small Claims).

Dollar Limit: Small Claims Division, $1,500; regular Justice Court, $5,000.

Where to Sue: Precinct where any defendant resides, act or omission occurred, or obligation was to be performed. A corporation "resides" wherever it is doing business.

Service of Process: Sheriff, adult approved by court, or registered or certified mail with return receipt requested.

Transfer: To regular Justice Court if defendant in Small Claims Division counterclaims over $1,500 or objects at least ten days before hearing (for right of appeal and jury). For counterclaims over $5,000, transfer is allowed to Superior Court.

Attorneys: Allowed in Small Claims Division only if both parties agree in writing.

Appeals: Not allowed in Small Claims Division. Allowed in Justice Court.

Evictions: No in Small Claims Division; yes in Justice Court.

Notes: (1) Defendant must answer within 20 days in writing or will lose by default.

(2) Equitable relief is available.

(3) No right to jury trial in Small Claims Division. Allowed in Justice Court.

(4) Assignees (collection agencies) are not allowed to sue in Small Claims Division. Allowed in Justice Court.

ARKANSAS

Urban: Municipal Court (Small Claims Division);

Rural: Justice of the Peace

Statutes: Arkansas Statutes Annotated, Secs. 16-17-601 through 614; Secs 16-19-401 through 1108; Constitution, Amendment 64.

Dollar Limit: $3,000.

Where to Sue: County where a defendant resides, act or omission occurred, or obligation was to be performed. A corporation "resides" wherever it is doing business.

Service of Process: Sheriff, constable (Justice of the Peace Court only); certified mail (Small Claims only). *Transfer:* In Small Claims, if the judge learns that any party is represented by an attorney, he or she must transfer to regular Municipal Court; no transfer provision in Justice of the Peace courts.

Attorneys: Not allowed (Small Claims); Allowed (Justice of the Peace).

Appeals: Allowed by either party within 30 days to Circuit Court for new trial.

Notes: (1) No assignees (collection agencies).

(2) Defendant must file written answer within 20 days of service if she's within the state, within 30 days if she's outside the state.

(3) No right of jury trial in Small Claims Division; allowed in Justice Court.

CALIFORNIA

Small Claims Division (Municipal or Justice Court)

Statutes: California Code of Civil Procedure Secs. 116.110 through 116.950.

Dollar Limit: $5,000, except that a plaintiff may not file a claim over $2,500 more than twice a year. $1,500 is the limit for suits involving a surety company.

Where to Sue: Judicial district where any defendant resides (or resided when promise or obligation was made), act or omission occurred, or obligation was to be performed. A corporation "resides" wherever it is doing business.

Service of Process: Sheriff, disinterested adult, or certified or registered mail.

Transfer: If defendant counterclaims over $5,000, case will be heard in higher court if the Small Claims Court agrees to the transfer.

Attorneys: Not allowed, except representing themselves.

Appeals: Allowed by defendant (or plaintiff who lost on a counterclaim) within 30 days to Superior Court for new trial. Plaintiff may not appeal on her claim, but can make a motion to correct clerical errors or where a decision is based on a legal mistake.

Evictions: No.

Notes: (1) Assignees (collection agencies) cannot sue in Small Claims Court.

(2) No jury trials allowed.

(3) Equitable relief is available.

(4) Small Claims advisor available at no cost.

(5) List of interpreters may be available; call court. If a party does not speak and understand English, she may have assistance in court, other than an attorney.

(6) Judge may make a "conditional judgment" to order the performance or cessation of actions by a party.

COLORADO

County Court (Small Claims Division)

Statutes: Colorado Revised Statutes: Secs. 13-6-401 through 13-6-416, and Colorado Rules of Civil Procedure (County Courts), Rule 411, Rules of Civil Procedure (Small Claims Courts) Rules 501 through 521.

Dollar Limit: $3,500

Where to Sue: County in which any defendant resides, is regularly employed, is a student at an institution of higher education or has an office for the transaction of business.

Service of Process: Sheriff, disinterested adult, or certified mail.

Transfer: Allowed by defendant who has a counterclaim over $3,500.

Attorneys: Allowed only if attorney is plaintiff or defendant, or full- time employee or one of the following with respect to these types of plaintiffs or defendants: general partner (partnership), officer (corporation), active member (corporation or association). If an attorney does appear as permitted above, the other party may have one also.

Appeals: Allowed by either party within 15 days to District Court, on law—not facts. Parties may agree before or at trial that there will be no appeal.

Evictions: No.

Notes: (1) Assignees (collection agencies) cannot sue in Small Claims Court.

(2) No plaintiff may file more than two claims per month in Small Claims Court; no more than 18 claims per year allowed.

(3) No jury trials allowed.

CONNECTICUT

Small Claims (Superior Court)

Statutes: Connecticut General Statutes Annotated: Title 51, Secs. 15, 349; Title 52, Secs. 259, 549a through 549d.

Dollar Limit: $2,000.

Where to Sue: County or geographical area where the defendant resides or does business, or where act or omission occurred, or obligation occurred.

Service of Process: Peace officer, disinterested adult, registered mail or regular first-class mail.

Transfer: Allowed by defendant to regular Superior Court procedure, if he/she has a counterclaim over $2,000.

Attorneys: Allowed; required for corporations.

Appeals: Not allowed.

Evictions: No.

DELAWARE

Justice of the Peace (No Small Claims System)

Statutes: Delaware Code Annotated: Title 10, Secs. 9301 through 9640. Civil Rules, Justice of the Peace Courts.

Dollar Limit: $5,000.

Where to Sue: Anywhere in the state.

Service of Process: Sheriff, constable, or certified mail.

Transfer: No provision.

Attorneys: Allowed.

Appeals: Allowed by either party within 15 days to Superior Court for new trial (on claims over $5).

Evictions: Yes.

Notes: (1) Party can demand jury trial if right to trial provided by statute. (2) Interest due on any cause of action may be added to the claim, even if adding it will make the amount exceed $5,000.

(3) *Counterclaims:* If defendant's counterclaim against Plaintiff exceeds $5,000, Plaintiff can still pursue the counterclaim in Small Claims Court. (There is no provision for transfer to another court). If defendant wins her counterclaim, she then has two options: (1) the court will note the outcome on the record and defendant can prosecute the cause of action in higher court, or (2) Defendant can waive the excess over $5,000 and take the $5,000 as her judgment.

DISTRICT OF COLUMBIA

Superior Court (Small Claims and Conciliation Branch)

Statutes: District of Columbia Code: Title 11, Secs. 1301 through 1323; Title 16, Secs. 3901 through 3910; Title 17, Secs. 301 through 307; and Superior Court Rules for Small Claims and Conciliation Branch.

Dollar Limit: $2,000.

Where to Sue: There is only one court in the District of Columbia.

Service of Process: U.S. Marshal, adult approved by court, or certified (with return receipt) or registered mail. Certified or registered mail is binding on defendant who refuses to accept letter.

Transfer: Transferable to regular Superior Court if justice requires, defendant's counterclaim affects interest in real property (land or housing), or either party demands a jury trial.

Attorneys or Certified Law Students: Allowed; required for corporations.

Appeals: To court of appeal by either party within three days.

Evictions: No.

Note: Parties may consent to arbitration rather than trial.

FLORIDA

Small Claims Procedure (County Court)

Summary Procedure (County Court)

Statutes: Florida Rules of Court: Small Claims, Rules 7.010 through 7.341.

Dollar Limit: $2,500 (Small Claims Court); $15,000 (County Court)

Where to Sue: County where a defendant resides, act or omission occurred, or contract entered into. Corporation resides in its place of "customary business."

Service of Process: Peace officer, adult approved by court, or (for Florida residents only) registered mail, return receipt.

Transfer: Allowed to regular County Court procedure only if defendant counterclaims over $2,500.

Attorneys: Allowed; if attorneys involved, parties may use discovery. Court may require assignees (collection agencies) to have attorneys.

Appeals: Motion for new trial within 10 days after return of verdict or filing of judgment; Appealable to Circuit Court by either party within 30 days on law—not facts.

Evictions: Yes.

Notes: (1) Either party may demand jury trial; plaintiff must make demand when filing suit; defendant must make demand within five days after service or notice of suit or at pre-trial conference.

(2) Defendant must file counterclaim in writing at least five days before appearance date.

GEORGIA

(Magistrate Court)

Statutes: Official Code of Georgia, Title 15-10-1 through 15-10-202.

Dollar Limit: $5,000.

Where to Sue: County where defendant resides.

Service of Process: Constable, official or person authorized by judge.

Transfer: To appropriate court if defendant's counterclaim over $5,000.

Attorneys: Allowed.

Appeals: To Superior Court of county for new trial.

Evictions: Yes.

Notes: (1) Courts may adopt local rules of procedure.

(2) No jury trials.

(3) Defendant must answer complaint (in writing or orally) within 30 days to avoid default.

(4) Equitable relief available.

HAWAII

Small Claims Division (District Court)

Statutes: Hawaii Revised Statutes, Title 34, Secs. 633-27 through 633-36.

Dollar Limit: $3,500; no limit in landlord-tenant residential deposit cases. For return of leased/rented personal property, the property must not be worth more than $3,500. Counterclaims up to $10,000.

Where to Sue: Judicial district in which the defendant or a majority of defendants reside, or act or omission occurred, or where rental premises situated.

Service of Process: Sheriff, County Chief of Police, certified (return receipt) or registered mail.

Transfer: If either party demands jury trial or the claim or counterclaim is over $5,000. Otherwise, only if plaintiff agrees.

Attorneys: Allowed (except in landlord-tenant deposit cases); also, with court permission, an attorney may represent another if he/she does not charge any fee.

Appeals: Not allowed.

Evictions: No.

Notes: (1) The state publishes a booklet on Small Claims Division procedures.

(2) Jury trials allowed.

(3) Cases limited to: recover money, recover rented personal property, recover shopping carts, or recover damages sustained in repossessing carts.

(4) No punitive damages.

(5) Equitable relief available in landlord-tenant cases.

IDAHO

Small Claims Department of Magistrate's Division
(District Court)

Statutes: Idaho Code: Secs. 1-2301 through 1-2315.

Dollar Limit: $3,000.

Where to Sue: County where the defendant resides or where claim arose. A corporation "resides" wherever it is doing business.

Service of Process: Sheriff, disinterested adult, or certified or registered mail, return receipt.

Transfer: No provision.

Attorneys: Not allowed.

Appeals: Allowed by either party within 30 days to Attorney Magistrate for new trial.

Evictions: No.

Notes: (1) Assignees (collection agencies) cannot sue in Small Claims Court.

(2) No jury trials allowed.

ILLINOIS

Small Claims (Circuit Court)

Statutes: Illinois Compiled Statutes: Supreme Court Rules 281 through 289; Ch. 735, Secs. 5/1-104 and 5/2-416.

Dollar Limit: $2,500 (Small Claims); $1,500 (Cook County "Pro Se").

Where to Sue: County in which any defendant resides, act or omission occurred. A corporation "resides" where it is doing business.

Service of Process: Sheriff, court-approved adult, certified or registered mail, return receipt.

Transfer: No provision.

Attorneys: Allowed except in Cook County "Pro Se" branch. Defendant may have one.

Appeals: Allowed by either party within 30 days to Appellate Court, on law—not facts.

Evictions: No.

Notes: (1) Court may order installment payments by judgment debtor if unpaid over three years.

(2) Either party may demand a jury trial in small claims only. (If jury is demanded in Cook County, "Pro se" case is transferred to Small Claims).

(3) Corporation may not appear as assignee.

INDIANA

Small Claims Court; Small Claims Docket

(Circuit Court, Superior Court and County Court)

Statutes: Indiana Statutes Annotated: Secs. 33-11.6-1-1 through 33-11.6-9-5 (Marion County Small Claims Court), 33-4-3-5 through 33-4-3-10 (Circuit Court), 33-5-2-2 through 33-5-2-7 (Superior Court), 33-10.5-1-4 (County Court).

Dollar Limit: $3,000 ($6,000 in Marion County).

Where to Sue: County in which any defendant resides or is employed, act or omission occurred, or obligation was incurred or was to be performed by defendant.

Service of Process: Personal service first; if unable, then registered or certified mail.

Transfer: Defendant may transfer to regular docket by requesting jury trial at least three days prior to the trial date noted on notice of claim—only in Small Claims Court.

Attorneys: Allowed.

Appeals: From Small Claims docket of other courts, same as from regular circuit court.

Evictions: Yes, if total rent due does not exceed $6,000.

Note: Defendant may request jury trial within 10 days following service of complaint (Circuit) if can show questions of fact requiring a jury determination (in Circuit, Superior and County Courts).

IOWA

Small Claims Docket (District Court)

Statutes: Iowa Code Annotated: Secs. 631.1 through 631.16.

Dollar Limit: $2,000.

Where to Sue: County in which any defendant resides, act or omission occurred, or obligation was to be performed.

Service of Process: Peace officer, disinterested adult or (except in eviction suits) certified mail.

Transfer: At judge's discretion if defendant counterclaims over the dollar limit.

Attorneys: Allowed.

Appeals: Allowed by either party to District Court upon oral notice at end of hearing or if filed written notice within 20 days of judgment. No new evidence on appeal.

Evictions: Yes.

Notes: (1) The defendant must file a written answer within 20 days after service is made, or will lose by default; a form for this purpose accompanies the summons.

(2) Replevin (an action to recover a specific item of property) may be granted if value of property is $2,000 or less.

(3) The Small Claims Docket has jurisdiction over orders and motions relative to collecting judgments from personal property, including garnishments, where the amount involved does not exceed $2,000.

KANSAS

Small Claims (District Court)

Statutes: Kansas Statutes Annotated: Secs. 61-2701 through 61-2713.

Dollar Limit: $1,000

Where to Sue: County in which defendant lives or county where plaintiff resides if defendant served there, or defendant's place of doing business or employment.

Service of Process: Personal service by sheriff or adult approved by court, certified mail.

Transfer: If the defendant counterclaims over $1,000 but within the dollar limit of the regular district court, judge may decide claim or let defendant reserve right to bring claim in court of competent jurisdiction.
Attorneys: Not allowed prior to judgment.
Appeals: Allowed by either party within 10 days to District Court for new trial.
Evictions: No.
(2) No person may file more than 10 claims in same court during any calendar year.

KENTUCKY

Small Claims Division (District Court)
Statutes: Kentucky Revised Statutes: Secs. 24A.200 through 24A.360.
Dollar Limit: $1,500.
Where to Sue: Judicial district in which the defendant resides or does business, or if corporation, county of corporate headquarters.
Service of Process: Certified or registered mail first; if that fails, then by sheriff or constable.
Transfer: Allowed to regular District Court or Circuit Court if defendant's counterclaim over $1,500 or if defendant demands a jury trial, or if judge deems matter too complex for Small Claims.
Attorneys: Allowed.
Appeals: Allowed by either party within 10 days to Circuit Court, on law—not facts.
Evictions: Yes.
Notes: (1) Collection agents, or agencies or lenders of money at interest cannot sue in Small Claims Court.
(2) No person may file more than 25 claims in one calendar year in any district court.
(3) *Jury trials:* Plaintiff no, but if defendant makes a written request for jury trial within at least seven days before hearing date, case is transferred to regular court.

LOUISIANA

Rural (Justice of the Peace);
Urban (City Court: Small Claims Division)
Statutes: Louisiana Statutes Annotated: Sec. 13:5200 through 13:5211; Code of Civil Procedure, Articles 4831, 4911 through 4925. Code of Civil Procedure Article 42.
Dollar Limit: $2,000.
Where to Sue: Parish in which the defendant resides. A corporation or partnership may also be sued in a parish or district in which a business office is located.
Service of Process: Certified mail with return receipt, or sheriff or constable, if certified mail is marked "unclaimed" or "refused."

Transfer: Small claims may be transferred to City Court procedure for any reason if defendant files written request within time allowed for filing answer to complaint; transfer by counterclaim ("reconventional demand") over the dollar limit. In Justice of the Peace Court, if demand asserted in amended or supplemental pleading exceeds jurisdictional amount, transfer to court of appropriate jurisdiction.

Attorneys: Allowed.

Appeals: Allowed by either party in Justice of the Peace Courts within 15 days to District Court for new trial. No appeal from Small Claims Division of City Court.

Evictions: Yes, regardless of the amount of monthly or yearly rent or rent for the unexpired term.

Notes: (1) Equitable relief is available in either court.

(2) Judge may award installment payments.

(3) Default taken in Justice of the Peace Court if answer not filed within 10 days of service.

(4) No class actions, summary proceedings, or executory proceedings allowed.

(5) Party may request arbitration.

MAINE

Small Claims (District Court)

Statutes: Maine Rules of Small Claims Procedure, Maine Revised Statutes Annotated: Title 14, Secs. 1901, 7481 through 7486.

Dollar Limit: $1,400

Where to Sue: District Court "division" in which the defendant resides or has place of business or where the transaction occurred or where registered agent resides if corporation.

Service of Process: Registered or certified mail, or personally.

Transfer: Allowed.

Appeals: Allowed by either party within 10 days to Superior Court.

Evictions: Yes.

Notes: (1) Equitable relief available but limited to orders to return, reform, refund, repair or rescind.

(2) Jury trial not allowed.

(3) Judges have power to refer cases to mediation. Mediators are available in all Maine courts, and handle a high percentage of contested cases.

MARYLAND

Small Claims Action (District Court)

Statutes: Annotated Code of Maryland: Courts and Judicial Proceedings Secs. 4-405, 6-403; Rules of Civil Procedure, District Court Rule 3-701; Rules-Appeals from District Courts Rule 1314e and 1312a.

Dollar Limit: $2,500.

Where to Sue: County in which any defendant resides, is employed, or does business, or where injury to person or property occurred. Corporation may be sued where it maintains principal office.

Service of Process: Sheriff or non-party, personally or by certified mail. If refused, clerk remails and service is presumed.

Transfer: To regular civil docket if counterclaim exceeds $2,500 for a jury trial.

Attorneys: Allowed.

Appeals: Allowed by either party within 30 days to Circuit Court for new trial.

Evictions: Yes, as long as the rent claimed does not exceed $2,500, exclusive of interests and costs.

MASSACHUSETTS

Small Claims Division (Boston—Municipal Court; Elsewhere—District Court)

Statutes: Massachusetts General Laws Annotated: Ch. 214, Secs. 1A, 2, 30; Ch. 218, Secs. 21 through 25, Ch. 93A, Sec. 9 (consumer complaints).

Dollar Limit: $2,000; no limit for action for property damage caused by a motor vehicle.

Where to Sue: Judicial district in which the plaintiff or defendant resides, is employed, or does business. Actions against landlords can also be brought in the district in which the property is located.

Service of Process: Sheriff, constable, or certified mail.

Transfer: Allowed only at court's discretion to regular civil docket.

Attorneys: Allowed.

Appeals: Allowed by defendant within 10 days to Superior Court for new trial ($100 bond required). Jury allowed on appeal.

Evictions: No.

Notes: (a) Generally:

    (1)   Equitable relief is available.

    (2)   Mediation is available at request of either party and with agreement of both parties.

  (b) For consumer complaints:

    (1)   Plaintiff must make demand 30 days before filing suit;

    (2)   Attorney's fees available.

    (3)   Triple damages available.

MICHIGAN

Small Claims Division (District Court)

Statutes: Michigan Compiled Laws Annotated: Secs. 600.8401 through 600.8427.

Dollar Limit: $1,750.

Where to Sue: County where defendant resides or where act or omission occurred.

Service of Process: Personal service, or court clerk's certified mail with return receipt.

Transfer: Either party may transfer to regular District Court procedure. Defendant's counterclaim over $1,500 will also cause transfer.

Attorneys: Not allowed, except on own behalf.

Appeals: Not allowed, except that if action is heard by District Court magistrate, parties can appeal to Small Claims Division for new trial within seven days.

Evictions: No.

Notes: (1) Assignees (collection agencies) cannot sue in Small Claims Court.

(2) No jury trial.

(3) Time payments allowed.

(4) Instruction sheet available from court.

(5) May not file more than five claims in one week.

MINNESOTA

Conciliation Court (County Court)

Statutes: Minnesota Statutes Annotated Section 487.30, District Court Rules 501 through 525.

Dollar Limit: 1993 - $6,000; July 1, 1994 - $7,500.

Where to Sue: County in which any defendant resides or automobile accident occurred. A corporation may be sued in any county in which it has "an office, resident agent, or business place."

Service of Process: Mail or personal service by clerk.

Transfer: To County Court on jury demand or defendant's counterclaim above jurisdictional limit.

Attorneys: Not allowed except with court's approval.

Appeals: To County Court for new trial or jury trial.

Evictions: No.

Notes: (1) If defendant counterclaims over jurisdictional limit and files in another court, clerk will strike the Small Claims case from calendar.

(2) Defendant must file counterclaim within five days of the trial date.

(3) *Student Loans:* As long as an educational institution has administrative offices in the county in which the conciliation court is located, it may bring actions to recover student loans even though the defendant is not a resident of that county, as long as (a) the student loans were originally awarded in that county; (b) overdue notice was sent by first-class mail to the last known address of borrower; (c) the notice states that a conciliation court action may be commenced in the county where the loan was awarded.

MISSISSIPPI

Justice Court

Statutes: Mississippi Annotated Code: Secs. 9-11-9 (amount), 9-11-27, 11-9-103 through 11-9-143, 11-51-85.

Dollar Limit: $1,000.

Where to Sue: District in which any defendant resides; if nonresident, where act or omission occurred, or obligation entered into. A corporation "resides" where its registered office is located.

Service of Process: Sheriff, constable, or disinterested adult (only in "emergency" with court's permission).

Transfer: No provision.

Attorneys: Allowed.

Appeals: Allowed by either party within 10 days to Circuit Court for new trial.

Evictions: No.

Notes: (1) Either party may demand a jury trial.

(2) Equitable remedy to recover a specific item of property (*replevin*) is allowed.

(3) Some help to collect judgments is available.

MISSOURI

Small Claims Court (Circuit Court)

Statutes: Annotated Missouri Statutes: Secs. 482.300 through 482.365. Missouri Rules of Court: Rules of Practice and Procedure in Small Claims Court, Rules 140.01 through 155.

Dollar Limit: $1,500.

Where to Sue: County in which any defendant resides, or act or omission occurred; county in which plaintiff resides and at least one defendant may be found. A corporation "resides" wherever an office or agent is located. Suit against corporation must be brought where defendant resides or the subject of the claim arose.

Service of Process: Certified mail, return receipt. If impossible, sheriff will serve.

Transfers: Allowed to regular Circuit Court if defendant counterclaims over $1,500, unless all parties agree to stay in Small Claims Court.

Attorneys: Allowed.

Appeals: Allowed by either party within 10 days for new trial before regular Circuit Court judge.

Evictions: No.

Notes: (1) Assignees (collection agencies) cannot sue in Small Claim Court.

(2) Only six claims allowed per plaintiff per 12 months.

(3) Jury trials not allowed.

(4) Each county may promulgate local rules.

(5) *Counterclaims:* Any time up to 10 days after service of process and before the hearing date, defendant may file a counterclaim against plaintiff.

MONTANA

Small Claims Court (Justice Court and District Court)

Statutes: Montana Code Annotated: Title 3, Chapter 12, Secs. 101 through 106 (District Court); Title 25, Chapter 34, Secs. 101 through 404; Title 25, Chapter 35, Secs. 501 through 807 (Justice Court).

Dollar Limit: $3,000.

Where to Sue: County or judicial district in which any defendant can be served.

Service of Process: Sheriff, constable. (Justice Court only—disinterested adult).

Transfer: Allowed by defendant to Justice Court if request filed within 10 days of receipt of complaint.

Attorneys: Not allowed, unless all parties present have attorneys.

Appeals: Allowed by either party within 30 days (District Court) for new trial. Within 10 days (Justice Court) on law, not facts.

Evictions: No.

Notes: (1) Small Claims must be based on contract, express or implied.

(2) Assignees (collection agencies) cannot sue in Small Claims Court.

(3) Maximum 10 claims per year.

(4) Defendant may request jury trial unless he counterclaims.

(5) Defendant's counterclaim (up to $2,500) arising out of the same transaction or occurrence must be served on plaintiff at least 72 hours before the hearing date.

NEBRASKA

Small Claims Court (County or Municipal Court)

Statutes: Revised Statutes of Nebraska: Secs. 25-2801 through 25-2807; 25-2728 through 25-2738 (appeals).

Dollar Limit: $1,800.

Where to Sue: County in which any defendant resides (or works, or can be found, if plaintiff lives there), or injury or property damage occurred. A corporation "resides" wherever it regularly does business through an office or agent.

Service of Process: Sheriff or certified mail, sent by clerk.

Transfer: Transferable to regular civil court on defendant's request or counterclaim over $1,500.

Attorneys: Not allowed.

Appeals: Allowed by either party within 30 days to District Court for new trial but no jury permitted. Attorneys allowed.

Evictions: No.

Notes: (1) Jury trials not available.

(2) Equitable relief available.

(3) Assignees (collection agencies) cannot sue in Small Claims Court.

(4) Plaintiff may not bring more than two claims in a week nor more than 10 in one year.

(5) *Transfers:* Defendant may request a transfer to the regular docket in order to have a jury trial by giving notice to the court at least two days before the hearing date.

NEVADA

Small Claims (Justice Court)

Statutes: Nevada Revised Statutes: Title 6, Secs. 73.010 through 73.060; and Justice Court Rules of Civil Procedure, Chapter XII, Rules 88 through 100.

Dollar Limit: $2500.

Where to Sue: City or township in which defendant resides, does business, or is employed.

Service of Process: Personal service by sheriff or constable, licensed process server, adult approved by court, Justice of the Peace, or registered or certified mail (mailed by court clerk), return receipt.

Transfer: No provision.

Attorneys: Allowed.

Appeals: Allowed by either party within 20 days to District Court, on law—not facts. New trial at court's discretion.

Evictions: No.

Note: Recovery of money only.

NEW HAMPSHIRE

Small Claims Actions (District or Municipal Court)

Statutes: New Hampshire Revised Statutes Annotated: Vol. 4C, Secs. 503:1 through 503:10; Rules of District and Municipal Court, Rules 4.1 through 4.28, 1.11.

Dollar Limit: $2,500.

Where to Sue: Town or district in which defendant resides or plaintiff resides, or act or omission occurred.

Service of Process: Certified mail sent by court or other court-approved method, return receipt.

Transfer: To Superior Court if claim plus counterclaim exceeds $2,500 or if case exceeds $500 and either party requests jury trial.

Attorneys: Allowed.

Appeals: Allowed by either party to Supreme Court, on law—not facts. Must be made within 30 days.

Evictions: No.

Note: Claims may not involve title (ownership) to real estate.

NEW JERSEY

Small Claims Section

(Special Civil Part of Law Division of Superior Court)

Statutes: New Jersey Rules of Court: Superior Court Rules, Law Division Special Civil Part Rule 6:1 through 6:12.

Dollar Limit: $1,500 in Small Claims; $7,500 in Regular Special Civil Court; Residential Security Deposits - $1,000 Small Claims, $5,000 Regular Special Civil Court.

Where to Sue: County in which any defendant resides. A corporation "resides" wherever it is actually doing business; if defendants do not reside in New Jersey, county where act or omission occurred.

Service of Process: Officers of the Special Civil Part, adult approved by court, or certified mail.

Transfer: Allowed to Civil Part if defendant counterclaims over $5,000 or demands jury trial.

Attorneys: Allowed.

Appeals: Allowed by either party within 45 days to Appellate Division of Superior Court, on law—not facts.

Evictions: No.

Notes: (1) The court will not hear cases involving personal injury or property damage except those resulting from auto accidents.

(2) Assignees (collection agencies) cannot sue in Small Claims Court.

(3) *Landlord-Tenant:* Small Claims Court has jurisdiction over landlord-tenant actions where the matter in dispute is the return of all or part of the security deposit.

NEW MEXICO

Metropolitan Court (Urban); Magistrate's Court (Rural)

Statutes: New Mexico Statutes: Annotated Secs 34-8A-1 through 12; 35-3-3 through 6; 35-8-1 and 2; 35-10-1 through 6; 35-13-2; Rules of Civil Procedure for the Metropolitan and Magistrate Courts.

Dollar Limit: $5,000 (Magistrate's Court); $5,000 (Metropolitan Court).

Where to Sue: County in which the defendant resides, may be found, or act or omission occurred.

Service of Process: By mail, and if no response, personal service by sheriff or disinterested adult.

Transfer: No provision.

Attorneys: Allowed.

Appeals: Allowed by either party within 15 days to District Court.

Evictions: Yes.

Notes: (1) Jury trial at either party's request; plaintiff must make jury trial request in the complaint and defendant must make request in the answer.

(2) Voluntary mediation program in Bernalillo County.

(3) No libel, slander or malicious prosecution.

(4) Small Claims Court also has jurisdiction over contested parking violations or operation of vehicle regulations.

NEW YORK

Small Claims [New York City Civil Court, Civil Courts outside of New York City, District Court in Nassau and Suffolk Counties (except 1st District), Justice Courts in rural areas.] See below for New York City Commercial Small Claims Court.

Statutes: Consolidated Laws of New York Annotated: Uniform Justice Court Act Secs. 1801 through 1814; NYC Civil Court Act Secs. 1801 through 1814; Uniform City Court Act Secs. 1801 through 1814; Uniform Rules for the NY State Trial Courts, Secs. 208.41 and 208.41-a.

Dollar Limit: $2,000.

Where to Sue: Political subdivision in which the defendant resides, is employed, or has a business office.

Service of Process: Certified mail (binding on defendant who refuses mail) or ordinary first class mail. If after 21 days not returned as undeliverable, then notice presumed.

Transfer: Allowed by court's discretion.

Attorneys: Allowed. Most large corporations must be represented by an attorney. Corporation defendant can defend self.

Appeals: Allowed by defendant within 30 days to County Court or Appellate Division, on law—not facts. Plaintiffs can appeal only on the ground that "substantial justice" was not done.

Evictions: No.

Notes: (1) Arbitration is available. Arbitrator's ruling unappealable.

(2) Assignees, corporations and partnerships cannot sue in Small Claims Court (exceptions: municipal corporations, public benefit corporations, school districts, school district public libraries).

(3) No counterclaim permitted in Small Claims action unless within the dollar limit.

(4) Section 1812 of the NYC Civil Court Act, Uniform City Court Act and the Uniform Justice Court Acts provide treble damages against judgment debtor who is sued in second action to enforce judgment, and who has unreasonably failed to pay within 30 days of first judgment *and* who has failed to pay at least in two small claims judgments recorded against him or her. Additional sanction against defaulting defendant whose liability arises from his or her business activities. Court will notify appropriate licensing and public certifying agencies or attorney general.

New York City Commercial Small Claims Court [NYC Civil Court Act, 1801-A to 1814-A] and Uniform City Court Act, 1801-A to 1814-A.

• only corporations, partnerships and associations can sue, they must sue for money only, and the jurisdictional amount is $2,000

• plaintiff must "reside" in NY

- defendant must reside, be employed, or have an office for transacting business in the county where suit is brought
- plaintiff can bring no more than five claims per month
- no assignees (collection agencies)

NORTH CAROLINA

Small Claims Actions (District Court)

Statutes: General Statutes of North Carolina: Chapter 7A, Secs. 210 through 232. Chapter 42, Sec. 26 through 36:2 (ejectments).

Dollar Limit: $3,000.

Where to Sue: County in which the defendant resides. A corporation "resides" where it "maintains a place of business."

Service of Process: Sheriff, registered or certified mail, adult approved by court. For evictions, sheriff may mail using ordinary first-class and then telephone or visit to arrange time to personally serve.

Transfer: No provision unless question of land title.

Attorneys: Allowed.

Appeals: Allowed by either party within 10 days to District Court for new trial. Jury trial allowed if request within 10 days of appeal's notice.

Evictions: Yes.

Notes: (1) Rules of evidence apply.

(2) Counterclaim that would make amount in controversy exceed $2,000 not allowed.

NORTH DAKOTA

Small Claims Court (County Court)

Statutes: North Dakota Century Code Annotated: Secs. 27.08.1 through 27.08.1-08.

Dollar Limit: $3,000.

Where to Sue: County where the defendant resides. If defendant is a corporation or partnership, where it has a place of business or where the subject of the claim arose.

Service of Process: Disinterested adult or certified mail.

Transfer: Defendant may transfer case to regular civil court procedure.

Attorneys: Allowed.

Appeals: Not allowed.

Evictions: No.

Notes: (1) No jury trial.

(2) Plaintiff may not discontinue once small claims process invoked; if plaintiff seeks to discontinue, then dismissal with prejudice. (i.e., no right to refile).

OHIO

Small Claims (Municipal and County Courts); County Court

Statutes: Ohio Revised Code Annotated: Title 19, Secs. 1925.01 through 1925.17, 1901, 1907; Rules of Civil Procedure (generally applicable).

Dollar Limit: $2,000 for claims; $3,000 in County Court.

Where to Sue: County in which the defendant resides, has place of business, or obligation occurred. Actions involving notes can be brought only were obligation was incurred.

Service of Process: Sheriff, certified mail by clerk, return receipt.

Transfer: Allowed from Small Claims to regular Civil Court procedure upon defendant's counterclaim over $2,000, upon request, or motion of court.

Attorneys: Allowed.

Appeals: To Court of Appeals within 30 days.

Evictions: No.

Notes: (1) Each plaintiff is limited to 24 claims per year.

(2) Municipal Court cases limited to recovery of personal property, taxes and money.

(3) No jury trials, except in County Court.

(4) No assignees except to recover taxes if appointed by authorized employee of state political subdivision.

OKLAHOMA

Small Claims (District Court)

Statutes: Oklahoma Statutes Annotated: Title 12, Secs. 1751 through 1773, 134, 139, 141.

Dollar Limit: $2,500.

Where to Sue: County in which the defendant resides, or obligation was entered into. In automobile or boat accident cases, where the accident occurred. A corporation may be sued in a county in which it is "situated" (i.e., has an office) or where the act or omission occurred.

Service of Process: Certified mail by clerk, return receipt. Plaintiff may request Sheriff or other disinterested adult.

Transfer: Allowed to regular District Court on a defendant's request or counterclaim over $2,500 unless both parties agree in writing to stay in Small Claims Court. Defendant must make a transfer request at least 48 hours prior to the time ordered for her appearance and answer.

Attorneys: Allowed, but can't charge more than 10% of judgment in uncontested cases.

Appeals: Allowed by either party within 30 days to Oklahoma Supreme Court, on law only—not facts.

Evictions: No.

Notes: (1) A jury trial may be demanded by either party.

(2) Suits to recover personal property are allowed.

(3) Small claims judgment becomes a lien on judgment debtor's real property.

(4) Assignees (collection agencies) not allowed to sue in Small Claims Court.

(5) Defendant must file any counterclaim at least 72 hours before appearance date.

(6) No suits for libel or slander.

OREGON

Small Claims Department (District or Justice Court)

Statutes: Oregon Revised Statutes: Secs. 46.405 through 46.560, 55.011 through 55.140.

Dollar Limit: $2,500.

Where to Sue: County where defendant resides or can be found; tort cases may be filed in county where injury occurred and contract cases may be filed in county where contract was to be performed.

Service of Process: Certified mail, return receipt, sheriff, adult approved by court.

Transfer: To regular docket or other appropriate court; counterclaim is more than $2,500 and defendant requests transfer; or, in District Court if defendant demands jury trial.

Attorneys: Not allowed without judge's consent.

Appeals: From District Court, no appeal. From Justice Court, allowed by defendant (or plaintiff, on counterclaim) within 10 days to Circuit Court for new trial.

Evictions: No.

Notes: (1) The defendant must respond (settle claim, request hearing or request jury trial) within 14 days or will lose by default.

(2) If greater than $200 claim, defendant may seek jury trial.

PENNSYLVANIA

Philadelphia—Philadelphia Municipal Court;

Everywhere else—District or Justice Court

Statutes: Pennsylvania Statutes Annotated: Title 42, Judiciary and Judicial Procedure, Secs. 1123, 1511 through 1516; Rules of Civil Procedure Governing District or Justice Court, Rules 201 through 325; Philadelphia Municipal Court Rules of Civil Practice, Rules 101 through 144.

Dollar Limit: $5,000 (Municipal Court); $8,000 (District or Justice Court).

Where to Sue: Where defendant can be served or, if corporation or partnership, where it regularly conducts business or has principal place of business, or where act or omission occurred.

Service of Process: Sheriff, constable, disinterested adult or registered or certified mail.

Transfer: If defendant counterclaims over dollar limit, he may bring suit in Court of Common Pleas within 30 days (Municipal Court); No provision (District or Justice Court).

Attorneys: Allowed.

Appeals: Allowed by either party within 30 days to Court of Common Pleas for new trial.

Evictions: Allowed.

Notes: (1) Either party can request a jury trial and case will be transferred.

(2) Judge may make award of installment payments.

(3) In Philadelphia, if claiming more than $2,000 for injury to self or property, will have to submit a verified (signed under oath) statement of claim.

RHODE ISLAND

Small Claims (District Court)

Statutes: General Laws of Rhode Island: Title 10, Chapter 16, Secs. 1 through 16; Title 9, Chapter 12, Sec. 10 (appeals).

Dollar Limit: $1,500.

Where to Sue: District where either party resides, unless plaintiff is corporation, then only where defendant resides.

Service of Process: Certified or registered mail first; if that fails, then by sheriff, constable, deputy, or adult approved by court. Certified or registered mail is binding on defendant who refuses letter.

Transfer: Allowed to regular District Court procedure on defendant's counterclaim over $1,500, provided the Small Claims judge decides that the counterclaim has merit.

Attorneys: Allowed; required for corporations, except close corporations.

Appeals: Allowed by defendant to Superior Court for new trial. Defendant right to appeal unavailable if plaintiff is consumer and defendant is manufacturer/seller whose failure to file answer in Small Claims Court results in default.

Evictions: No.

Notes: (1) Actions for contracts (including sale of personal property) and damages resulting from a retail sale or delivery of services to a member of the general public.

(2) Judge may order judgment to be paid in installments.

SOUTH CAROLINA

Magistrate's Court (No Small Claims Procedure)

Statutes: Code of Laws of South Carolina: Title 22, Chapter 3, Secs. 10 through 320; Title 15, Chapter 7, Sec. 30; Rules of Civil Procedure 3, 82; and Title 18, Chapter 7, Sec. 20.

Dollar Limit: $2,500.

Where to Sue: County or township where defendant resides. An insurance company "resides" where it is doing business.

Service of Process: Sheriff or disinterested adult.

Transfer: Check with clerk of court. Counterclaims over $2,500 must be transferred to the docket of common pleas.

Attorneys: Allowed.

Appeals: To County or Circuit Court, on law—not facts. Party may make motion for new trial within five days, and may appeal within 25 days after motion denied.

Evictions: Yes.

Notes: (1) Either party may request jury trial.

(2) Defendant must answer within 20 days of service.

SOUTH DAKOTA

Small Claims Procedure (Circuit or Magistrate's Court)

Statutes: South Dakota Compiled Laws Annotated: Title 15, Chapter 39, Secs. 45 through 78.

Dollar Limit: $4,000.

Where to Sue: County in which any defendant resides, or injury or property damage occurred. A corporation "resides" at its principal place of business.

Service of Process: Certified or registered mail first, return receipt; service this way is binding on defendant who refused to accept and sign for the letter. If undeliverable, then service must be made by sheriff, or disinterested adult, county resident.

Transfer: Allowed at judge's discretion on defendant's demand for jury trial (must include affidavit saying jury needed because facts are complex).

Attorneys: Allowed.

Appeals: Not allowed.

Evictions: No.

TENNESSEE

Court of General Sessions (No Specific Small Claims Procedure)

Statutes: Tennessee Code Annotated: Title 16, Chapter 15, Secs. 501 through 713; Title 19, Chapters 1 through 3.

Dollar Limit: $10,000; $15,000 in counties where population is over 700,000.

Where to Sue: District nearest to defendant's residence. For debt collection, where defendant is non-resident, suit can be bought where plaintiff resides. Eviction suits brought where property is located.

Service of Process: Sheriff, deputy sheriff, constable, or certified mail.

Transfer: No provision.

Attorneys: Allowed.

Appeals: Allowed by either party to Circuit Court for new trial.

Evictions: Yes.

Note: Tennessee has no actual Small Claims system, but sessions are normally conducted with relatively informal "equitable" rules.

TEXAS

Small Claims Court (Justice Court)

Statutes: Texas Government Code Secs. 28.001 through 28.055. Rules of Civil Procedure for Justice Courts, Rule 523-591.

Dollar Limit: $5,000.

Where to Sue: Precinct in which the defendant resides or obligation was to be performed. Corporations and associations may be sued where they have representatives.

Service of Process: Sheriff, constable, certified mail.

Transfer: No provision.

Attorneys: Allowed.

Appeals: Allowed by either party within 10 days to County Court for new trial (only for cases where amount in controversy exceeds $20).

Evictions: No.

Notes: (1) No assignees (collection agencies) or lenders of money at interest may sue in Small Claims Court.

(2) A jury trial may be demanded by either party.

(3) *Default judgments:* If a default judgment is entered against either defendant or plaintiff, that person has 10 days to file a written motion to show good cause for setting aside dismissal or default judgment for failure to appear.

UTAH

Small Claims (Circuit or Justice Court)

Statutes: Utah Code Annotated: Secs. 78-6-1 through 78-6-15.

Dollar Limit: $5,000.

Where to Sue: County in which the defendant resides or act or omission occurred. Corporation can be sued where has office or place of business.

Service of Process: Sheriff or disinterested adult.

Transfer: No provision.

Attorneys: Allowed.

Appeals: Either party may appeal for a new trial by filing within 10 days of notice of entry of judgment. The Circuit Court will try the appeal in accordance with Small Claims Court procedures, except that a record of the trial will be maintained.

Evictions: No.

Notes: (1) Assignees (collection agencies) cannot sue in Small Claims Court.

(2) Either party may demand jury trial.

(3) Utah has evening hour sessions.

(4) Defendant must counterclaim at least two days before trial.

VERMONT

Small Claims Procedure (District Court)

Statutes: Vermont Statutes Annotated: Title 12, Secs. 405, 5531 through 5538; District Court Civil Rule 80.3.

Dollar Limit: $2,000.

Where to Sue: Territorial unit in which any defendant or plaintiff resides, or act or omission occurred.

Service of Process: Sheriff, constable, disinterested adult (with court's permission), or certified mail, return receipt.

Transfer: Defendant may transfer by demanding jury trial.

Attorneys: Allowed.

Appeals: Allowed by either party within 30 days to Superior Court on law only—not facts.

Evictions: No.

Notes: (1) Defendant must give written answer within 20 days of service or will lose by default.

(2) Counterclaims over $2,000 allowed; however, recovery will be limited to $2,000.

(3) Defendant may request jury trial.

VIRGINIA

Small Claims Court (District Court) in all larger counties; otherwise regular District Court

Statutes: Code of Virginia: Secs. 16.1-76 through 16.1-118.1; 16.1-122.1 through 16.1-122.7.

Dollar Limit: $1,000 in Small Claims; $10,000 in District Court.

Where to Sue: District in which any defendant resides, is employed, or regularly conducts business, where act or omission occurred, or where property is located.

Service of Process: Sheriff or adult approved by court.

Transfer: Allowed.

Attorneys: Not allowed unless bringing their own suit.

Appeals: Allowed by either party within 10 days (on cases over $50) to Circuit Court for new trial; either party may request jury trial.

Evictions: Yes.

Note: No jury trials allowed.

WASHINGTON

Small Claims Department (District Court)

Statutes: Revised Code of Washington Annotated: Title 3, Sec. 66.040, Title 12, Secs. 40.010 through 40.120; Washington Court Rules Part V (Justice Court Civil Rules), Rule 73.

Dollar Limit: $2,500.

Where to Sue: County where any defendant resides. Corporation resides where it transacts business or has an office.

Service of Process: Sheriff or deputy, constable, disinterested adult, or certified or registered mail.

Transfer: Allowed if corporate plaintiff is represented by lawyer and defendant requests transfer to regular civil docket.

Attorneys or Paralegals: Not allowed without judge's consent, unless the case was transferred from regular civil court.

Appeals: No appeal by a party who requested Small Claims Court if the claim was under $1,000. Otherwise, within 14 days to Superior Court for new trial.

Evictions: No.

Notes: (1) Defendant with counterclaim over $2,000 must sue on it separately.

(2) May sue only to recover money.

(3) Court may order judgment payment plan if the debtor is present in court.

WEST VIRGINIA

Magistrate's Court

Statutes: West Virginia Code: Chapter 50, Secs. 2-1 through 6-3, Chapter 56, Sec. 1-1, Rules of Civil Procedure for Magistrate's Courts, Rules 1-21.

Dollar Limit: $3,000.

Where to Sue: County in which any defendant resides or can be served; also where act or omission occurred. West Virginia corporations reside at principal office; other corporations where they do business.

Service of Process: Sheriff or disinterested adult (clerk prepares summons and forwards to sheriff).

Transfer: Allowed if all parties agree to remove to Circuit court, or by any party for claims over $300. Also allowed at magistrate's discretion if defendant requests transfer in her answer or within a reasonable time.

Attorneys: Allowed.

Appeals: Allowed by either party within 20 days to Circuit Court for new trial.

Evictions: Yes.

Notes: (1) Defendant must give written answer in 20 days (30 days if service was made on attorney authorized to accept service for defendant) or lose by default. Time limit is five days for eviction action.

(2) Jury trial may be demanded by either party if claim over $20 or possession of real estate involved.

(3) The deposition (recorded questions and answers) of a witness unable to attend may be taken.

WISCONSIN

Small Claims (Circuit Court)

Statutes: Wisconsin Statutes Annotated: Secs. 799.01 through 799.45, 421.401.

Dollar Limit: $2,000. No limit on eviction suits.

Where to Sue: County where claim arose or in which any defendant resides or does substantial business. If defendant is a state agency or official, Dane County. If a claim arose from consumer transaction, county where consumer sought or acquired the property, services, money or credit which is the subject of the claim, or where the consumer signed the contract.

Service of Process: Except for evictions, summons mailed by court clerk, return receipt requested. For evictions, personal service required.

Transfer: Allowed to regular County Court procedure on defendant's counterclaim over $2,000.

Attorneys: Allowed.

Appeals: Allowed by either party within 45 days to Court of Appeals, on law—not facts. No appeal from default judgment. Appeal in eviction action must be initiated within 15 days of judgment.

Evictions: Yes.

Note: (1) Either party may request jury trial.

(2) A motion for a new trial must be made within 20 days of judgment.

WYOMING

County Court or Justice of the Peace Court

Statutes: Wyoming Statutes Annotated: Code of Civil Procedure Secs. 1-21-201 through 1-21-205; 5-5-101 through 5-5-175; Rules of Civil Procedure for Justice of the Peace Courts, Rules 1 through 8.

Dollar Limit: $2,000. County Court, $7,000.

Where to Sue: County in which the defendant resides or can be served for personal injury in county where accident occurred. If defendant is Wyoming corporation, in county where corporation is situated or has principal office or place of business; for nonresident corporation, where cause of action arose or plaintiff resides.

Service of Process: Sheriff or deputy, deputized process server, certified or registered mail, court-approved adult. Court can serve, within county, by registered mail.

Transfer: Allowed.

Attorneys: Allowed. If one party gets one, the other may, if desired, have a continuance to obtain counsel.

Appeals: Allowed by either party within 10 days to District Court on law only—not facts.

Evictions: Yes.

Notes: (1) Either party may demand jury trial.

(2) Arbitration is available in some circumstances.

Index

Before You Go to Court— Look Here for More Help

Winning in Small Claims Court
Audio Cassette Tape—50 Minutes
Attorney Ralph Warner with Joanne Greene. 1st National ed.

This tape guides through all the major issues involved in preparing and winning a small claims court case—deciding if there is a good case, assessing whether you can collect if you win, preparing your evidence and arguing before the judge.
$14.95/TWIN

How to Win Your Personal Injury Claim
By Attorney Joseph Matthews. 1st National ed.

Armed with the right information anyone can handle a personal injury claim. This step-by-step guide will show you how to evaluate what your claim is worth, negotiate with the insurance company, obtain a full and fair settlement, and save for yourself what you would pay an attorney.
$24,95/PICL

Neighbor Law
By Attorney Cora Jordan. 1st National ed.

Answers common questions about the subjects that most often trigger disputes between neighbors; fences, trees, boundaries and noise. It explains how to find the law and resolve disputes without a nasty lawsuit.
$14.95/NEI

Legal Research
By Attorneys Stephen Elias and Susan Levinkind. 3rd National ed.

A valuable tool on its own or as a companion to just about any Nolo book. Legal Research gives easy-to-use, step-by-step instructions on how to find legal information. Learn how to find and research a case, read statutes and administrative regulations and make Freedom of Information Act Requests.
$19.95/LRES

Represent Yourself in Court: How to Prepare & Try a Winning Case
By Attorneys Paul Bergman & Sara Berman-Barrett. National 1st ed.

Handle your own civil court case from start to finish without a lawyer with the most thorough guide to contested court cases ever published for the non-lawyer. Covers all aspects of civil trials including lining up persuasive witnesses, presenting testimony, cross examining witnesses and even picking a jury.
$29.95/RYC

To order any of these books:
Call us at 1-800-992-6656 or fill out and mail or
fax us the order form in the back of this book.

C A T A L O G

...more books from NoloPress

Estate Planning & Probate

Plan Your Estate
Covers every significant aspect of estate planning and gives detailed, specific instructions for preparing a living trust. Includes all the tear-out forms and step-by-step instructions to let you prepare an estate plan designed for your special needs. Good in all states except Louisiana.
$19.95/NEST

Make Your Own Living Trust
Find out how a living trust works, how to create one, and how to determine what kind of trust is right for you. Contains all the forms and instructions you need to prepare a basic living trust to avoid probate, a marital life estate trust (A-B trust) to avoid probate and estate taxes, and a back-up will. Good in all states except Louisiana.
$19.95/LITR

Who Will Handle Your Finances if You Can't?
Give a trusted person legal authority to handle your financial matters if illness or old age makes it impossible for you to handle them yourself. Create a durable power of attorney for finances with the step-by-step instructions and fill-in-the-blank forms included in this book.
$19.95/FINA

Nolo's Simple Will Book
It's easy to write a legally valid will using this book. Includes all the instructions and sample forms you need to name a personal guardian for minor children, leave property to minor children or young adults and update a will when necessary. Good in all states except Louisiana.
$17.95/SWIL

LAW FORM KITS

Nolo's Law Form Kit: Wills
All the forms and instructions you need to create a legally valid will.
$14.95/KWL

AUDIO CASSETTE TAPES

Write Your Will
60 minute audio tape
This tape answers the most frequently asked questions about writing a will and covers all key issues.
$14.95/TWYW

5 Ways to Avoid Probate
60 minute audio tape
Provides clear, in-depth explanations of the principal probate avoidance techniques.
$14.95/TPRO

SOFTWARE

WillMaker ®
Make your own legal will and living will (healthcare directive) — and thoroughly document your final arrangements—with WillMaker 5. WillMaker's easy-to-use interview format takes you through each document step-by-step. On-line legal help is available throughout the program. Good in all states except Louisiana
WINDOWS $69.95/WIW5
DOS $69.95/WI5
MACINTOSH $69.95/WM5

Nolo's Personal RecordKeeper
Finally, a safe, accessible place for your important records. Over 200 categories and subcategories to organize and store your important financial, legal and personal information, compute your net worth and create inventories for insurance records. Export your net worth and home inventory data to Quicken®.
DOS $49.95/FRI3
MACINTOSH $49.95/FRM3

Nolo's Living Trust
Put your assets into a trust and save your heirs the headache, time and expense of probate with this easy-to-use software. Use it to set up an individual or shared marital trust, transfer property to the trust, and change or revoke the trust at any time. Its manual guides you through the process, and legal help screens and an on-line glossary explain key legal terms and concepts. Good in all states except Louisiana.
MACINTOSH $79.95/LTM1

Business/Workplace

The Legal Guide for Starting & Running a Small Business
An essential resource for every small business owner. Find out how to form a sole proprietorship, partnership or corporation, negotiate a favorable lease, hire and fire employees, write contracts and resolve disputes.
$22.95/RUNS

Sexual Harassment on the Job: What it is and How To Stop it.
An invaluable resource both for employees experiencing harassment and for employers interested in creating a policy against sexual harassment and a procedure for handling complaints.
$14.95/HARS

How to Write a Business Plan
This book will show you how to write the business plan and loan package necessary to finance your business and make it work.
$19.95/SBS

Your Rights in the Workplace
Comprehensive guide to workplace rights —from hiring to firing.
$15.95/YRW

Marketing Without Advertising
Outlines practical steps for building and expanding a small business without spending a lot of money on advertising.
$14.00/MWAD

The Partnership Book
Shows you step-by-step how to write a solid partnership agreement that meets your needs.
$24.95/PART

Software Development: A Legal Guide
Book with Disk-DOS
This book explores the legal ins and outs of copyright, trade secret and patent protection and shows how to draft software development agreement and employment contracts. All contracts and agreements included on disk.
$44.95/SFT

The Independent Paralegal's Handbook
Provides legal and business guidelines for anyone who wants to go into business as an independent paralegal helping consumers with routine legal tasks.
$24.95 PARA

How to Form a Nonprofit Corporation
Shows you step-by-step how to form a nonprofit corporation. Includes forms for the Articles, Bylaws and Minutes along with complete instruction for obtaining federal 501(c)(3) tax exemptions and benefits.
$24.95/NNP

How to Form Your Own Corporation
These books contain the forms, instructions and tax information you need to incorporate a small business yourself and save hundreds of dollars in lawyers' fees.
California $29.95/CCOR
New York $24.95/NYCO
Texas $29.95/TCOR
How to Form Your Own Corporation is also available with incorporation forms on disk for these states:
New York . DOS $39.95/NYCI, Mac. $39.95/NYCM
Texas DOS $39.95/TCI
Florida DOS $39.95/FCCO

The Neighborhood

Dog Law
A practical guide to the laws that affect dog owners and their neighbors.
$12.95/DOG

Safe Homes, Safe Neighborhoods: Stopping Crime Where You Live
Learn how you and your neighbors can work together to protect yourselves, your families and property from crime.
$14.95/SAFE

Money Matters

Stand Up to the IRS
Gives detailed strategies on surviving an audit, appealing an audit decision, going to Tax Court and dealing with IRS collectors.
$21.95/SIRS

How to File for Bankruptcy
Trying to decide whether or not filing for bankruptcy makes sense? This book contains an overview of the process and all the forms plus step-by-step instructions you need to file for Chapter 7 Bankruptcy.
$25.95/HFB

Money Troubles: Legal Strategies to Cope with Your Debts
Essential for anyone who has gotten behind on bills. It shows how to obtain a credit file, negotiate with creditors, challenge wage attachments, contend with repossessions and more.
$16.95/MT

Simple Contracts for Personal Use
Contains clearly written legal form contracts to buy and sell property, borrow and lend money, store and lend personal property, release others from personal liability, or pay a contractor to do home repairs. Includes agreements to arrange child care and other household help.
$16.95/CONT

LAW FORM KITS

Nolo's Law Form Kit: Personal Bankruptcy
All the forms and instructions you need to file for Chapter 7 bankruptcy.
$14.95/KBNK

Nolo's Law Forms Kit: Rebuild Your Credit
Provides strategies for dealing with debts and rebuilding your credit.
$14.95/KCRD

Nolo's Law Form Kit: Power of Attorney
Create a conventional power of attorney to assign someone you trust to take of your finances, business, real estate or children when you are away or unavailable. Provides all the forms with step-by-step instructions.
$14.95/KPA

Nolo's Law Form Kit: Loan Agreements
Provides all the forms and instructions necessary to create a legal and effective promissory note.
$14.95/KLOAN

Nolo's Law Form Kit: Buy and Sell Contracts
Step-by-step instructions and all the forms necessary for creating bills of sale for cars, boats, computers, and other personal property.
$9.95/K CONT

Family Matters

Nolo's Pocket Guide to Family Law
Here's help for anyone who has a question or problem involving family law—marriage, divorce, adoption or living together.
$14.95/FLD

Divorce & Money

Explains how to evaluate such major assets as family homes and businesses, investments, pensions, and how to arrive at a division of property that is fair to both sides.
$21.95/DIMO

The Living Together Kit

A detailed guide designed to help the increasing number of unmarried couples living together understand the laws that affect them. Sample agreements and instructions are included.
$17.95/LTK

A Legal Guide for Lesbian and Gay Couples

This book shows lesbian and gay couples how to write a living-together contract, plan for medical emergencies, understand the practical and legal aspects of having and raising children and plan their estates. Includes forms and sample agreements.
$21.95/LG

Divorce: A New Yorker's Guide to Doing it Yourself

Step-by-step instructions and all the forms you need to do your own divorce and save thousands of dollars in legal fees.
$24.95/NYDIV

How to Do Your Own Divorce

These books contain all the forms and instructions you need to do your own uncontested divorce without a lawyer.
California $21,95/CDIV
Texas $17.95/TDIV

Trademark:
How to Name Your Business & Product

Learn how to choose a name or logo that others can't copy, conduct a trademark search, register a trademark with the U.S. Patent and Trademark Office and protect and maintain the trademark.
$29.95/TRD

Patent It Yourself

From the patent search to the actual application, this book covers everything including the use and licensing of patents, successful marketing and how to deal with infringement.
$36.95/PAT

The Copyright Handbook

Provides forms and step-by-step instructions for protecting all types of written expression under U.S. and international copyright law. $24.95/COHA

Beat the Nursing Home Trap: A Consumer's Guide to Choosing and Financing Long-Term Care (formerly Elder Care)

This practical guide shows how to protect assets, arrange for long-time care, evaluate nursing home insurance and understand Medicare, Medicaid and other benefit programs.
$18.95/ELD

Social Security, Medicare & Pensions

Offers invaluable guidance through the current maze of rights and benefits for those 55 and over.
$15.95/SOA

Legal Research: How to Find and Understand the Law

A valuable tool on its own or as a companion to just about every other Nolo book. Gives easy-to-use, step-by-step instructions on how to find legal information.
$19.95/LRES

Nolo's Law Form Kit: Hiring Child Care & Household Help

All the necessary forms and instructions for fulfilling your legal and tax responsibilities. Includes employment contracts, applications forms and required IRS forms.
$14.95/KCHLD

How to Get a Green Card: Legal Ways to Stay in the U.S.A.

This book clearly explains the steps involved in getting a green card. It covers who can qualify, what documents to present, and how to fill out all the forms and have them processed. Tear-out forms included.
$19.95/GRN

order form

CODE	QUANTITY	ITEM	UNIT PRICE	TOTAL

DATE DUE

Subtotal

Tax

Handling per item

(ii)

TOTAL

Name

Address (UPS to street address;

for faster service, use these numbers

Monday-Friday, 8am to 5pm Pacific
ORDER LINE   1-800-992-
CUSTOMER SERVICE   1-510-549-
FAX YOUR ORDER   1-800-645-0

METHOD OF PAYMENT

☐ Check enclosed   ☐ VISA   ☐ Ma

Account #

Send to

NOLO PRESS, 950 PARKER STREET, BERKELE
Allow 2-3 weeks for delivery. PRICES SUBJECT TO CHANGE.

visit our store

If you live in the Bay Area, be sure to visit the Nolo Press Bookstore on the corner of 9th & Parker
Streets in west Berkeley. You'll find our complete line of books and software—all at a discount.
Call 1-510-704-2248 for hours.

NSCC